INTERNETWORKING IPv6
WITH CISCO ROUTERS

McGraw-Hill
Computer Communications Titles

Amos/Minoli   *IP Applications with ATM*, 0-07-042312-1

Data Communications Handbook, 0-07-005147-X

Relay Networks: Specifications & Implementation, 2/e,

TCP/IP and Related Protocols, 3/e, 0-07-913282-0

Charles   *LAN Blueprints: Engineering It Right*, 0-07-011769-1

Chiong   *Internetworking ATM for the Internet and Enterprise Networks*, 0-07-011941-4

Chiong   *SNA Interconnections: Bridging and Routing SNA in Hierarchical, Peer, and High-Speed Networks*, 0-07-011486-2

Dhawan   *Mobile Computing: A Systems Integrator's Handbook*, 0-07-016769-9

Dziong   *ATM Network Resource Management*, 0-07-018546-8

Feit   *TCP/IP: Architecture, Protocols & Implementation with Ipv6 and IP Security, 2/e*, 0-07-021389-5

Goralski   *ADSL and DSL Technologies*, 0-07-024679-3

Goralski   *SONET: A Guide to Synchronous Optical Networks*, 0-07-024563-0

Goralski   *Introduction to ATM Networking*, 0-07-024043-4

Huntington-Lee/Terplan/Gibson   *HP's OpenView: A Manager's Guide*, 0-07-031382-2

Kessler   *ISDN: Concepts, Facilities, and Services, 3/e*, 0-07-034249-0

Kumar   *Broadband Communications*, 0-07-035968-7

Matusow   *SNA, APPN, HPR and TCP/IP Integration*, 0-07-041051-8

McDysan/Spohn   *ATM: Theory and Applications*, 0-07-060362-6

Mukherjee   *Optical Communication Networks*, 0-07-044435-8

Muller   *Network Planning Procurement and Management*, 0-07-044362-9

Russell   *Signaling System #7*, 0-07-054991-5

Sackett/Metz   *ATM and Multiprotocol Networking*, 0-07-057724-2

Saunders   *The McGraw-Hill High Speed LANs Handbook*, 0-07-057199-6

Simoneau   *Hands-On TCP/IP*, 0-07-912640-5

Smith   *Virtual LANs: A Guide to Construction, Operation, and Utilization*, 0-07-913623-0

Spohn   *Data Network Design, 2/e*, 0-07-060363-4

Summers   *ISDN Implementor's Guide*, 0-07-069416-8

Taylor   *The McGraw-Hill Internetworking Handbook*, 0-07-063399-1

Taylor   *McGraw-Hill Internetworking Command Reference*, 0-07-063301-0

Terplan   *Effective Management of Local Area Networks, 2/e*, 0-07-063639-7

Yarborough   *Building Communications Networks with Distributed Objects*, 0-07-072220-X

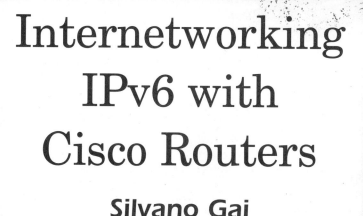

Internetworking IPv6 with Cisco Routers

Silvano Gai

Translated by Antonella Caporello

www.ip6.com

McGraw-Hill
New York • San Francisco • Washington, D.C. • Auckland
Bogotá • Caracas • Lisbon • London • Madrid • Mexico City
Milan • Montreal • New Delhi • San Juan • Singapore
Sydney • Tokyo • Toronto

Library of Congress Cataloging-in-Publication Data

Gai, Silvano.
    Internetworking IPv6 with Cisco routers / Silvano Gai ; translated
by Antonella Caporello.
        p.   cm.— (The McGraw-Hill series on computer communications)
    Includes bibliographical references and index.
    ISBN 0-07-022836-1
    1. TCP/IP (Computer network protocol)   2. Computer networks—
Management.   I. Title.   II. Series.
    TK5105.585.G35   1998
    004.6'2—dc21   98-5075
                                                                          CIP

McGraw-Hill

A Division of The **McGraw·Hill** Companies

1 2 3 4 5 6 7 8 9 0   FGR/FGR   9 0 3 2 1 0 9 8

ISBN 0-07-022836-1

*The sponsoring editor for this book was Steven Elliot and the production
supervisor was Sherri Souffrance. It was set in Century Schoolbook by Douglas
& Gayle, Limited.*

Printed and bound by Quebecor / Fairfield.

McGraw-Hill books are available at special quantity discounts to use as
premiums and sales promotions, or for use in corporate training programs.
For more information, please write to Director of Special Sales, McGraw-Hill,
11 West 19th Street, New York, NY 10011. Or contact your local bookstore.

This book is printed on recycled, acid-free paper containing a minimum of 50%
recycled de-inked fiber.

To Antonella
with all my love, yesterday, today, forever

CONTENTS

Contents

Contents

PREFACE

We reject kings, presidents, and voting.
We believe in rough consensus
and running code

IEFT Credo

Dave Clark, 1992

This book originates from my firm belief that *Internet Protocol* (IP) will be the only layer 3 protocol to survive in the future. The present version of IP is identified by version number four, from which it derives its complete name IPv4.

IPv4 has been a standard since it was designed in September, 1981, and in these years, it has proven to be a simple and scalable protocol. Both the Internet and all Intranets are based on it. Because it is 16 years old, IPv4, although not even obsolete, is becoming dated. In the early 1990s, the *Internet Engineering Task Force* (IETF) began to design the new version of the IP protocol that became a standard in December, 1995, with the acronym IPv6.

IPv6 (also called IPng) has new and important features that will make it, in my opinion, the only layer 3 protocol of the new millennium. Among these features, the most important are undoubtedly a simple and rational design that allows it to overcome all IPv4 limits, a practically infinite addressing space, the possibility to auto-configure hosts, an efficacious support for security and mobility of nodes, a design more suitable to transport real-time traffic, and the possibility to implement a gradual and painless transition from IPv4 to IPv6.

The year of IPv6 testing has been 1997, and during 1998 IPv6 will be included as a standard feature in operating systems, in network devices, in management systems, and so on. This will trigger the transition of the Internet and of Intranets to IPv6, which will be completed at the dawn of the new century.

The migration from IPv4 to IPv6 can be implemented node by node, and this migration will allow us to benefit immediately from the many advantages of IPv6 while maintaining the possibility to communicate with IPv4 users or peripherals. Therefore, we have no reason to delay updating to IPv6 because new developments on networks, starting in 2000, will concern IPv6 only.

IPv6 will be the only protocol used in the Internet and in Intranets, and in fact, it will eliminate the distinction between these types of networks!

I tried to write this book in a simple and understandable style, using my experience in higher education for undergraduate and graduate students in the field of computer networks. The book starts from basic subjects, and it is therefore suitable to people dealing with these topics for the very first time. The book covers all the most important theoretical and practical aspects of the IPv6 protocol and of other protocols related to it (for example, ICMPv6, RIPv6, OSPFv6, BGP4+) with detailed and precise information derived from international standards (RFC: Request For Comment). I tried to place at the readers' disposal updated material compliant with most updated standards and, in some cases, to describe which are the proposals for future standards.

The main goal of this book is to help small companies to become more competitive on the international market and network managers to be better prepared and aware of ongoing changes.

From February to October, 1997, I spent a sabbatical at Cisco Systems, Inc., in San Jose, CA. These months of research offered me the chance to improve my knowledge of computer networks, and I decided to translate the first Italian version of the book into English, to update it accordingly for the most recent developments and to add a new chapter on the Cisco approach to IPv6.

I wish to express my particular thanks to Martin McNealis, Cisco Systems, for his contribution to the chapter on "Cisco and IPv6" and to Antonio Lioy from Politecnico di Torino, author of the chapter "Security Features of IPv6".

Overview

During the years between the end of the second millennium and the beginning of the third one, computer networks will benefit from the availability of many new technologies, including ATM, Gigabit Ethernet, and virtual LANs. The organization of the Internet and of Intranets will have a strong evolution thanks to the adoption of the new IPv6 protocol.

But what is IPv6? IPv6 is the new version of the *IP protocol* (Internet Protocol) on which the Internet and many Intranets are based. The work for IPv6 standardization began in 1991, and the main part was completed within 1996 with the publication of *RFCs* (Requests For Comments), standards that exactly define IPv6. During the standardization phase, this new protocol was indicated also by the terms *IPng* (IP new generation) and *IPv7*. What happened to IPv5? It lost the race, and therefore everyone agreed not to use that version number.

This book moves from the author's firm belief that, in the interim, IP will be the only layer 3 protocol to survive.

This didactic text provides a global overview of the protocol organization, of its functions, and of problems related to its adoption "in the field." In this sense, this book cannot and will not replace standard RFCs, to which readers must refer to resolve their doubts if they want to get into further details or they must deal with the design of IPv6-based plants, products, networks, and so on.

1.1   Why IPv6?

The answer is simple: "The Internet is becoming a victim of its own success." Probably many of you have heard this sentence repeated many times lately, but what does it really mean?

Ordinary users see the Internet through its applications they use daily for their work—from electronic mail, which has become user-friendly thanks to application software such as Eudora and Pegasus, to the navigation on WWW servers with powerful browsers such as Netscape or Microsoft Explorer, which today are frequently enriched with Java applets. In general, users have had a great deal of success with all Internet applications, even the more simple ones such as FTP or Telnet, and many companies have decided to reorganize their networks on the Internet model by creating Intranets.

The worldwide success of the Internet and of Intranets keeps pace with the success of the network architecture called *Internet Protocol Suite*, best known as TCP/IP, on which they are based.

In particular, the present IP protocol (Internet Protocol) is a protocol standardized in 1981 by RFC 791[1]; therefore, this protocol is a little dated even if it is a cornerstone of the architecture. To avoid confusion, in the following text we will indicate the present IP protocol that has version number 4 with the acronym *IPv4*, the new protocol with the acronym *IPv6*, and we will simply use *IP* to indicate what is common to both versions.

IP handles the decoupling of applications from transmission networks; that is, it enables users to use their preferred applications independently from the underlying network technology (see Figure 1-1).

Moreover, IP allows users to use different technologies in different parts of the network—for example, LANs (Ethernet, Token Ring, FDDI) inside buildings and frame relay or ATM public services for the geographic part of the same network.

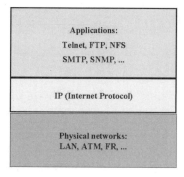

Figure 1-1
Internet Protocol (IP)

IPv4 achieves this result by providing a service with the following main characteristics:

- *Universal addressing:* Each IPv4 network interface has a unique worldwide address with 32 bits.

- *Best effort:* IPv4 performs its best effort to deliver packets, but it doesn't guarantee anything at the upper layer, neither in terms of percentage of delivered packets nor in terms of time used to execute the delivery. In short, IPv4 doesn't have a built-in concept of *Quality of Service* (QoS).

These two characteristics, which have been points of strength for IPv4 up to now, risk becoming its main limits and forcing the introduction of IPv6. Let's look at the reasons.

1.1.1   Why a New Address Scheme?

We have already seen that IPv4 addresses take up 32 bits, which means that in total about 4 billion addresses are available and, because 4 billion computers don't exist in the world, understanding the reasons that the Internet is running out of addresses is not immediately apparent. We must search for the reasons in the IPv4 address structure and in assignment procedures, which cause a significant number of assigned addresses to be unused.

In fact, IPv4 addresses are not assigned one by one (a procedure clearly impossible for organizational reasons), but by "networks." Networks belong to three different classes:

- Class A: 128 available networks, each one with about 16 million addresses

■ Class B: About 16,000 available networks, each one with about 65,000 addresses

■ Class C: About 2 million available networks, each one with 254 addresses

In January 1996, 92 class A networks, 5655 class B networks, and 87,924 class C networks were assigned. This data shows that the main problem is related to class B networks, which, for their intermediate size, are more suitable to be assigned to organizations. In fact, class A networks are too wide, and only 36 are left to be assigned, whereas class C networks are too small. Table 1-1 shows the growth trend of networks and addresses.

The problem of IPv4 address exhaustion was realized in 1991. In that year, the requests for address assignments began to grow more rapidly than any expectations. It was a historic moment when the Internet became the only network for everybody. And when we say *everybody,* we really mean everybody: public and private companies, government and private administrations, universities and research centers, and above all, private citizens. This use was made possible by ISPs (Internet Service Providers)

Table 1-1

Growth in time of networks and IPv4 addresses

Date	Host	Networks of Class:		
		A	B	C
Jan 97	16,146,000			
Jun 96	12,881,000			
Jan 96	9,472,000	92	5655	87,924
Jul 95	6,642,000	91	5390	56,057
Jan 95	4,852,000	91	4979	34,340
Oct 94	3,864,000	93	4831	32,098
Jul 94	3,212,000	89	4493	20,268
Jan 94	2,217,000	74	4043	16,422
Oct 93	2,056,000	69	3849	12,615
Jul 93	1,776,000	67	3728	9,972
Apr 93	1,486,000	58	3409	6,255
Jan 93	1,313,000	54	3206	4,998

that provide low-cost connections to the Internet through telephone lines first by using modems and, more recently, ISDN access. A further turning point is very recent: the introduction of xDSL and "cable modems" to provide all domestic users with high-speed connections to the Internet (faster than 1 Mbps).

In 1991, forecasts were that class B addresses would be used up within 1994. To face this dramatic forecast and to leave a reasonable amount of time for the development and the migration to IPv6, the IETF (Internet Engineering Task Force), the committee responsible for technical decisions for IP and for the Internet, decided to assign not only class B networks, but also blocks of class C "adjacent" networks. For example, an organization with 100 computers with a growth forecast to 500 computers could be assigned, instead of a class B network, a block of four class C networks for a total of about 1000 addresses.

This new and more conservative policy of address assignment moves forward the moment in which IPv4 addresses will be exhausted: Some very uncertain forecasts identify a date between 2005 and 2015.

There is no rose without a thorn, as an old saying goes, and also this addressing scheme immediately generates problems on routers that are forced to maintain routing information for each network. In fact, if an organization is assigned a class B network, routers must have only one routing entry, but if it is assigned 16 class C networks, routers must have 16 different routing entries, using 16 times more memory for routing tables. To avoid this problem, the CIDR (Classless InterDomain Routing)[2] was introduced in 1992, which in substance means that the concept of network class at the routing table level is eliminated.

In the end, the suggestion is that all Intranets use the same addresses, and to this purpose the RFC 1597[3] was issued, later replaced by the RFC 1918[4], assigning Intranets a class A network (the 10.0.0.0) and some class B and C networks.

At this point, it should be clear that IPv6 needs a new addressing scheme with the following characteristics:

- A higher number of bits so that the addressing space is not subject to further exhaustion

- A more flexible hierarchical organization of addresses that doesn't use the concept of classes, but the CIDR mechanism

- A scheme for address assignment aimed to minimize the size of routing tables on routers and to increase the CIDR performance

- Global addresses for the Internet and local addresses for Intranets

1.1.2   Best Effort: Is It Enough?

IPv4 is a connectionless protocol. This means that it transmits each packet independently from other ones, specifying in the packet header IPv4 addresses of the source and of the destination. The packet is neither marked as belonging to a flow or to a connection, nor numbered in any way. Therefore, it is neither possible to correct errors at this level nor to understand whether a packet has been delivered, or if so, what was the delivery time. This kind of service is called "best effort" because every IPv4 node performs at its best to deliver the packet in the minimum time, but it cannot guarantee if and when the delivery will happen.

Best effort connectionless protocols can be implemented easily and have a limited and constant overhead. These characteristics allowed IPv4 to become popular—and eventually the only surviving layer 3 protocol.

Nevertheless, the availability of new high-speed ATM networks guaranteeing the QoS[5], on the one hand, and the need to develop new multimedia applications requiring a guaranteed QoS, on the other hand, have led to discussions of whether "best effort" choice is still to be considered the best one for IPv6.

The IETF has already recognized the lack of the concept of QoS as a limit of IP, and it has developed an additional protocol, called RSVP (Resource reSerVation Protocol)[6], to allocate resources on routers and make them suitable to guarantee the QoS for IPv4-based applications that explicitly require a given QoS through RSVP.

IPv6, while remaining faithful to the IPv4 connectionless origin, introduces the concept of flow as a better integration mechanism toward QoS concepts and with RSVP.

1.2   Requirements to Be Met by IPv6

Up to now, we have discussed reasons to switch from IPv4 to IPv6, and we have caught a glimpse of some characteristics that differentiate IPv6 from IPv4. The question to be answered now is: Which characteristics do we want to maintain, which ones do we want to eliminate, and which new ones do we want to introduce?

A risk that the IETF has always taken into consideration is the "second generation syndrome," which consists of adding everything that users ask with the risk of obtaining a slow, not manageable, and useless protocol.

Let's inspect the main expectations that emerged about IPv6[7].

1.2.1   An Address Space to Last Forever

The expectation here mainly depends on what we mean by the term *forever*. A proposal could be to have an IPv6 address for every potential Internet user. We can estimate that the world population will reach 10 billion people and assume that each person will have more than one computer because, in the future, home appliances, electro-medical devices, and electrical devices in general will be computers. Today, we already have available domestic lighting systems in which lamps have an address and are turned on and off by messages sent by switches on a service bus. In the future, Internet users might want to order from outside their homes that an oven begin to cook a turkey, or to receive a message from their home alarms to detect a possible intrusion, or to control their Internet browsers using remote-controlled video cameras. The examples are diverse; cellular telephones with Java terminals inside already appear on the market. An estimate of 256 IPv6 addresses for each planet inhabitant is not unrealistic.

A more drastic proposal is to try to estimate the number of IPv6 addresses based on the number of atoms in the universe, keeping in mind that you only need about an atom to build a computer. But, be careful not to exaggerate; in fact, having more addresses means a greater length of IPv6 address fields, and because both the source and the destination address must be transported within each IPv6 packet header, this means more overhead.

On the other hand, everybody agrees to define an addressing space that is not subject to exhaustion in the future.

Besides the number of addresses to be assigned, considering the efficiency of the assignment scheme is also important. An accurate study by Christian Huitema[8] proposes to define the efficiency of address assignment H as the ratio between the logarithm in base 10 of the number of used addresses and the address bits number.

$$H\ 5\ \frac{\log_{10}\ (\text{address number})}{\text{bits number}}$$

In a scheme with a maximum efficiency rate, all addresses are used; therefore, H is equal to the base 10 logarithm of 2 (that is, H = 0.301). An analysis of real addressing schemes shows that H varies between 0.22 and 0.26.

The final decision is to predict one million billion networked computers (10^{15}) that, with H equal to 0.22 (the worst case), require 68-bit addresses. Because the address, for implementation reasons, must be a multiple of 32 bits, it has been opted for having the IPv6 address on 128 bits (that is, 16 bytes or 4 words of 32 bits).

1.2.2   Multicast and Anycast Addresses

Besides Layer 3 unicast addresses (described previously), IPv4 also utilizes multicast or class D addresses for applications that require group communications such as video conferencing on the Internet. The concept of multicast addresses is also handled in IPv6.

IPv6 also introduces a new type of address called *anycast*. These addresses also are group addresses in which the only member of the group to respond is the "closest" to the source. The use of anycast addresses is potentially very interesting because the closest router, the closest name server, or time server can be accessed by an anycast address.

1.2.3   To Unify Intranets and the Internet

IPv6 must provide a unified addressing scheme for the Internet and for Intranets, overcoming temporary IPv4 solutions (RFC 1597[3] and RFC 1918[4]). For this purpose, besides global addresses, site addresses and link local addresses also have been developed. Site addresses should be used for network nodes inside Intranets, whereas link local addresses are used to identify nodes attached to a single link (small networks without a router).

Lastly, addresses with embedded IPv4, OSI NSAP, and Novell IPX addresses have been developed.

1.2.4   Using LANs Better

When IPv4 operates on a LAN, it frequently needs to determine the relationship between an IPv4 address and a MAC address, and vice versa. IPv4 performs this function through an auxiliary protocol called *ARP* (Address Resolution Protocol)[9] that utilizes broadcast MAC layer transmissions. A broadcast packet is received by all stations and causes an interruption on all stations, including those not using the IP protocol. This ineffectiveness must be corrected in IPv6 by using a "neighbor discovery" method on LAN more efficient than ARP and utilizing multicast, not broadcast, transmissions. In fact, a station can determine at the network adapter level which multicast to receive, while it is obliged to receive all broadcasts.

1.2.5   Security

The security in IPv4 is today managed through particular routers or computers performing the role of *firewalls*. They cannot solve intrinsic IPv4 security problems, but they can counterbalance many computers' operating system weaknesses and the superficial management of security that frequently exists at a single computer level.

IPv6 is not necessarily requested to improve the security state of the art, but it will not make the situation worse. As a matter of fact, the IETF defined a series of encryption and authentication procedures that will be available in the IPv6 protocol in the beginning. These procedures will also be implemented in a compatible way in IPv4.

Moreover, IPv6 has a careful management of *Source Routing*, that is, of the possibility to determine at source station level the path to be followed by an IP packet. This function, already available in IPv4 but not always implemented or active, is frequently exploited by hackers to try to bypass firewalls.

Many network administrators will undoubtedly find in the availability of standard security procedures one of the main reasons for migrating to IPv6.

1.2.6 Routing

Routing is clearly one of the central themes in the design of a protocol expected to route packets on the future Internet. If we consider IPv4 routing as a starting point, we can see that routing tables of Internet routers tend to explode. In fact, if the CIDR is not used, every single network must be announced by an entry in routing tables. The CIDR introduction[2] allows us to announce a block of networks with contiguous addresses (for example, 195.1.4.0, 195.1.5.0, 195.1.6.0, and 195.1.7.0) as a unique entry by specifying how many bits must be considered as significant (in our example, 195.1.4.0/22, which is each network with the first 22 bits equal to 195.1.4.0).

In any case, the CIDR can do little if it is not connected to the address assignment. In fact, if addresses are assigned to ISPs (Internet Service Providers) and by them to users, the CIDR works properly because, from a theoretical point of view, all addresses of a single ISP can be announced by a unique entry. We can think of a form of hierarchical routing accompanied also by a hierarchical kind of address assignment bound to the network topology. At the root of the hierarchical tree, we can think of an address assignment by continents; then within a continent, an assignment by ISPs; then by organizations; and eventually by networks within organizations. This model minimizes tables on routers, allowing the CIDR to aggregate addresses first by user, then by ISP, and eventually by continent, but this model has a big limit: The users don't have any more addresses permanently assigned to them.

If we consider how the IPv4 address assignment is managed nowadays, an organization can contact authorities such as INTERNIC (Northern America), APNIC (Asia and Pacific) and RIPE-NCC (Europe) to obtain addresses that the organization will use independently from the ISP it will be connected to. This way, the organization can change ISPs without changing addresses. With IPv6, when an organization changes ISPs, it necessarily must change addresses. An organization may even have to change addresses because two ISPs have merged or separated; therefore, the organization must change addresses even if it doesn't want to.

The address assignment model based on the network topology is acceptable in IPv6 only if autoconfiguration mechanisms (plug and play) are available (that is, networks dynamically assign addresses to stations).

So far, we have talked about computation of routing tables used for default routing toward a given destination. IPv6 also addresses the possibility of having policy routing and QoS (in this context called *ToS*, or *Type of Service*). An example of routing based on a particular policy is one that determines the transmission of packets to a given destination on a path determined also by the source address (this was impossible in Ipv4).

The IPv6 routing must also provide good support for mobility—for example, to those users who, by means of a portable PC and a cellular phone, can connect themselves to the Internet in different places.

1.2.7   A Good Support for ATM

The great industrial effort related to the development of *ATM* (Asynchronous Transfer Mode)[5] will make this technology one of the most important actors in future wide area and local area networks. IPv6 designers, well aware of this fact, tried to improve the support of ATM in IPv6. But what are ATM's peculiarities? ATM is an NBMA (Non-Broadcast Multiple Access) network, and it guarantees the QoS.

An NBMA network[10] is a multipoint access network that doesn't provide a simple mechanism to transmit a packet to all other stations. IPv4 has been designed to work either on point-to-point channels that have only two endpoints or on local networks that have multiple access, but where a packet transmission to a single station or to all stations has exactly the same cost. Other NBMA networks are, for example, X.25 and Frame Relay (if equipped with signaling), but the need to provide a good IP support on NBMA networks emerged only with ATM because of the role that this technology will play in the future.

Guaranteeing the QoS means associating to each data flow a given set of quality requirements. For example, if the data flow has been generated by a file transfer, that the loss rate is equal to zero is very important, whereas the delay to which packets are subject along the path is irrelevant. If the data flow is generated by an audio or video source, a certain rate of loss of data can be tolerated (we can understand audio and video signals also if uncompleted), but guaranteeing limited and less variable delays from a packet to another is fundamental.

We must also remember that the QoS can be used only if it is requested by applications, an action that today's applications don't perform. We need to foresee that applications request the QoS through a protocol like RSVP[6] (see Section 1.2.2) and that this one, by jointly operating with IPv6, transforms the QoS request into a QoS request for the ATM network (see Figure 1-2).

Figure 1-2
Handling of QoS requests

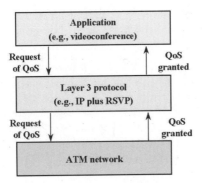

Figure 1-2
Handling of QoS requests

1.2.8 The Concept of Flow

To simplify the implementation of IPv6 on ATM and the QoS management, we need to introduce the concept of *flow*. A flow is a sequence of packets in some way correlated (for example, because they have been generated by the same application) and that therefore must be treated coherently by the IP layer. Packets belong to the same flow on the basis of parameters like the source address, the destination address, the QoS, the accounting, the authentication, and the security.

No relationships exist between the concept of flow and other concepts such as TCP connection; for example, a flow can contain several TCP connections. Moreover, we must emphasize that the introduction of the concept of flow occurs on a protocol that is and remains connectionless (also frequently called a *datagram*); therefore, flows do not have the same purposes of connection-oriented protocols—for example, correction of errors. In general, a flow can have as its destination either a single station or a group of stations; therefore, we can have either unicast or multicast flows.

After the concept of flow has been introduced, we can introduce the flow label concept by which we will mark packets or datagrams by reserving a special field in the IPv6 header. In this way, IPv6 has the possibility, at the moment it receives a packet, to know to which flow it belongs by examining its flow label and, as a result, to know the packet needs in terms of QoS.

1.2.9 Priorities

Even if an application doesn't request a QoS, differentiating the traffic generated by principal applications as a function of their real-time requirements is possible. For this purpose, a 4-bit "priority" field has been introduced in the IPv6 header to differentiate 16 potential traffic priorities. Up to now, priorities have been defined for news, e-mail, FTP, NFS, Telnet, X, routing, and SNMP protocols.

1.2.10   Plug and Play

In Section 1.3.1, we saw how IPv6 needs autoconfiguration (or plug and play) mechanisms to manage addresses that can change in the long run. Moreover, manual management is inconvenient because an IPv6 address requires that 32 hexadecimal digits be written (for example, **FEDC:BA98: 1234:5678:0BCA:9987:0102:1230**).

The *DHCP* (Dynamic Host Configuration Protocol)[11], available on some IPv4 implementations, has been considered a good starting point. The idea is to develop a DHCPv6 protocol that allows the automatic configuration of hosts and subnetworks, the learning of default routers, and through an interaction with the DNS (Domain Name Service)[12], also an automatic configuration of host names.

The implementation of the DHCPv6 on all IPv6 hosts will allow network administrators to reconfigure addresses by operating on the primary DHCPv6 server.

1.2.11   Mobility

As we already mentioned, an increasing number of Internet users don't work at their office desks anymore but work while traveling. Mobile users are usually equipped with portable PCs with the PCMCIA network card, which connects them to a cellular telephone or to a public network via radio.

IPv4 doesn't provide any support for mobility. In fact, every computer has a fixed address that belongs to a network. If the computer is connected to a different network, packets sent to it continue to reach the original network, and there they are lost.

Clearly, providing support for mobility is a main requirement for IPv6: It has been estimated that, in Northern America, there will be from 20 to 40 million mobile users in 2007. Also, this requirement is one of the more complex to be met, as it has to deal with a range of problems, starting from those related to radio transmission (reliability, roaming, hand-off) to those related to IP protocols (identification, addressing, configuration, routing) to security problems.

The solution that is taking shape predicts that mobile users will have two addresses: the first one "permanent" on their organization's network and the second one "dynamic" depending on the point from which they are connected in a given moment. The organization's firewall, when the users are traveling, acts as "proxy" for the permanent address and creates a safe tunnel toward the dynamic address.

1.2.12 Transition from IPv4 to IPv6

Many users will consider the transition to IPv6 as something they must resign themselves to so that they can obtain the potential advantages discussed previously. But people, like me, who have experienced other transitions know that, even if such transitions are well planned, they can easily end up as a "blood bath." Changing the network software is similar to changing the operation system version: This step potentially brings forward some incompatibilities and causes the need to update both the hardware and the software.

The IETF decided to design a migration strategy based on a "dual-stack" approach, but this approach will be a field in which computer and network vendors will fight strongly to simplify users' lives and to win market share. In fact, very few users will be able to migrate at a given moment; many organizations will have a transition period lasting months or even years, during which IPv6 must coexist with IPv4.

For this reason, the IETF decided that IPv4 and IPv6 will be two different protocols with two corresponding and separated protocol stacks. When a station receives a frame from its local network, the *Protocol Type* allows it to distinguish whether the frame contains an IPv4 or an IPv6 packet, with the same mechanisms that allow it to distinguish between IPv4 and Decnet packets today. In fact, we know that IPv4 packets have a protocol type equal to 0800H (800 Hexadecimal), and IPv6 packets have a protocol type equal to 86DDH.

Therefore, the first field of IPv4 and of IPv6 packets, representing the protocol version (that can assume values 4 or 6), will remain unused because the IPv4 stack will receive only IPv4 packets and the IPv6 stack will receive only IPv6 packets.

One of the critical steps in the transition will be the parallel management of IPv4 and IPv6 addresses. A timely updating of DNS servers will be necessary, followed by the updating of DHCP servers. A dual-stack station will use the IPv4 address (32 bits wide) to communicate with other IPv4 stations, and it will use the IPv6 address (128 bits wide) to communicate with other IPv6 stations.

For this approach to be successful, IPv6 islands must be interconnected. This connection will be implemented through a series of tunnels on the Internet, and therefore on IPv4, that will form a layered network called *6-Bone*. This approach is based on the positive experience of *Mbone*, the network used for video conferencing on the Internet, that has been successfully implemented following the same philosophy.

6-Bone will grow and some islands will directly interconnect using IPv6, without needing tunnels. An increasing number of machines will communicate by using IPv6; then the end of IPv4 will arrive, when all computers running only the IPv4 protocol stack will lose their direct global connectivity to the Internet.

1.3   Choice Criteria

The need to meet all these requirements reveals how difficult the choice of the new IPv6 has been, because this protocol will be entrusted with the destiny of the Internet and Intranets. The previously listed requirements are joined by another one to maintain the critical router loop simply. The *critical router loop* is the set of code lines that route most packets, all those packets that don't have particular requests apart from reaching the destination. The critical router loop determines the router's performance more than any other part of the code, and a careless addition of all the new requested and previously mentioned functions will complicate the situation too much.

For this reason, IPv6 designers Steven Deering and Robert Hinden decided to take to themselves a famous maxim by Antoine de Saint-Exupery, the author of *The Little Prince*, a nice book that I suggest everybody read, about architectural simplicity:

> The architectural simplicity
> In each thing, you reach the perfection, not when there is nothing left to add, but when there is nothing left to take off.
>
> *Antoine de Saint-Exupery*

The result is a protocol with an extremely pure design and a small header with few fields. In fact, the IPv4 header (see Figure 1-3) consists of 24 bytes, 8 of which are used for IPv4 addresses and the remaining 16 bytes by 12 additional fields.

The IPv6 header (see Figure 1-4) has only 40 bytes, 32 of which are used for IPv6 addresses and the remaining 8 bytes by 6 additional fields.

And what about all the fields needed to implement many new additional functions? They have been inserted in various *extension headers*

Figure 1-3
The IPv4 header

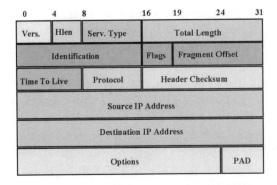

0	4	8	16	19	24	31

Vers.	Hlen	Serv. Type	Total Length			
Identification			Flags	Fragment Offset		
Time To Live		Protocol	Header Checksum			
Source IP Address						
Destination IP Address						
Options					PAD	

Figure 1-4
The IPv6 header

Version	Priorit.	Flow Label	
Payload Length		Next Header	Hop Limit
Source Address			
Destination Address			

that are present only if the function is effectively requested. In this way, most packets pass very quickly through critical router loops, and only packets with particular requests receive a more sophisticated treatment that provides for the extension header's analysis. In any case, many extension headers have "end-to-end" functions; therefore, they don't need to be processed by routers, but only by source and destination nodes. (A typical example is represented by the encryption extension header.)

1.4 The Path Toward Standardization

The path toward standardization formally began in 1992, when the IETF, during a meeting in Boston, issued a "call for proposal" for IPv6 and many working groups were created.

The main proposals for IPv6 are described in the following subsections.

1.4.1   TUBA

The proposal known as TUBA (TCP and UDP over Bigger Addresses)[13] suggested the adoption of the ISO/OSI 8473 CLNP protocol to replace IPv4, trying in this way to create a fusion *in extremis* between the OSI world and the Internet world. This solution would have allowed users to have at their disposal OSI NSAP 20-byte addresses and a common platform on which OSI transport protocols, such as TP4 and the cited TCP and UDP, could be used.

The main censure made against CLNP by the Internet world was that it had been copied 10 years before from IPv4 by introducing some depreciatory modifications.

Supporters of the TUBA proposal, in the first two years of discussions, remained faithful to the original CLNP project, refusing to introduce innovative aspects such as multicasting, mobility, and QoS for reasons of incompatibility with the OSI installed base (of secondary importance). This stubbornness brought about the failure of the TUBA proposal, later followed by a general failure of the OSI CLNP.

1.4.2   IPv7, TP/IX, CATNIP

In 1992, Robert Ullmann advanced the proposal of a new IP protocol called IPv7. The proposal was re-elaborated in 1993 and assumed the name of TP/IX to indicate the will to change both the IP protocol and the TCP protocol at the same time. The proposal contained interesting ideas about speed packet processing and a new routing protocol called RAP. In 1994, the proposal had a further evolution, trying to define a unique format for IP, CLNP, and IPX packets, and assumed the new name of CATNIP[14]. CATNIP would have been a common platform supporting several transport protocols such as OSI/TP4, TCP, UDP, and SPX. Layer 3 addresses adopted by CATNIP were of OSI/NSAP type.

1.4.3   IP in IP, IPAE

IP in IP was a proposal made in 1992, designed to use two IPv4 layers to limit the address shortage at the Internet level: a layer to implement a worldwide backbone and a second layer within limited areas. In 1993, the proposal was developed further and was called IPAE (IP Address Encapsulation) and accepted as a transition solution toward SIP.

1.4.4 SIP

SIP (Simple IP) was proposed by Steve Deering in November 1992. It was based on the idea of bringing IP addresses to 64 bits and to eliminate some obsolete IPv4 details. This proposal was immediately accepted by many companies who appreciated its simplicity.

1.4.5 PIP

PIP (Paul's Internet Protocol), a proposal by Paul Francis, introduced significant innovations on the front of routing by allowing an efficient policy routing and mobility implementation. In September 1993, PIP merged with SIP, thus creating SIPP.

1.4.6 SIPP

SIPP (Simple IP Plus)[15] tried to combine the implementation simplicity of SIP and the routing flexibility of PIP. SIPP was designed to work efficiently on high-performance networks, such as ATM, but also on low-performance networks, such as wireless networks. SIPP has a small size header and 64-bit addresses.

The header coding is particularly emphasized. With SIPP, the header can be efficiently elaborated by routers and can be extended to insert new options in the future.

1.5 The Evaluation

A comparative evaluation of the last three proposals (CATNIP, SIPP, and TUBA) brought about the results shown in Table 1-2.

Table 1-2

Comparative analysis of three proposals for IPv6

	CATNIP	SIPP	TUBA
Complete specification	no	yes	mostly
Simplicity	no	no	no
Scale	yes	yes	yes
Topological flexibility	yes	yes	yes
Performance	mixed	mixed	mixed
Robust service	mixed	mixed	yes
Transition mechanisms	mixed	no	mixed
Media independence	yes	yes	yes
Connectionless service (datagram)	yes	yes	yes
Configuration simplicity	unknown	mixed	mixed
Security	unknown	yes	mixed
Name uniqueness	mixed	mixed	mixed
Standards access	yes	yes	mixed
Multicast support	unknown	yes	mixed
Extensibility	unknown	mixed	mixed
Availability of service classes	unknown	yes	mixed
Mobility support	unknown	mixed	mixed
Control protocol	unknown	yes	mixed
Tunneling support	unknown	yes	mixed

1.6   The Final Decision

The decision made in June 1994 was to adopt SIPP as a base for IPv6 with the modification of the address length from 64 to 128 bits.

1.7   Conclusion

The point of no return has been passed, a new IP protocol is at last a standard, and it will be a main actor in our future. Some competitors have been defeated, and among them the worst defeat was to OSI CLNP. But now it is time to forget *ifs* and *buts* and to begin to work on these new standards. Currently, RFCs from **17** to **36** are already available.

REFERENCES

[1]J. Postel, *RFC 791: Internet Protocol*, September 1981.

[2]V. Fuller, T. Li, J. Yu, K. Varadhan, *RFC 1519: Classless Inter-Domain Routing (CIDR): An Address Assignment and Aggregation Strategy*, September 1993.

[3]Y. Rekhter, B. Moskowitz, D. Karrenberg, G. de Groot, *RFC 1597: Address Allocation for Private Internets*, March 1994.

[4]Y. Rekhter, B. Moskowitz, D. Karrenberg, G. J. de Groot, E. Lear, *RFC 1918: Address Allocation for Private Internets*, February 1996.

[5]Uyless Black, *ATM: Foundation for Broadband Networks*, Prentice Hall, 1995.

[6]B. Braden, L. Zhang, D. Estrin, S. Herzog, S. Jamin, *RSVP: Resource ReSerVation Protocol (RSVP)— Version 1 Functional Specification*, Work in progress, January 1996.

[7]S.O. Bradner, A. Mankin, *IPng: Internet Protocol Next Generation*, Addison-Wesley, 1995.

[8]C. Huitema, *IPv6: The New Internet Protocol*, Prentice-Hall, 1996.

[9]D.C. Plummer, *RFC 826: Ethernet Address Resolution Protocol: On converting network protocol addresses to 48 bit Ethernet address for transmission on Ethernet hardware*, November 1982.

[10]J. Heinanen, R. Govindan, *RFC 1735: NBMA Address Resolution Protocol (NARP)*, December 1994.

[11]R. Droms, *RFC 1541: Dynamic Host Configuration Protocol*, October 1993.

[12]P.V. Mockapetris, *RFC 1035: Domain names—implementation and specification*, November 1987.

[13]R. Callon, *RFC 1347: TCP and UDP with Bigger Addresses (TUBA), A Simple Proposal for Internet Addressing and Routing*, June 1992.

[14]M. McGovern, R. Ullmann, *RFC 1707: CATNIP: Common Architecture for the Internet*, October 1994.

[15]R. Hinden, *RFC 1710: Simple Internet Protocol Plus White Paper*, October 1994.

[16]S. Bradner, A. Mankin, *RFC 1752: The Recommendation for the IP Next Generation Protocol*, January 1995.

[17]C. Partridge, *RFC 1809: Using the Flow Label Field in IPv6*, June 1995.

[18]IAB, IESG, *RFC 1881: IPv6 Address Allocation Management*, December 1995.

[19]S. Deering, R. Hinden, *RFC 1883: Internet Protocol, Version 6 (IPv6) Specification*, December 1995.

[20]R. Hinden, S. Deering, *RFC 1884: IP Version 6 Addressing Architecture*, December 1995.

[21]A. Conta, S. Deering, *RFC 1885: Internet Control Message Protocol (ICMPv6)*, December 1995.

[22]S. Thomson, C. Huitema, *RFC 1886: DNS Extensions to support IP version 6*, December 1995.

[23]Y. Rekhter, T. Li, *RFC 1887; An Architecture for IPv6 Unicast Address Allocation*, December 1995.

[24]R. Hinden, J. Postel, *RFC 1897: IPv6 Testing Address Allocation*, January 1996.

[25]R. Elz, *RFC 1924: A Compact Representation of IPv6 Addresses*, April 1996.

[26]R. Gilligan, E. Nordmar, *RFC 1933: Transition Mechanisms for IPv6 Hosts and Routers*, April 1996.

[27]T. Narten, E. Nordmark, W. Simpson, *RFC 1970: Neighbor Discovery for IP Version 6 (IPv6)*, August 1996.

[28]S. Thomson, T. Narten, *RFC 1971: IPv6 Stateless Address Autoconfiguration*, August 1996.

[29]M. Crawford, *RFC 1972: A Method for the Transmission of IPv6 Packets over Ethernet Networks*, August 1996.

[30]M. Crawford, *RFC 2019: Transmission of IPv6 Packets Over FDDI*, October 1996.

[31]D. Haskin, E. Allen, *RFC 2023: IP Version 6 over PPP*, October 1996.

[32]D. Mills, *RFC 2030: Simple Network Time Protocol (SNTP) Version 4 for IPv4, IPv6 and OSI*, October 1996.

[33]Y. Rekhter, P. Lothberg, R. Hinden, S. Deering, J. Postel, *RFC 2073: An IPv6 Provider-Based Unicast Address Format,* January 1997.

[34]G. Malkin, R. Minnear, *RFC 2080: RIPng for IPv6*, January 1997.

[35]R. Gilligan, S. Thomson, J. Bound, W. Stevens, *RFC 2133: Basic Socket Interface Extensions for IPv6,* April 1997.

[36]D. Borman, *RFC 2147: TCP and UDP over IPv6 Jumbograms,* May 1997.

2

An Overview
of IPv6

This second chapter is meant to provide a general overview of the IPv6 protocol and of the way network layer protocols operate. These descriptions are partly valid also for other protocols such as IPv4[1] or ISO 8473[2] (the connectionless OSI protocol); the aim is to introduce readers to routing problems on the Internet and Intranets. The following chapters will examine further the different aspects mentioned in this chapter and the details of how the IPv6 protocol operates. This approach has the disadvantage of introducing repetition in the general treatment, but I hope it will allow readers to have a general overview of the protocol, in which the different aspects can be inserted after a more thorough analysis.

2.1   Terminology

Before discussing the treatment of IPv6, let me introduce terms used in standards[3]:

- *node*: A device that implements IPv6.
- *router*: A node that forwards IPv6 packets not explicitly addressed to itself.
- *host*: Any node that is not a router.
- *upper layer*: A protocol layer immediately above IPv6—for example, transport protocols such as TCP and UDP, control protocols such as ICMP, routing protocols such as OSPF, or lower layer protocols being tunneled over IPv6 such as IPX and AppleTalk.
- *link*: A communication facility or medium over which nodes can communicate at the Data Link layer—that is, at layer 2 of the ISO/OSI reference model. Examples of links are Ethernet, PPP, X.25, Frame Relay, and ATM, or tunnels over other protocols such as IPv4 or IPv6 itself.
- *neighbors*: Nodes attached to the same link.
- *interface*: A node's attachment to a link.
- *address*: An IPv6 layer identifier for an interface or a set of interfaces.
- *packet*: An IPv6 layer PDU (Protocol Data Unit)—that is, the IPv6 header plus the payload.
- *datagram*: A synonym for *packet*.
- *link MTU*: The Maximum Transmission Unit—that is, the maximum packet size in octets (bytes) that can be conveyed unfragmented over a link.
- *path MTU*: The minimum link MTU of all the links in a path between a source node and a destination node.

2.2   Architecture of a Network

The terminology introduced in the preceding sections allows us to understand that, in general, an IPv6 network will be formed by a certain number of *routers* interconnected with a partially meshed topology, as shown in Figure 2-1.

Figure 2-1
An example of a network

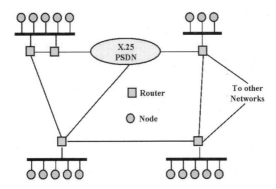

The choice of a partially meshed topology is justified by reasons of re-liability. In fact, the mesh has alternative paths that can be used in case of fault. *Hosts* are generally interconnected to routers through *LANs* (lo-cal area networks)[4].

2.3 Addresses and Names

To reach all nodes in a network, the first problem to be solved is the unique identification of each node. IPv6 assigns a 128-bit numerical *address* to each network interface[5]. Nevertheless, in most cases, users find referring to a node using a *name* more convenient than using *a numerical address*. The name and the address of a system have the same purpose: the unique identification of an interface within the network. Nevertheless, the address is thought to interact with routing mechanisms and is therefore numeri-cal, whereas the name is thought to be more easily remembered by the users and is therefore alphanumerical and mnemonic. Maintaining a bi-univocal relation between names and addresses is clearly necessary, and doing so is more complex than one might think. In fact, in a small network, each computer maintaining a file with this relationship is foreseeable, but with the growth of network sizes, adopting a distributed database, called DNS (*Domain Name Service*), is essential[6].

If we want to use IP to build a worldwide computer network like the Internet, the addresses must be unique at the worldwide level. This requirement was already met by IPv4 addresses, but IPv6 extends the addresses to cope with the growth of the Internet and Intranets. This uniqueness is typically obtained through organizations that assign sets of addresses to end users.

These sets are called *networks* in IPv4 and can be subdivided into smaller sets, called *subnetworks*, through a parameter called a *netmask*. IPv4 requires that each link be associated to a subnetwork[*] so that checking whether two nodes are connected to the same link is easy; they are connected if their IP addresses belong to the same subnetwork.

In IPv6, the address organization is similar, but with two important differences:

■ Addresses are longer (128 bits in IPv6 compared to 32 bits in IPv4).

■ The concept of netmask is replaced by the concept of prefix. The prefix indicates how many bits are used to identify the subnetwork.

For example, in an IPv6 address with a prefix equal to 80, 80 bits will be used to identify the subnetwork and 48 bits to identify nodes within the subnetwork.

2.4   Routers and Internetworking

When a user wants to use an application on a given computer, that user can request it on the network by specifying the name of the computer; the network consults the Domain Name Service and extracts the IPv6 address of the remote computer. The address of the destination computer becomes the key element to determine the most suitable routing to reach the remote node. A first check made by the sender is whether the destination is connected to the same physical network of the sender; in this case, the transmission can occur directly. In the opposite case, an operation of *internetworking* is essential; the sender forwards the packet, and the router attends to its delivery.

The router's main task is precisely to route messages on the network. The chosen routing technique depends on the adopted network architecture. Connectionless protocols, such as IPv4, IPv6, IPX, DECnet, OSI-CLNP, and so on, use a technique known as *routing by network address*. A node is addressed by writing in the layer 3 packet (ISO/OSI reference model) its address, which must be unique on the network. Each router

---

[*]As a matter of fact, many IPv4 implementations release this original constraint, that it is preferable to observe to obtain better performance; this constraint has been reintroduced in IPv6.

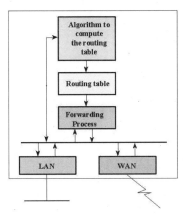

Figure 2-2
Routers internal architecture

uses this address as an index in its routing table and determines the path on which the packet must be retransmitted.

At this point, the important role of the *routing table* present on routers should be explained (see Figure 2-2).

When a packet reaches a router through a local or a geographical network interface, the router passes the packet to its *forwarding process*, which extracts the source address, uses this address to examine the routing tables, and decides on which interface to retransmit the packet.

2.5 The Routing Table

The routing table of an IPv6 router contains one *entry* for each subnetwork reachable from the router itself. A general scheme for a routing table organization[7] is shown in Figure 2-3. Routing tables can be written manually or computed automatically by appropriate protocols such as RIP[8] or OSPF[9].

In the example shown in Figure 2-3, we decided to use the name of the *subnetwork* itself, not its extended address. In the case of IPv6, for example, an address of the type **FEDC:BB87:0:0:0:0:0:0/80**, which is the address of a subnetwork with an 80-bits prefix (the syntax of IPv6 addresses will be explained in Chapter 4), can be associated to the name Delta.

Likewise, for the *Next Hop* field, for example, the Router-4 could have address **FEDC:BB87:0:0:0:0800:2B3C:4D73**.

The *Type* field indicates the type of reachability associated to the subnetwork. *Direct* indicates that the router has an interface directly connected to the subnetwork; *Static* indicates that a routing rule to reach the

Figure 2-3
Example of a routing
table

Subnetwork	Next Hop	Type	Cost	Age	Status
Alpha	-	Direct	1	-	UP
Tau	-	Direct	1	-	DOWN
Beta	-	Direct	1	-	UP
Delta	Router-27	RIP	10	27	UP
Omega	Router-5	OSPF	5	13	UP
Gamma	Router-4	Static	2	-	UP

subnetwork has been written manually; *RIP* and *OSPF* indicate that the subnetwork reachability has been learned by the router through an appropriate protocol.

The *Age* field specifies the left validity in seconds, and it is significant only for entries associated to subnetworks whose reachability information has been learned through protocols for the automatic computation of the routing table. In fact, dynamic entries must be periodically updated.

The *Status* field indicates the entry's state. In our example, the router interface associated to the subnetwork Tau is down; therefore, the associated reliability information is not usable.

The router forwarding process uses the routing table for each packet by searching in the subnetwork column for which subnetwork the destination address belongs and then by routing the packet to the associated Next Hop. Note that Direct entries don't have a Next Hop because the router has an interface directly connected to those subnetworks and can therefore directly reach all the subnetwork nodes by link layer (also called layer 2 or Data Link layer) transmission (IPv6 terminology).

2.6   Layer 2 and Layer 3 Addresses

Until now, we have referred to 128-bit IPv6 addresses, corresponding to ISO/OSI reference model layer 3 or network layer addresses. Nevertheless, when a packet must be routed on a subnetwork, the transmission must occur at layer 2, which is at the link layer. Therefore, we must know and use layer 2 addresses. In the case of LANs, these addresses are the 48-bit MAC addresses; in the case of ATM, the 20-octet ATM addresses; and in the case of the point-to-point channels, they do not exist.

The need for two types of addresses can be summarized as follows:

■ The link layer address is used to identify the final destination of a packet within a physical network (IP subnetwork).

■ The layer 3 address is used to identify the final destination of a packet within the whole network.

Different methodologies are available to maintain the mapping between link layer addresses and layer 3 addresses within a subnetwork. The best known is based on the ARP (Address Resolution Protocol)[10], which is adopted by IPv4 but not by IPv6, which uses the newer Neighbor Discovery[11] protocol.

The example shown in Figure 2-4 explains the role of the two types of addresses. Suppose that we want to transmit a packet from the host B to the host A. The transmission occurs in the following four phases, through three different packets identified with (a), (b), and (c) in Figure 2-4:

1. The host B generates an IPv6 packet with destination address equal to A and source address equal to B; this packet will remain unchanged until it reaches the destination. B checks whether A is on the same LAN, and if this is not true, B sends the message to R2 by inserting the IPv6 packet into a layer 2 envelope with a destination link address equal to R2 and source link address equal to B (packet (a)).

2. The router R2 receives the packet (a) and uses its routing table to decide to retransmit the packet on the point-to-point WAN link. In this case, as we are in the presence of a point-to-point channel, the presence of link layer addresses in the packet (b) is not necessary.

Figure 2-4
Link and IPv6 addresses

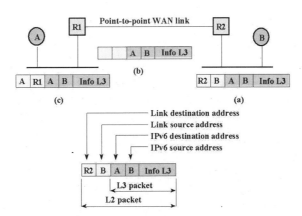

3. The router R1 receives the packet (b) and decides to retransmit it to A through the LAN. By using the Neighbor Discovery algorithm, it discovers the link layer address of A starting from its IPv6 layer address and then executes the transmission of the packet (c).

4. The host A receives the packet (c) and, because the IPv6 destination address is equal to its layer 3 address, it doesn't send the packet further in the network but passes it to its upper layers.

2.7   Neighbor Discovery

To manage the interaction between different nodes connected to the same link (for example, to the same LAN), IPv6 uses ICMP (Internet Control Message Protocol)[11, 12] messages.

These messages have the following three purposes:

- ▓ To allow hosts to know which routers are present on a link. This capability is implemented through periodical multicast transmission of the ICMP *Router Advertisement* packet. Router Advertisement messages are transmitted by routers and received by all the hosts connected to a link that stores, in this way, the presence of routers in a local cache.

- ▓ To allow hosts to learn through *Routing Redirect* packets which is the best router through which a node outside the link can be reached.

- ▓ To allow all nodes (hosts and routers) to learn mappings between IPv6 addresses and link addresses through *Neighbor Solicitation* and *Neighbor Advertisement* messages.

Figure 2-5 shows the five types of packets and their direction.

2.7.1   Router Advertisement

Routers use Router Advertisement messages to advertise their presence on all links to which they are connected. This process can happen periodically or as a response to a *Router Solicitation* message. Router Advertisement messages contain several parameters relevant to the link, among which are addresses, prefixes, and so on.

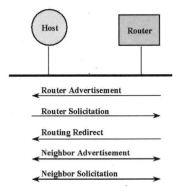

Figure 2-5
Neighbor discovery
messages

These types of messages allow hosts to learn all routers present on a given link automatically, and they overcome one of the main IPv4 limits: the manual configuration of a default router.

Router Advertisement messages are used by hosts to build their *Default Router List* automatically.

2.7.2 Router Solicitation

When the interface of a host becomes active, it can send a Router Solicitation message to request all routers connected to the link to send a Router Advertisement message immediately, without waiting for the periodical transmission.

2.7.3 Routing Redirect

When a host must communicate for the first time with a destination on a subnetwork to which the host is not directly connected, it must choose a default router from its Default Router List and send the packet to it. The chosen router cannot represent the best choice and be forced to route the packet toward another router on the same link from which it received the packet. In this case, the chosen router, besides correctly delivering the packet, generates a Routing Redirect message to signal to the host that there is, on the same link, a router that represents a best choice toward the final destination.

The host, when receiving a Routing Redirect message, updates its *Destination Cache*, storing the best path.

2.7.4   Neighbor Solicitation

A Neighbor Solicitation message is sent by a node to discover the link layer address of another node or to check whether another node is still reachable through the address stored in the cache. This message is also used in the autoconfiguration phase to detect the presence of duplicated addresses.

2.7.5   Neighbor Advertisement

A Neighbor Advertisement represents the response to a Neighbor Solicitation message. A node can periodically send this type of message as well. When a node receives this type of message, it updates its *Neighbor Cache*, which contains the mapping between IPv6 and layer 2 addresses.

The Neighbor Advertisement message, with the Neighbor Solicitation message, replaces the IPv4 ARP[10] protocol.

2.8   Encapsulation of IPv6 on LANs

IPv6 must coexist on LANs with many other protocols, one of which is IPv4. For a long time, IPv6 designers discussed how to implement this co-existence, by mainly analyzing the following two options:

1. To consider IPv6 as an evolution of IPv4 and therefore to maintain, at the local network level, the *Protocol Type* equal to that of IPv4 (that is, 0800 hexadecimal). This solution entails IPv4 and IPv6 packets being distinguished by the *Version* field (that is, by the first four bits of the IP packet). (See Figures 1-3 and 1-4.)

2. To consider IPv6 as a new protocol completely different from IPv4 and therefore to assign a *Protocol Type* different from that of IPv4.

The latter solution was chosen because it is more robust and reliable during the migration from IPv4 to IPv6, when both protocols will be active at the same time. The new assigned Protocol Type, 86DD (hexadecimal), and the LAN encapsulation are shown in Figure 2-6.

The solution (b) can be used on all IEEE 802 (IEEE 802.3, 802.5, FDDI, and so on) LANs; it anticipates that after the MAC header (MAC-DSAP, MAC-SSAP, and Length), the LAN LLC header will be present in its SNAP

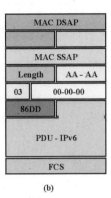

Figure 2-6
Encapsulations of
IPv6 on LANs

(a)   (b)

variant (see Chapter 5 of *Reti Locali: dal Cablaggio all'Internetworking*[4]). The solution (a) is used only on Ethernet and IEEE 802.3 LANs, but it is very important because of the wide diffusion of this type of network.

2.9   Impact of IPv6 on Upper Layers

The TCP/IP network architecture is not perfectly layered; therefore, the replacement of the IPv4 protocol with the IPv6 protocol has an impact also on upper layers (for example, TCP and UDP) up to involved applications (for example, Telnet, FTP, SMTP).

The first aspect to be considered is that applications allow us to specify the destination node by using its IP address or its name. In the latter case, applications use the Domain Name Service to map the name into the corresponding address.

In both cases, they must be modified to manage new IPv6 addresses on 128 bits.

These addresses are typically passed to TCP and UDP transport protocols, which must be updated, too. In the case of TCP (Transmission Control Protocol)[13], modifications are even more substantial. In fact, TCP also uses source and destination IP addresses as connection identifiers; therefore, its data structures must be updated.

In general, enabling TCP and UDP to work is necessary either if the network layer is IPv4 or if it is IPv6. In fact, we can realistically think that, during the transition period, many hosts will support both IPv4 and IPv6 at the same time.

2.10   Modifications to Sockets

To update all applications, even those written by end users and not only those belonging to operating systems, redefining sockets so that they are both IPv4 and IPv6 compatible is necessary.

To accomplish this task, *Basic Socket Interface Extensions for IPv6*[14] supplies new definitions to be used with operating systems derived from Berkeley UNIX (4.x BSD); these definitions can be implemented on all other operating systems.

2.10.1   New Macro Definition

First, a new macro called **AF_INET6** has been defined in **<sys/socket.h>** with the purpose of differentiating the original data structure **sockaddr_in** from the new data structure **sockaddr_in6**. In parallel, a new macro called **PF_INET6** (Protocol Family) has been defined, and its value is set equal to **AF_INET6**.

2.10.2   Definition of the Data Structure for IPv6 Addresses

The data structure that will contain an IPv6 address has been defined in the file **<netinet/in.h>** in the following way:

```
struct in6_addr {
        u_char  s6_addr[16];   /* IPv6 address */
}
```

This data structure contains a set of 16 elements, each 8 bits long, unsigned, that together form the 128-bit IPv6 address.

The structure **in6_addr** is used to build the new structure **sockaddr_in6**, which is used to contain the address of a socket and is defined in the following way:

```
struct sockaddr_in6 {
    u_short    sin6_family;     /* AF_INET6 */
    u_short    sin6_port; /* Transport layer port # */
```

```
    u_long    sin6_flowinfo;/* IPv6 flow information */
    struct in6_addr sin6_addr;       /* IPv6 address */
};
```

2.10.3   The socket() Function

Application programs use the socket() function to create a socket descriptor that represents the endpoint of a communication. Parameters passed to the socket() function indicate which protocol must be used and which is the address's format. For example, to create a TCP connection on IPv4, a call of the following type is used:

```
s = socket (PF_INET, SOCK_STREAM, 0);
```

The value PF_INET is used as the first parameter of the socket() function to request the creation of a socket on IPv4. If we want to create the same connection but use IPv6, we need to specify PF_INET6 as the first parameter:

```
s = socket (PF_INET6, SOCK_STREAM, 0);
```

2.10.4   Interoperability

To guarantee the usability of all current applications, the new API (Application Programming Interface) must be compatible with the old one either at the source level or at the binary level. This means that an old application can continue to create TCP and UDP sockets on IPv4 by specifying the PF_INET parameter in the socket() function. In general, creating any combination of TCP and UDP communications on IPv4 and IPv6 also within the same process must be possible.

2.10.5   Mapping Names into Addresses and Vice Versa

To map names into addresses and vice versa, the decision was to adopt what was defined by the standard POSIX 1003.1g (Protocol Independent Interfaces)[15]—that is, getaddrinfo() functions (for mapping names into addresses) and getnameinfo() functions (for mapping addresses into names). These two functions were designed by IEEE to be independent from the protocol and are therefore suitable to meet IPv6 needs.

2.10.6   Mapping Binary Addresses into ASCII Addresses and Vice Versa

Each time we need to interact with human users, we need to translate an address's numerical format into a textual format or vice versa. To do so, we can use the two new library functions that have been defined:

`inet_pton()` (from a textual format to numerical a format)

`inet_ntop()` (from a numerical format to a textual format)

2.11   Domain Name Service (DNS) Modifications

The calls to functions `getaddrinfo()` and `getnameinfo()` cannot be executed if the Domain Name Service is not upgraded, allowing it to store IPv6 addresses.

First, a new type of record "AAAA"[16] has been added. The name of this new record (AAAA) was derived from the one used to memorize IPv4 (A) addresses; because IPv6 addresses are four times bigger than IPv4 addresses (128 bits instead of 32), the decision was to use four A's.

Therefore, if, in DNS, we write configuration files mapping from the name into the IPv4 address as

```
HOST1.POLITO.IT IN A 130.192.253.252
```

we write the same operation from the name into the IPv6 address as

```
HOST1.POLITO.IT IN AAAA 4321:0:1:2:3:4:567:89ab
```

The DNS must also provide opposite definitions—that is, of mapping addresses into names. To define the mapping from an IPv4 address into a name, we use a PTR record, for example, with reference to the previous case:

```
252.253.192.130.IN-ADDR.ARPA. PTR HOST1.POLITO.IT
```

Because the ARPA domain is obsolete, it has been decided to define the second layer IP6 domain under the first layer INT domain. With reference to the preceding example, the rule to map an IPv6 address into the corresponding name is as follows:

```
b.a.9.8.7.6.5.0.4.0.0.0.3.0.0.0.2.0.0.0.1.0.0.0.0.0.0.0.1.2.
3.4.IP6.INT.  PTR HOST1.POLITO.IT
```

2.12   DHCP Servers

In practice, the length of IPv6 addresses makes their use by end users impossible. End users will work on IPv6 using only names, and these names will be converted into addresses by DNSs. Also, network managers will be confronted with the addresses' lengths, so they must adopt the necessary support tools for the network configuration. In particular, configuring IPv6 addresses not directly on hosts, but on DHCP (Dynamic Host Configuration Protocol)[17] servers, will become common. Hosts, when bootstrapping, will interact with DHCP servers to configure their addresses and their prefixes (the subnetworks).

In practice, DHCP servers are databases that contain relationships between link addresses (typically LANs' MAC addresses) and IPv6 addresses, whereas DNS servers contain relationships between IPv6 addresses and names. Because both types of servers (DNS and DHCP) will be practically mandatory with IPv6 and because both of them share IPv6 addresses, integrated solutions for DHCP and DNS servers based on a common database should be preferred.

REFERENCES ▬ ▬ ▬ ▬ ▬ ▬ ▬ ▬

[1]J. Postel, *RFC 791: Internet Protocol*, September 1981.

[2]IS 8473, *Information processing systems—Data communications— Protocol for providing the connectionless-mode network service*, ISO, 1988.

[3]S. Deering, R. Hinden, *RFC 1883: Internet Protocol, Version 6 (IPv6) Specification*, December 1995.

[4]S. Gai, P.L. Montessoro, P. Nicoletti, *Reti Locali: dal Cablaggio all'Internetworking*, SSGRR (Scuola Superiore G. Reiss Romoli), 1995.

[5]R. Hinden, S. Deering, *RFC 1884: IP Version 6 Addressing Architecture*, December 1995.

[6]S. Thomson, C. Huitema, *RFC 1886: DNS Extensions to support IP version 6*, December 1995.

[7]G. Bennett, *Designing TCP/IP Internetworks*, Van Nostrand Reinhold.

[8]G. Malkin, *RFC 1723: RIP Version 2—Carrying Additional Information*, November 1994.

[9]J. Moy, *RFC 1583: OSPF Version 2*, March 1994.

[10]D.C. Plummer, *RFC 826: Ethernet Address Resolution Protocol: On converting network protocol addresses to 48 bit Ethernet address for transmission on Ethernet hardware*, November 1982.

[11]T. Narten, E. Nordmark, W. Simpson, *RFC 1970: Neighbor Discovery for IP Version 6 (IPv6)*, August 1996.

[12]A. Conta, S. Deering, *RFC 1885: Internet Control Message Protocol (ICMPv6)*, December 1995.

[13]J. Postel, *RFC 793: Transmission Control Protocol*, September 1981.

[14]R.E. Gilligan, S. Thomson, J. Bound, *Basic Socket Interface Extensions for IPv6*, IETF, April 1996.

[15]IEEE, *Protocol Independent Interfaces*, IEEE Std 1003.1g, DRAFT 6.3., November 1995.

[16]S. Thomson, C. Huitema, *RFC 1886: DNS Extensions to support IP version 6*, December 1995.

[17]R. Droms, *RFC 1541: Dynamic Host Configuration Protocol*, October 1993.

3

IPv6 Headers

This third chapter provides a more detailed overview of IPv6 packet headers. In the first part, the basic IPv6 header will be described, and in the following sections, extension headers will be presented. (Extension headers are additional headers that can be present in the IPv6 packet.) Some of these optional headers will be described in more detail in the following chapters, and the prominent problems related to IPv6 addresses will be discussed in Chapter 4.

3.1   The IPv6 Header

The IPv6 header was introduced in Chapter 1, but it is shown again in Figure 3-1 for convenience.

We can begin to understand IPv6 better by inspecting its header's fields.

3.1.1   Version

The 4-bit *Version* field contains the number 6. This field is the same size as the IPv4 version field that contains the number 4. Nevertheless, the use of this field is limited because IPv4 and IPv6 packets are not distinguished on the basis of the value contained in it, but as a function of a different protocol type present in the layer 2 envelope (for example, Ethernet or PPP). See, for example, Section 2.9, which describes the encapsulation of IPv6 into LANs and differences with the analogous IPv4 encapsulation.

3.1.2   Priority

The 4-bit *Priority* field in the IPv6 header can assume 16 different values. It enables the source node to differentiate packets it generates by associating different delivery priorities to them. These 16 possible values are further divided into two groups: from 0 through 7 and from 8 through 15.

Values 0 through 7 are used to specify the priority of traffic for which the source is providing traffic control. A typical example is the traffic of

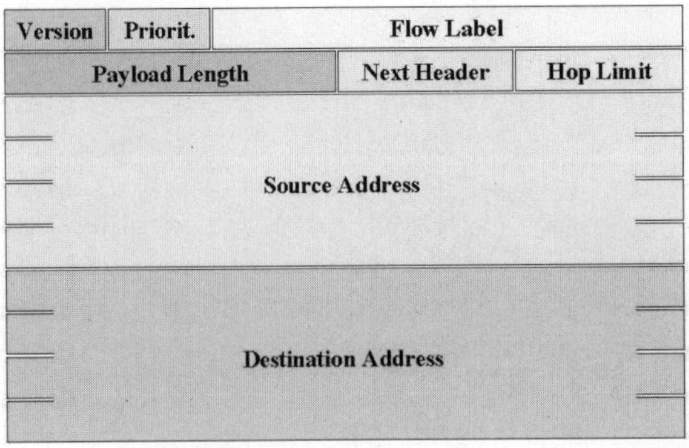

Figure 3-1
The IPv6 header

Version	Priorit.	Flow Label		
Payload Length			Next Header	Hop Limit
Source Address				
Destination Address				

applications that use TCP and its congestion control mechanisms based on variable sizes of windows.

RFC 1883[1] proposes the association between priorities and applications shown in Table 3-1.

Values 8 through 15 are used to specify the priority of traffic that does not back off in response to congestion. A typical example is represented by real-time packets like those associated with the transmission of films or sound. Priority 8 is associated with those packets that the network will discard first under conditions of congestion (for example, high-fidelity video traffic), and priority 15 is associated with those packets that the sender will discard at the end, only if absolutely necessary (for example, low-quality telephone audio traffic).

3.1.3 Flow Label

The 24-bit *Flow Label* field in the IPv6 header can be used by a source to label a set of packets belonging to the same flow. A flow is uniquely identified by the combination of the source address and of a nonzero Flow Label. Multiple active flows may exist from a source to a destination (with the same source address but with nonzero and different Flow Labels) as well as traffic that is not associated with any flow (carrying a Flow Label of zero).

In Section 1.3.8, we learned that a flow is a sequence of packets in some way correlated (for example, generated by the same application) and sharing parameters such as the source and destination address, the QoS, the

Table 3-1

Associations between priorities and applications

Priorities	Applications
0	Uncharacterized traffic
1	"Filler" traffic (for example, netnews)
2	Unattended data transfer (for example, e-mail)
3	Reserved for future purposes
4	Attended bulk transfer (for example, FTP, NFS)
5	Reserved for future purposes
6	Interactive traffic (for example, Telnet, X-Windows)
7	Internet control traffic (for example, routing protocols, SNMP)

accounting, authorizations, the authentication, and the security. Flows can be unicast (from a node toward another node) or multicast (from a node toward a set of nodes).

Packets belonging to the same flow must be coherently handled by IPv6 routers. The way to handle packets belonging to a given flow can be specified by information within the packets themselves or conveyed by a control protocol such as RSVP (Resource reSerVation Protocol)[2].

RFC 1883[1] specifies that problems related to flows, at the time the RFC itself was published, are still experimental and subject to change when requirements for the Internet flow handling will become clearer. In the meanwhile, nodes that cannot support the function of the Flow Label field are required to set the field to zero when originating a packet, pass the field on unchanged when forwarding a packet, and ignore the field when receiving a packet.

The Flow Label assigned to a flow is a numeric value randomly chosen by the source node from the range 1 to FFFFFF (hexadecimal). This value must be different from Flow Labels in use on the source node or used in the recent past. All packets belonging to the same flow must be sent with the same source address, destination address, priority, and Flow Label. Moreover, if any Hop-by-Hop or Routing extension headers are present (see Section 3.2), they must be the same in all packets belonging to the same flow.

When routers receive the first packet of a new flow, they can process the information carried by the IPv6 header and by Hop-by-Hop and Routing extension headers, "remember" the result (for example, on which interface packets must be retransmitted) in a cache memory, and then apply the result to all other packets belonging to the same flow (with the same source address and the same Flow Label), by reading it directly from the cache memory.

RFC 1883[1] specifies that the cache memory lifetime is limited to 6 seconds, independent from the presence of traffic. For example, let's suppose that a router has in its cache a rule for the flow identified by the source address A and by the Flow Label 37. After 6 seconds, the rule expires; the first packet reaching the router with source address A and Flow Label 37 will be entirely processed and will reestablish the rule, in most cases equal to the previous one.

3.1.4 Payload Length

The 16-bit *Payload Length* field contains the payload length—that is, the length of the data field following the IPv6 header, in octets. Because it is a 16-bit field, the maximum length of an IPv6 packet payload is 64 Kbytes. If a wider data field is needed, a Jumbo Payload extension header can be used (see Section 3.2.4). The presence of a Jumbo Payload is indicated by the value zero in the Payload Length field.

3.1.5 Next Header

The 8-bit *Next Header* field identifies the type of header immediately following the IPv6 header and located at the beginning of the data field (payload) of the IPv6 packet.

The two most common kinds of Next Headers are clearly TCP (6) and UDP (17), but many other headers are possible. The format adopted for this field is the one proposed for IPv4 by RFC 1700[3]; it is summarized in Table 3-2 where appropriate integration for IPv6 has been inserted. The Next Header field is generally the same as the IPv4 Protocol field.

3.1.6 Hop Limit

The 8-bit *Hop Limit* field is decremented by one by each node (typically a router) that forwards a packet. If the Hop Limit field is decremented to zero, the packet is discarded. The main function of this field is to identify and to discard packets that are looping because of erroneous routing information. Clearly, between two IPv6 nodes, we cannot have more than 255 hops (links), which means no more than 254 routers.

3.1.7 Source Address

The 128-bit *Source Address* field contains the IPv6 address of the node originating the packet. The IPv6 address format, which is specified by RFC 1884[4], will be discussed in Chapter 4 of this book.

3.1.8 Destination Address

The 128-bit *Destination Address* field contains the IPv6 address of the node recipient of the packet. If a Routing header is present, this address is not that of the ultimate recipient (see Section 3.3.5).

Table 3-2

Possible values for
the Next Header
field

Decimal Value	Keyword	Protocol
0		Reserved (IPv4)
0	HBH	Hop-by-Hop option (IPv6)
1	ICMP	Internet Control Message (IPv4)
2	IGMP	Internet Group Management (IPv4)
3	GGP	Gateway-to-Gateway Protocol
4	IP	IP in IP (IPv4 encapsulation)
5	ST	Stream
6	TCP	Transmission Control
8	EGP	Exterior Gateway Protocol
9	IGP	Any private interior gateway
16	CHAOS	Chaos
17	UDP	User Datagram
29	ISO-TP4	ISO Transport Protocol Class 4
36	XTP	XTP
43	RH	Routing header (IPv6)
44	FH	Fragmentation header (IPv6)
45	IDRP	Inter-Domain Routing Protocol
46	RSVP	Reservation Protocol
50	ESP	Encapsulating Security Payload
51	AH	Authentication header (IPv6)
54	NHRP	NBMA Next Hop Resolution Protocol
58	ICMP	Internet Control Message (IPv6)
59	Null	No next header (IPv6)
60	DOH	Destination Options header (IPv6)
80	ISO-IP	ISO Internet Protocol (CLNP)
83	VINES	VINES
88	IGRP	IGRP
89	OSPF	OSPF (Open Shortest Path First)
93	AX.25	AX.25 Frames

3.1.9   Examples of IPv6 Packets

Appendix B shows some examples of IPv6 packets captured with a Rad-com RC100 protocol analyzer. In particular, Section B.3 shows a TCP packet, and Section B.4 shows a UDP packet.

3.2   Extension Header

The IPv4 header has space for some optional fields requiring a particular processing of packets. These optional fields are not used often, and they can deteriorate router performance remarkably because their presence must be checked for each packet. IPv6 replaces optional fields with *extension headers*. Extension headers are based on the principle that most of the packets need a very simple processing, and therefore basic fields of the IPv6 header are sufficient (see Figure 3-1). Packets requiring additional information at the network layer can encode this information in additional headers that can be placed in a header between the IPv6 header and the upper layer header. Headers are connected by the Next Header field (see Section 3.2.5) to form a chain similar to the one shown in Figure 3-2.

An IPv6 packet can have no extension headers, one extension header, or several extension headers. The few existing extension headers will be described later in this chapter.

Each extension header has a length equal to a multiple of 8 octets (64 bits).

A full implementation of IPv6 must include support for the following extension headers:

- Hop-by-Hop Options
- Routing (Type 0)

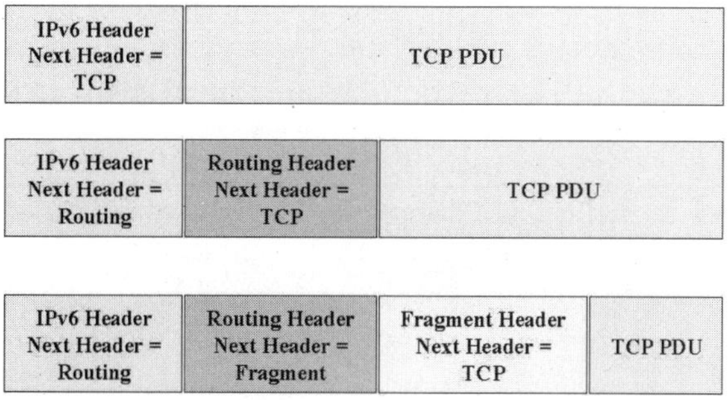

Figure 3-2
Extension headers

- Fragment
- Destination Options
- Authentication
- Encapsulating Security Payload

3.2.1 Extension Headers Order

Extension headers must be processed in the order they appear in the packet. Most extension headers will be processed only by the destination node (for example, those related to security); therefore, they do not affect the router's performance.

The only type of extension header to be processed by all nodes along its delivery path is the Hop-by-Hop Options header (see Section 3.2.3), which, if present, must immediately follow the IPv6 header. Its presence is indicated by the value zero in the Next Header field of the IPv6 header (see Table 3-2).

When more than one extension header is used in the same packet, RFC 1883[1] recommends that those headers appear in the following order:

- IPv6 header
- Hop-by-Hop Options header
- Destination Options header (see note 1)
- Routing header
- Fragment header
- Authentication header
- Encapsulating Security Payload header
- Destination Options header (see note 2)
- Upper layer header

Each extension header should occur at most once, with the only exception being the Destination Options header, which can occur twice in different positions (see notes 1 and 2).

NOTE 1: _For options to be processed by all nodes whose address appears in the IPv6 Destination Address field and in the Routing header._

NOTE 2: *For options that must be processed only by the final destination of the packet.*

3.2.2 Options

Among extension headers previously listed, the Hop-by-Hop Options header and the Destination Options header carry variable numbers of options. These options, which are encoded in a format called *TLV (Type-Length-Value),* are shown in Figure 3-3.

The three fields that appear in the described option have the following meanings:

- *Option Type* is an 8-bit unsigned integer; it identifies the type of option.
- *Option Data Length* is an 8-bit unsigned integer that contains the length of the Option Data field in octets.
- *Option Data* is a variable length field that contains the option-type specific data.

The Option Type field assigns a particular meaning to the three highest order bits, as shown in Figure 3-4.

In particular, the two highest order bits (*Action*) specify the action that must be taken if the processing IPv6 node doesn't recognize the option type. These bits can have the following values:

00   Skip over this option and continue to process eventual subsequent options.

01   Discard the packet.

10   Discard the packet, regardless of whether the packet destination address is multicast; the source node is notified by an ICMP packet.

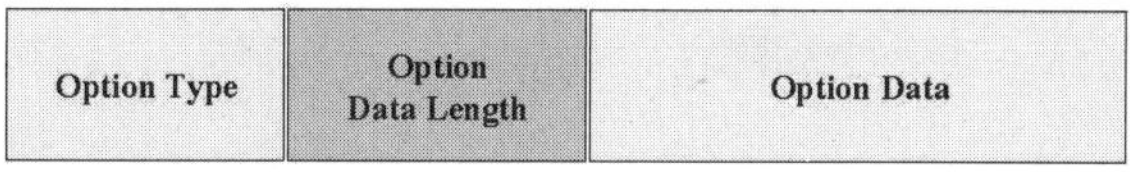

Figure 3-3
TLV Options (Type-Length-Value)

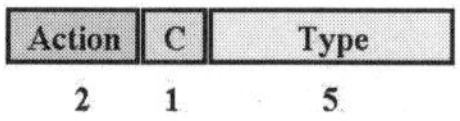

Option Type	Option Data Length	Option Data

Figure 3-4
Detail of the Option Type field

Action	C	Type
2	1	5

11   Discard the packet, and only if its destination address is not multicast, the source node is notified by an ICMP packet.

The third bit *C* (Change) specifies whether the Option data can change *en route* to the packet's final destination:

0   Option data cannot change en route.

1   Option data can change en route.

Two *padding* options are used, when necessary, to align subsequent options. They are shown in Figure 3-5.

The (a) option, which is called *Pad1,* is used to insert one octet of padding into the Options area of a header, and the (b) option, which is called *PadN,* is used to insert two or more octets of padding in the Options area of a header.

3.2.3   Hop-by-Hop Options Header

The Hop-by-Hop Options header is used to carry optional information that must be examined by every node along a packet delivery path. This type of header must immediately follow the IPv6 header, and its presence is identified by a value zero in the Next Header field of the IPv6 header. Its format is shown in Figure 3-6.

The 8-bit *Next Header* field has the same meaning as the field with the same name in the IPv6 header (see Section 3.1.5).

The 8-bit *Hdr Ext Len* (Header Extension Length) field contains the length of the Hop-by-Hop Options header in 8-octet units (64 bits), not in-

Figure 3-5
Padding options

Figure 3-6
Hop-by-Hop Options header

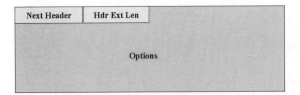

cluding the first 8 octets. Expressing the length this way can appear extravagant, but it speeds up IPv6 implementations.

In fact, remember that extension headers have lengths in multiples of 8 octets (64 bits), and they obviously cannot be empty; therefore, they are almost always 64 bits long. (This condition is indicated by the value zero in the Hdr Ext Len field.) For example, if the Hop-by-Hop Options header is 256 octets long, the Hdr Ext Len value is 3. This coding simplifies the implementation because it avoids continued testing on the Hdr Ext Len value's validity. If the header length were measured in octets, the values 0, 1, 2, 3, 4, 5, 6, 7, 9, and so on would not be valid!

The *Options* field has a variable length, and it contains one or more TLV options (see Section 3.2.2).

In addition to the Pad1 and PadN options, we will define the Jumbo Payload option.

3.2.4   The Jumbo Payload Option

As we've already seen in Section 3.1.4, the choice to have a 16-bit Payload Length field limits the IPv6 payload length to 65,535 octets. The Jumbo Payload option can be used to exceed this limit.

This option requires a $4n + 2$ alignment, where n can be any natural number. This means that the option can begin with octets 2, 6, 10, 14, and so on. The format of the Jumbo Payload option is shown in Figure 3-7.

The 8-bit *Option Type* field contains the value 194, which indicates the Jumbo Payload option. The 8-bit *Option Data Length* field contains the value 4, which indicates that 4 octets of data will follow—that is, the *Jumbo Payload Length* field. The last one indicates the packet length in octets, excluding the IPv6 header but including the Hop-by-Hop Options header. This length must be more than 65,535 octets.

The Payload Length field of the IPv6 header must be set to zero in every packet that carries the Jumbo Payload option. The Jumbo Payload option is not consistent with the Fragment header (see Section 3.3.6); therefore, they cannot both be present in the same IPv6 packet.

Figure 3-7
The Jumbo Payload
option

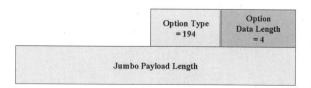

| Option Type = 194 | Option Data Length = 4 |
| Jumbo Payload Length | |

If an IPv6 implementation doesn't support the Jumbo Payload option, it cannot have an interface to a link whose link MTU is greater than 65,575 octets (40 octets of the IPv6 header plus 65,535 octets of Payload).

3.2.5 Routing Header

The Routing header is used by an IPv6 source to specify a list of intermediate nodes that a packet has to traverse on the path to its destination. The specification can be for each node on the path binding (*Strict*) or not (*Loose*). This header supports a function very similar to the IPv4 packet Source Route option.

The Routing header is identified by a Next Header value of 43 (see Table 3-2). The Routing header can be of different types, but currently RFC 1883[1] specifies only the type zero, whose organization is shown in Figure 3-8.

The 8-bit *Next Header* field uses the same values as the field with the same name in the IPv6 header (see Section 3.1.5).

The 8-bit *Hdr Ext Len* (Header Extension Length) field contains the length of the Routing header in 8-octet (64-bit) units, not including the first 8 octets. In the case of a Type 0 Routing header, the Hdr Ext Len value must be less than or equal to 46, equal to twice the number of addresses in the header itself, and therefore even. In fact, the first 64 bits contain the fixed part of the Type 0 Routing header (Next Header, Hdr Ext Len, Routing Type, Segment Left, Reserved, and Strict/Loose Bit Map), and each address has 128 bits—that is, two times 64 bits.

Figure 3-8
Type 0 Routing header

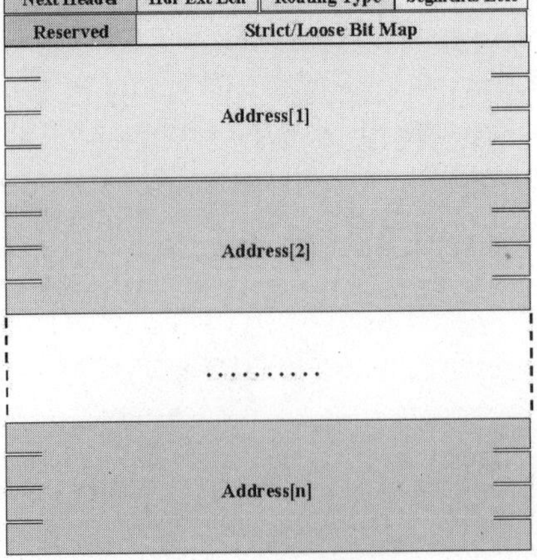

The 8-bit *Routing Type* field always contains, in this case, the zero value. Different values can be used in the future to support new types of Routing headers.

The 8-bit *Segments Left* field contains the number of explicitly listed intermediate nodes still to be visited on the path to the destination—that is, the number of addresses not yet used. The maximum legal value for this field is 23.

The 8-bit *Reserved* field is reserved for future uses. It must be set to zero for transmission and ignored on reception.

The 24-bit *Strict/Loose Bit Map* field is a mask containing a Strict/Loose bit for each address. If the *Strict/Loose* bit associated with an address is zero, then the address must be treated as *Loose;* if equal to 1, the address must be treated as *Strict*.

Each *Address* field is 128 bits long, and up to 23 Address fields can be used. They contain IPv6 addresses of nodes to be traversed along the path to the destination. Nodes are visited in the order Address[1] ... Address[*n*].

When a Routing header is processed by a node, the node checks whether the Segment Left field is different from 0, and if so, it extracts the following address and the Strict/Loose bit associated with the address. If the bit indicates that the address must be treated in the Strict way, the node checks that the address belongs to an adjacent node (a neighbor on one of the links), and it delivers the packet on the interface associated with that adjacent node; if the node is not adjacent, the packet is discarded. If the bit indicates that the address must be treated in the Loose way, the node examines its routing tables and routes the packet to the address.

The complete flowchart of the Routing header management procedure can be found in Section A.1 of Appendix A, and an example of routing is shown in Section A.2.

3.2.6   Fragment Header

The management of fragmentation in IPv4 is rather different from the management in IPv6. In fact, one of the IPv4 router's tasks is to fragment a packet if its size is too large to fit the MTU of the link on which it must retransmit the packet. For example, if an IPv4 router receives a 4000-octet packet from an FDDI ring and must retransmit it on an Ethernet network with an MTU link of 1500 octets, the router fragments the packet into three packets with sizes less than or equal to 1500 octets. This IPv4 function can be deactivated by setting the *don't fragment* bit to 1 in the IPv4 header.

Figure 3-9
Fragment header

Next Header	Reserved	Fragment Offset	Res	M
Identification				

IPv6 routers always operate as if the don't fragment bit were equal to 1. When they receive a packet whose size exceeds the MTU link, they discard the packet and signal this fact to the source (through an ICMP packet), by indicating what is the maximum length that can be accepted for the packet. The source node will appropriately fragment the packet before retransmitting it.

The fragmentation can be implemented in IPv6 only by the source node through an extension header and in particular by a Fragment header. The Fragment header is processed only by the destination node and ignored by nodes along the path. The Fragment header (see Figure 3-9) is identified by the value 44 in the Next Header field.

The 8-bit *Next Header* field uses the same values as the field with the same name in the IPv4 header (see Section 3.1.5).

The 8-bit *Reserved* field is reserved for future uses. It is initialized to zero for transmission and is ignored on reception.

The 13-bit *Fragment Offset* field contains the offset of the data following this header relative to the start of the fragmentable part of the original packet (before fragmentation), in 8-octet (64-bit) units.

The 2-bit *Res* field is reserved for future uses. It must be set to zero for transmission and ignored on reception.

The 1-bit *M* (More fragments) field indicates whether a fragment is the last in a packet (M = 0) or not (M = 1).

The 32-bit *Identification* field contains a unique identification of the packet generated by the node that executes the fragmentation. Its aim is to simply identify all fragments belonging to the same packet.

3.2.7   The Fragmentation Process

To better understand the use of the Fragment header, let's see how an IPv6 host manages a fragmentation process. The first point to understand is that an IPv6 packet consists of a fragmentable part and an unfragmentable part (see Figure 3-10).

The unfragmentable part consists of the IPv6 header plus other headers that must be processed by all nodes along the path—that is, extension headers up to and including the Routing header.

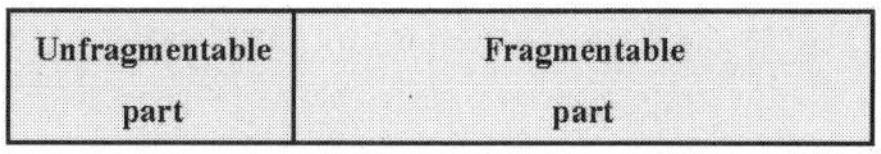

Figure 3-10
An IPv6 header be-
fore fragmentation

Figure 3-10
An IPv6 header be-
fore fragmentation

Unfragmentable part	Fragmentable part

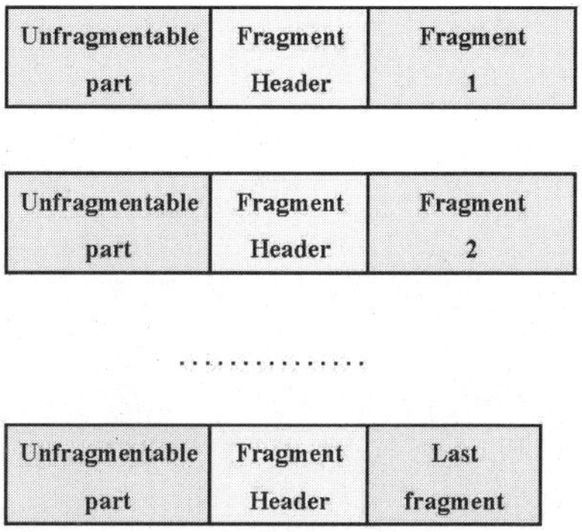

Figure 3-11
Packets resulting
from a fragmentation

Unfragmentable part	Fragment Header	Fragment 1

Unfragmentable part	Fragment Header	Fragment 2

. . . .

Unfragmentable part	Fragment Header	Last fragment

The fragmentable part consists of the rest of the packet—that is, extension headers that must be processed only by the destination node and
the IPv6 payload. This part is divided into fragments that are multiples
of 8 octets (with the possible exception of the last one). A Fragment header
is put before each fragment, and fragments are transmitted as separate
IPv6 packets, as illustrated in Figure 3-11.

The unfragmentable part, which is repeated in each packet, is equal to
the original unfragmentable part with two exceptions:

■ The Payload Length field of the IPv6 header reflects the new
length.

■ The Next Header field of the last header of the unfragmentable
part is set to 44 to indicate the Fragment header presence.

3.2.8   Destination Options Header

The Destination Options Header is used to carry additional information that
must be processed only by the destination node or nodes, not by each node
on the routing path of the packet. This kind of header is identified by a Next
Header field value of 60 (see Table 3-2). It has been decided to create only
one type of header for all destination options because the Next Header field
is limited to 8 bits, and therefore only 256 values are totally available. The
Destination Options header structure is illustrated in Figure 3-12.

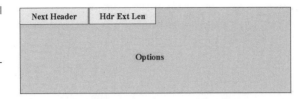

Figure 3-12
Destination Options
header

The 8-bit *Next Header* field uses the same values as the field with the same name in the IPv4 header (see Section 3.1.5).

The 8-bit *Hdr Ext Len* (Header Extension Length) field contains the length of the Destination Options header in 8-octet (64-bit) units, not including the first 8 octets.

The variable-length *Options* field contains one or more TLV-encoded options (see Section 3.1.2).

The only options specified by RFC 1883[1] that can be part of a Destination Options header are the Pad1 and the PadN (see Figure 3-5). RFC 1888[6] specifies an option called NSAP (see Section 4.7.9) that can be part of a Destination Options header.

3.2.9 No Next Header

The value 59 in the Next Header field of the IPv6 header or any extension header indicates that nothing follows that header. If the Payload Length field of the IPv6 header indicates the presence of other octets after the header, they must be ignored and retransmitted unchanged.

3.2.10 Security Header

Two extension headers, like the Destination Options header, are used to carry additional information that must be processed only by the destination node or nodes, not by each node on the routing path of the packet. These two headers, which are dedicated to security problems, are called the Authentication header and the Encapsulating Security Payload header.

The Encapsulating Security Payload header is indicated by the value 50 in the Next Header field (see Table 3-2).

These headers will be described in Chapter 8, which is dedicated to security problems.

3.3   Size of IPv6 Packets

RFC 1883[1] explicitly recommends that, to allow IPv6 to operate correctly, each link must have an MTU greater than or equal to 576 octets. If any link cannot meet this constraint, it must provide fragmentation mechanisms at the link layer, typically at layer 2 of the ISO/OSI reference model.

Links that have a configurable MTU must be configured to have an MTU greater than or equal to 576 octets.

It is recommended that IPv6 nodes implement Path MTU discovery[5] to use MTUs greater than 576 octets. However, very simple nodes, with restricted IPv6 implementations, can simply send packets not longer than 576 octets and be certain that, fitting the MTU path, they will be delivered.

REFERENCES

[1]S. Deering, R. Hinden, *RFC 1883: Internet Protocol, Version 6 (IPv6) Specification*, December 1995.

[2]B. Braden, L. Zhang, D. Estrin, S. Herzog, S. Jamin, *RSVP: Resource ReSerVation Protocol (RSVP)—Version 1 Functional Specification*, Work in progress, January 1996.

[3]J. Reynolds, J. Postel, *RFC 1700: Assigned Numbers*, October 1994.

[4]R. Hinden, S. Deering, *RFC 1884: IP Version 6 Addressing Architecture*, December 1995.

[5]J.C. Mogul, S.E. Deering, *RFC 1191: Path MTU discovery*, November 1990.

[6]J. Bound, B. Carpenter, D. Harrington, J. Houldsworth, A. Lloyd, *RFC 1888: OSI NSAPs and IPv6*, August 1996.

4

IPv6 Addresses

As we have already seen in Chapter 1 (Section 1.2.1), the main innovation of IPv6 addresses lies in their size: *128 bits!*

With 128 bits, 2^{128} addresses are available, which is approximately 10^{38} addresses or, more exactly,

```
340.282.366.920.938.463.463.374.607.431.768.211.456
```

addresses[1]. If we estimate that the earth's surface is 511.263.971.197.990 square meters, the result is that 655.570.793.348.866.943.898.599 IPv6 addresses will be available for each square meter of earth's surface—a number that would be sufficient considering future colonization of other celestial bodies!

On this subject, we suggest that people seeking good humor read RFC 1607, "A View From The 21st Century," [2] which presents a "retrospective" analysis written between 2020 and 2023 on choices made by the IPv6 protocol designers.

4.1   The Addressing Space

IPv6 designers decided to subdivide the IPv6 addressing space on the basis of the value assumed by leading bits in the address; the variable-length field comprising these leading bits is called the *Format Prefix* (FP)[3]. The allocation scheme adopted is shown in Table 4-1.

Table 4-1

Allocation of the IPv6 addressing space

Allocation	Prefix (binary)	Fraction of Address Space
Reserved	0000 0000	1/256
Unassigned	0000 0001	1/256
Reserved for NSAP addresses	0000 001	1/128
Reserved for IPX addresses	0000 010	1/128
Unassigned	0000 011	1/128
Unassigned	0000 1	1/32
Unassigned	0001	1/16
Aggregatable global unicast addresses	001	1/8
Unassigned	010	1/8
Unassigned	011	1/8
Reserved for Geographic-based addresses	100	1/8
Unassigned	101	1/8
Unassigned	110	1/8
Unassigned	1110	1/16
Unassigned	1111 0	1/32
Unassigned	1111 10	1/64
Unassigned	1111 110	1/128
Unassigned	1111 1110 0	1/512
Link Local addresses	1111 1110 10	1/1024

From the first examination of the table, we can see that only 15 percent of the addressing space is initially used by IPv6, thus leaving 85 percent of the addressing space unassigned for future uses.

The format prefixes 001 through 111, except for Multicast Addresses (1111 1111), are all required to have 64-bit interface identifiers in EUI-64 format (see Section 4.10 for definitions).

Reserved addresses must not be confused with Unassigned addresses. They represent 1/256 of the addressing space (FP = 0000 0000) and are used for *unspecified* addresses (see Section 4.6.6), *loopback* (see Section 4.6.7), and *IPv6 with embedded IPv4* addresses (see Section 4.6.8).

Other reserved addresses are *NSAP* addresses (FP = 0000 001) that represent 1/128 of the addressing space and can be derived from ISO/OSI *Network Service Access Point* (NSAP) addresses. A proposal in this direction is specified by RFC 1888 [3] and described in Section 4.6.9.

In the same way, a space for *IPX* addresses is reserved (FP = 0000 010) equal to 1/128 of the addressing space. These addresses can be derived from Novell IPX addresses (see Section 4.6.10).

The last type of reserved address is the *Geographic-based* address (FP = 100), which is the most similar to the present IPv4 addresses from the management point of view. The Geographic-based address was conceived to be assigned to the end user on the basis of the user's geographic location. This kind of address didn't gain much popularity because it potentially causes the routing table's explosion problems mentioned in Section 1.2.6. Of the addressing space, 1/8 is reserved for Geographic-based addresses (see Section 4.6.3), but they have been removed from the last IETF draft on Addressing Architecture.

The following unicast addresses are certain to be used from the beginning:

- Aggregatable Global Unicast addresses (FP = 001), which represent 1/8 of the addressing space; they will be described in Section 4.6.2.

- Link Local addresses (FP = 1111 1110 10), which represent 1/1024 of the addressing space; they will be described in Section 4.6.4.

- Site Local addresses (FP = 1111 1110 11), which represent 1/1024 of the addressing space; they will be described in Section 4.6.5.

- Multicast addresses (FP = 1111 1111), which represent 1/256 of the addressing space; they will be described in Section 4.8.

4.2   Syntax of IPv6 Addresses

IPv4 addresses are 32 bits (4 octets) long. When they are written, each octet is the representation of an unsigned integer, and the 4 octets are written as four decimal numbers divided by three dots (. . .). For example:

    130.192.1.143

For IPv6 addresses, defining a similar syntax is necessary, taking into account that IPv6 addresses are four times longer. The syntax standardized by RFC 1884 [3] recommends considering 128 bits (16 octets) of the IPv6 address as eight unsigned integers on 16 bits and writing each number with four hexadecimal digits; we divide each number from the preceding one and from the following one by using a colon (:). For example:

    FEDC:BA98:7654:3210:FEDC:BA98:7654:3210

The preceding example clarifies the difficulty of the manual management of IPv6 addresses and the need for DHCP and DNS servers (as discussed in Section 2.13). Some IPv6 designers see some advantages in the users' difficulty remembering and writing IPv6 addresses: this way, users will be forced to use names more and more, and addresses will become a problem more internal to the network and functional to the routing of packets.

Nevertheless, the preceding example is not completely realistic; the following are more realistic examples of addresses:

    1080:0000:0000:0000:0008:0800:200C:417A
    0000:0000:0000:0000:0000:0000:0A00:0001

Clearly, more compressed forms of representation are easier for these kinds of addresses. One shortcut derives from the fact that we do not need to write the leading zeros in each group of digits; for example, we can write 0 instead of 0000, 1 instead of 0001, 20 instead of 0020, and 300 instead of 0300. If we apply this shortcut, the two preceding addresses become

    1080:0:0:0:8:800:200C:417A
    0:0:0:0:0:0:A00:1

A further simplification is represented by the symbol ::, which replaces a series of zeros. By applying this shortcut, the two preceding addresses become

    1080::8:800:200C:417A
    ::A00:1

Note that the preceding shortcut can be applied only once to an address. We make the assumption that the IPv6 address has a fixed length so that we can compute how many zeros have been omitted. This shortcut can be applied either to the center of the address (as in the case of the first address), or to the leading (as in the case of the second address) or trailing zeros.

If we consider the case of multicast, loopback, or unspecified addresses, we realize how useful this shortcut is. In fact, the extended form of these addresses results in the following:

`FF01:0:0:0:0:0:0:43`   A multicast address

`0:0:0:0:0:0:0:1`   The loopback address

`0:0:0:0:0:0:0:0`   The unspecified address

They can be represented in compressed form as follows:

`FF01::43`   A multicast address

`::1`   The loopback address

`::`   The unspecified address

A special case is valid for addresses such as `0:0:0:0:0:0:A00:`. The six leading zeros indicate that it is an IPv6 address with an embedded IPv4 address (see Section 4.6.8). In particular, this IPv6 address is associated with the IPv4 address `10.0.0.1`. Only in this case can a mixed IPv4/IPv6 notation be used. In its extended form, the resulting address is

`0:0:0:0:0:0:10.0.0.1`

and in compressed form, the address is

`:::10.0.0.1`

The representation of IPv6 prefixes is similar to the way IPv4 addresses' prefixes are written in CIDR notation. An IPv6 address prefix is represented by the notation

`ipv6-address/prefix-length`

where `ipv6-address` is any of the notations described in this section and `prefix-length` is a decimal value specifying the length of the prefix in bits.

For example, to indicate a subnet with an 80-bit prefix, we use the following notation:

`1080:0:0:0:8::/80`

Note that in this case the three central zeros cannot be eliminated because the notation `::` has already been used once at the end of the address.

For example, the 60-bit prefix

`12AB00000000CD3`

has the following legal representations:

`12AB:0000:0000:CD30:0000:0000:0000:0000/60`

`12AB::CD30:0:0:0:0/60`
`12AB:0:0:CD30::/60`

However, the following representations are not legal:

`12AB:0:0:CD3/60`	Because we can drop leading zeros but not trailing zeros within any 16-bit chunk of the address
`12AB::CD30/60`	Because the address to the left of / expands to `12AB:0000:0000:0000:0000:000:0000:CD30`
`12AB::CD3/60`	Because the address to the left of / expands to `12AB:0000:0000:0000:0000:000:0000:0CD3`

The node address and its prefix can be combined as shown here. The lines

```
node address: 12AB:0:0:CD30:123:4567:89AB:CDEF
prefix: 12AB:0:0:CD30::/60
```

can be abbreviated as

`12AB:0:0:CD30:123:4567:89AB:CDEF/60`

4.3   Types of IPv6 Addresses

As we already saw in Section 2.2, interfaces are addressable in IPv6. More precisely, we can say that a 128-bit IPv6 address is associated with an interface or to a set of interfaces. In particular, RFC 1884 [3] identifies three types of IPv6 addresses:

■ *Unicast:* This type is the address of a single interface. A packet forwarded to a unicast address is delivered only to the interface identified by that address.

- *Anycast:* This type is the address of a set of interfaces typically belonging to different nodes. A packet forwarded to an anycast address is delivered to only one interface of the set (the nearest to the source node, according to the routing metric).

- *Multicast:* This type is the address of a set of interfaces that typically belong to different nodes. A packet forwarded to a multicast address is delivered to all interfaces belonging to the set.

The main differences between IPv4 and IPv6 addresses are the appearance of anycast addresses in IPv6 and the disappearance of IPv4 broadcast addresses, replaced by IPv6 multicast addresses.

4.4   The Addressing Model

We have already learned that addresses belong to interfaces, not to nodes. A node can be identified by any unicast address associated with its interfaces. An IPv6 unicast address refers to a single interface. A single interface can be assigned more addresses of the same type or of different types (unicast, anycast, or multicast). The following are two exceptions to this model:

1. A single IPv6 address can be assigned to a group of interfaces belonging to a node if IPv6 implementation treats that group as a single interface when presenting packets to the IP layer. This capability is useful in fault tolerant systems, in which the presence of only one interface can represent a single point of failure, or to implement a mechanism for load sharing over multiple physical interfaces.

2. Routers can have *unnumbered* interfaces—that is, without any addresses. This can be the case for interfaces on point-to-point links where the presence of addresses is not essential. This setup can simplify a router's configuration, but its use is discouraged from the management point of view because explicitly referring to an interface is not possible if the interface is not associated with a unicast address.

IPv6 assumes that a subnet (or subnetwork, see Section 2.4) is associated with a link (or communication channel, see Section 2.2). More subnets can be associated with the same link, but a subnet cannot be associated with more than one link.

4.5   Assignment of IPv6 Addresses

We have already seen that IPv6 addresses will be unique at a worldwide level, and this uniqueness implies the existence of one or more organizations to assign these addresses.

RFC 1881 [6] specifies that the IPv6 addressing space must be managed in the Internet community's interest through a small central authority availing itself of the cooperation of peripheral authorities.

The Internet community decided that the appropriate entity to perform the role of central authority would be the *Internet Assigned Numbers Authority* (IANA). The IANA will base the IPv6 addressing space management on suggestions coming from the *Internet Architecture Board* (IAB) and from the *Internet Engineering Steering Group* (IESG).

The IANA will delegate to regional and other local registries the task of making specific address allocations to network service providers and other subregional registries. Individuals and organizations can obtain address allocations directly from the appropriate regional (or other) registry or from their service providers.

The IANA will try to prevent monopolies and instances of abuse.

The IANA will develop a plan for the initial IPv6 address allocation, including a provision for the automatic allocation of IPv6 addresses to holders of IPv4 addresses. IANA will also develop mediation and appeals procedures concerning delegation and revocation.

The IANA has already identified three local authorities to collaborate with for IPv6 address allocation:

■ RIPE-NCC (Réseaux IP Européens Network Coordination Centre) for Europe

■ INTERNIC (Internet Network Information Center) for Northern America

■ APNIC (Asian and Pacific Network Information Center) for Asian and Pacific countries

4.6   Unicast Addresses

IPv6 unicast addresses are continuous, bit-wise, maskable addresses similar to IPv4 addresses with *Classless Inter-Domain Routing* (CIDR) [7], as described in Section 1.2.1. We have already seen that the following types of unicast addresses have been specified: Aggregatable Global Unicast,

Geographic-based, IPv4, NSAP, IPX, Link Local, Site Local, nonspecified, and loopback. They will be described in this section. Additional address types will be defined later.

IPv6 nodes may have little knowledge of the internal structure of an IPv6 address. In the simplest case, a node may consider an IPv6 address as a 128-bit string (see Figure 4-1).

A slightly more sophisticated node may have a vision of the IPv6 address structured into two parts by means of the prefix that identifies the subnet (see Figure 4-2).

Routers can have even more sophisticated visions of the address and know other boundaries. The sophistication level of routers depends on what position routers hold in the routing hierarchy.

4.6.1   Example of a Unicast Address

An example of a unicast address format that will likely be common on LANs is the one that allows us to identify the node within the subnet from its 48-bit *MAC address*. Even if, until now, MAC addresses have been assigned on 48 bits, the *EUI-64* standard introduces MAC addresses on 64 bits to be used in the future (see Section 4.10). To be compliant with this standard, IPv6 uses identifiers on 64 bits from the beginning interface (see Figure 4-3).

The *subscriber ID* identifies the set of addresses allocated to a given organization. The *subnet ID* divides this set into several subnets (in this case, the prefix will be 64 bits). The 48-bit MAC address is extended to 64 bits using the EUI-64 rules, and the address is used to identify the inter-

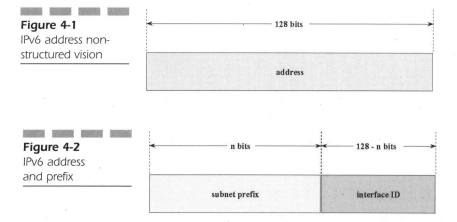

Figure 4-1
IPv6 address non-structured vision

128 bits

address

Figure 4-2
IPv6 address
and prefix

n bits   128 - n bits

subnet prefix   interface ID

Figure 4-3
Example of a unicast
address

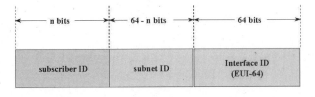

Figure 4-4
Two hierarchical lev-
els

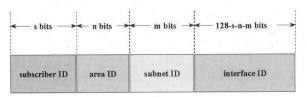

face within the subnet. The use of the MAC address makes possible a very
simple form of address autoconfiguration: The interface can learn the first
64 bits from the router and autoconfigure its address by linking the 64
bits derived from its MAC address to them. In case the interface doesn't
have a MAC address, other forms of layer 2 addresses can be used—for
example, *E.164* addresses (ISDN numbers) for public network interfaces.

If the organization is particularly wide, it can decide that only one level
of internal hierarchy is not enough and to configure two hierarchy levels:
area and subnet. This solution is shown in Figure 4-4. Using an interface
ID smaller than 64 bits may be desirable to leave more space for *area ID*
and *subnet ID* fields.

Anyhow, the main partition remains the one between the interface address and the remaining part of the address. In fact, as we saw in Section
2.5, when a node forwards a packet, it checks whether the destination address is reachable through one of its interfaces—that is, whether the destination node is connected to one of its links. To execute this operation,
knowing the length of the subnet prefix independently from existing hierarchical levels is essential. This number is

```
n = 128 - length(interface address)
```

according to the description in Figure 4-2.

4.6.2 Aggregatable Global Unicast Addresses

Aggregatable Global Unicast addresses are specified in *IP Version 6 Addressing Architecture* [16]. These addresses, which are characterized by FP
= 001, are illustrated in Figure 4-5.

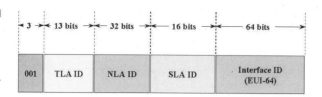

Figure 4-5
An Aggregatable
Global Unicast ad-
dress

The *Top-Level Aggregation IDentifier* (TLA ID) field is assigned to an organization providing public transit topology. It is specifically not assigned to an organization providing only leaf or private transit topology. The IANA will assign small blocks of TLA ID to IPv6 registries. At present, four registries exist; see Table 4-2.

The *Next-Level Aggregation IDentifier* (NLA ID) field is used by organizations assigned a TLA ID to create an addressing hierarchy and to identify sites (the ISP users).

The *Site-Level Aggregation IDentifier* (SLA ID) field is used by users assigned a TLA ID to create an addressing hierarchy within the sites, and this usually includes the subnet identifier.

This kind of assignment satisfies most users who can have at their disposal 64 thousand subnets, each one of practically unlimited size.

A discussion of problems related to Aggregatable Global Unicast addresses can be found in Section 7.6 and in RFC 1887 [8], where the connection between routing and addressing is examined, either within a domain or between different domains.

The Unicast addresses to be used in the IPv6 testing phase are detailed in Section A.4 of Appendix A.

4.6.3 Geographic-Based Addresses

Geographic-based addresses have been studied and proposed in the SIP project (see Section 1.5.4), but a final decision about them has not yet been made because ISPs strongly oppose them. In the latest IETF drafts, they are no longer present.

So that we can deploy these addresses, the world must be subdivided into continents, then into regions, and then into metropolitan areas. All ISPs that serve a given area must interconnect to route packets correctly. In this way, addresses can be directly allocated to end users who maintain the addresses even if they change ISPs. The ISPs' opposition is based on the complexity of routing table management.

Table 4-2

Current registries

Scope	Authority
Multiregional	IANA
Europe	RIPE-NCC
Northern America	INTERNIC
Asia and Pacific	APNIC

Geographic-based addresses have not yet been definitively abandoned, as shown by the fact that they have been allocated 1/8 of the IPv6 addressing space (FP = 100). Nevertheless, at the moment, there are no plans to use them.

For a discussion of advantages and drawbacks of Aggregatable Global Unicast and Geographic-based solutions, see Chapter 7.

4.6.4 Link Local Addresses

Link Local addresses (FP = 1111 1110 10) are designed to be used on each link for address autoconfiguration and for neighbor discovery functions. Their format is illustrated in Figures 4-6 and 4-7.

Suppose we have a small LAN with a few PCs connected and without a router; in this case, Link Local addresses turn out to be the only addresses we need.

Let's consider, for example, a PC with an IEEE 802.3 board with MAC address `08-00-02-12-34-56`. If we assume that the 48-bit MAC address is used as the interface ID, the PC's IPv6 Link Local address is

`FE80:0000:0000:0000:0000:0800:0212:3456`

or its compressed form is

`FE80::800:0212:3456`

In contrast, if we assume that the 64-bit EUI-64 (see Section 4.10) address is used as the interface ID, the PC's IPv6 Link Local address is

`FE80:0000:0000:0000:0A00:02FF:FE12:3456`

or its compressed form is

`FE80::A00:2FF:FE12:3456`

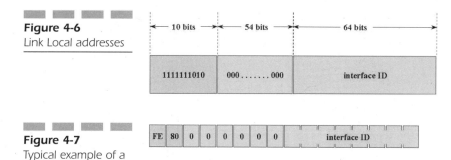

Figure 4-6
Link Local addresses

Figure 4-7
Typical example of a
Link Local address

Remember that routers must never retransmit IPv6 packets that have a Link Local address as a source address.

4.6.5   Site Local Addresses

Site Local (FP = 1111 1110 11) addresses are designed to replace IPv4 addresses defined by RFCs 1597 [9] and 1918 [10] (see Section 1.3.3) for use in Intranets. Site Local addresses are therefore ideal for organizations not (yet) connected to the global Internet. They do not need any form of registration, and they have a format (see Figure 4-8) that makes replacing them with Aggregatable Global Unicast addresses simple when global connectivity to the Internet is desired.

The typical format of a Site Local address is illustrated in Figure 4-9.

A network using Site Local addresses can be complex because the presence of the subnet field on two octets allows us to have up to 64 thousand different subnets, each one with practically unlimited size.

A router with an IEEE 802.3 interface and MAC address `00-00-0C-12-34-56` connected to subnet 17 will have, on that interface, the following Site Local IPv6 address (using the 48-bit MAC address as the interface identifier):

FEC0:0000:0000:0000:0011:0000:0C12:3456

Its compressed form is as follows:

FEC0::11:0:C12:3456

If the EUI-64 MAC address is used (see Section 4.10) as the interface identifier, the resulting Site Local address is as follows:

FEC0:0000:0000:0011:0200:0CFF:FE12:3456

                                              Chapter Four

Figure 4-8
Site Local addresses

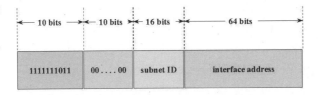

Figure 4-9
Typical example of a
Site Local address

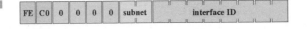

Here is its compressed form:

FEC0::11:200:CFF:FE12:3456

Again, remember that routers must never retransmit outside the site; IPv6 packets having a Site Local address as the source address. They must obviously retransmit these packets between different subnets of the same site.

4.6.6 The Unspecified Address

The address `0000:0000:0000:0000:0000:0000:0000:0000` is also called the *unspecified address,* and it can be written in the compressed form `::`. It must never be assigned to any interface because it indicates the absence of an IPv6 address. It can be used as a source address by a node during the configuration phase, when the node itself is trying to discover its IPv6 address. Also, the unspecified address must never be used as the destination address or in the Routing header (see Section 3.2.5).

4.6.7 The Loopback Address

The address `0000:0000:0000:0000:0000:0000:0000:0001` is also called the *loopback address* (its compressed form is `::1`), and it is used by a node to send an IPv6 packet to itself. It must never be assigned to any interface.

A node must never transmit outside itself any IPv6 packets with a loopback address as the source or destination address.

4.6.8 IPv6 Addresses with Embedded IPv4 Addresses

The transition mechanism from IPv4 to IPv6 includes a mechanism to dynamically tunnel IPv6 packets over the IPv4 routing infrastructure. (See Chapter 12 for details about the transition to IPv6.) IPv6 nodes that use this technique are assigned special IPv6 unicast addresses that carry an IPv4 address in the low-order 32 bits, as shown in Figure 4-10. These addresses are called *IPv4-compatible IPv6 addresses.*

An example of this type of address is the following:

```
::130.192.252.27
```

A second type of IPv6 address that holds an embedded IPv4 address is called an *IPv4-mapped IPv6 address* (see Figure 4-11). This second type of address is used to represent the address of an IPv4-only node in IPv6. An example of this type of address is the following:

```
::FFFF:130.192.252.27
```

4.6.9 NSAP Addresses

Today, the use of IPv6 addresses derived from ISO/OSI NSAP (FP = 0000 001) addresses is still under consideration, and a proposal in this direction is specified by RFC 1888 [4]. NSAP addresses are binary strings up to

Figure 4-10
IPv4-compatible IPv6 address

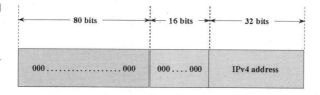

Figure 4-11
IPv4-mapped IPv6 address

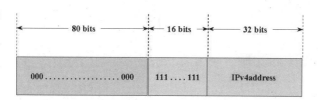

20 octets long defined in the OSI project by the standard ISO 8348 [12]. In the past, they held a certain interest because some organizations decided to adopt the layer 3 connectionless protocol ISO 8473 [11], which uses these addresses. NSAP addresses allow seven possible subformats, most of which are obsolete. Three subformats have been resumed and are used currently by the ATM [13] to address layer 2 ATM stations; they are illustrated in Figure 4-12.

At first glance, we can see that deriving IPv6 addresses starting from NSAP addresses (see Figure 4-13) clearly creates some problems because NSAP addresses (160 bits) are longer than IPv6 addresses (128 bits). These problems have three possible solutions:

1. To create a rule to map NSAP fields into IPv6 address fields; this solution is possible because not all NSAP fields have been used.

2. To truncate the NSAP and use it for routing while the complete NSAP address is transported inside a Destination option (see Section 3.2.8); for this purpose, a NSAPA option has been defined and is identified by the value 195 in the Option Type field (see Section 3.2.2).

3. To use a normal IPv6 address for the routing and to transport the complete NSAP inside a Destination option as in the previous case.

Considering the limited impact that, in our honest opinion, these types of addresses will have in the future, we will not discuss them further here. For a more detailed treatment, see RFC 1888 [4].

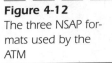

Figure 4-12
The three NSAP formats used by the ATM

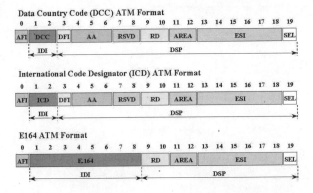

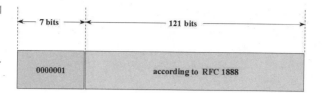

Figure 4-13
IPv6 address drawn
from a NSAP address

← 7 bits →	← 121 bits →
0000001	according to RFC 1888

4.6.10   IPX Addresses

The network operating system Novell Netware is undoubtedly one of the most diffused in the field of PC networks. This network software can support several layer 3 (network) protocols, but the preferential protocol is *Internetwork Packet Exchange* (IPX) [14]. IPX is a connectionless protocol that assigns addresses to interfaces and is therefore very similar to IP. Addresses, which have the format shown in Figure 4-14, consist of two parts: Six octets contain the interface address (very frequently the MAC address), and four octets contain the segment ID.

The concept of *segments* is similar to the concept of *subnets* in IP. Because an IPX address is globally 80 bits long, implementing a relationship with IPv6 addresses (FP = 0000 010) that have 121 bits available for this purpose creates no problems (see Figure 4-15).

Nevertheless, at present no standard specifies how to implement this solution.

4.7   Anycast Addresses

We discussed the role of anycast addresses in Sections 1.3.2 and 4.3. Nevertheless, we must say that today we have little experience with the management of these addresses. Anycast addresses don't have separate addressing spaces (no particular FP value identifies anycast addresses); they simply are unicast addresses (belonging to one of the formats described in Section 4.6) assigned to more than one interface. When an anycast address is assigned to an interface, it must be explicitly configured to know that it is an anycast address; this information is usually specified by a qualifier at the time of the assignment.

Figure 4-14
IPX address

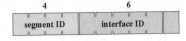

Figure 4-15
IPv6 address drawn
from an IPX address

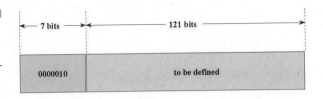

One possible use of anycast addresses is to identify a set of routers belonging to a given ISP, or all routers connected to a given subnet, or all border routers toward other domains.

For each anycast address, a prefix P identifies the topological region in which all interfaces belonging to that anycast address reside. Within this region—that is, this set of subnets—each interface associated with the anycast address must be advertised as a separate entry in a router's routing tables (see Section 2.6) so that the "nearest" interface belonging to the anycast set can be identified.

If the prefix P is null, the members of the set may have no topological locality. In this case, the anycast address must be advertised as a separate outing entry throughout the entire Internet, which presents a severe scaling limit on how many such "global" anycast sets can be supported.

After considering these "youthful" problems of anycast addresses, RFC 1884 [3] imposes the following two restrictions on the use of IPv6 anycast addresses:

■ Anycast addresses must not be used as source addresses on IPv6 packets.

■ Anycast addresses must not be assigned to IPv6 hosts—that is, they can be assigned to IPv6 routers only.

The only anycast address defined up till now is the *Subnet router anycast address;* its format is shown in Figure 4-16. Its intended use is to identify a set of routers connected to a given link. The *subnet prefix* must coincide with the prefix of the subnet associated with the link. A packet forwarded to the Subnet router anycast address will be delivered by a router connected to that link.

All routers are required to receive packets forwarded to the Subnet router anycast address on all the subnets on which they have interfaces.

n bits	128 - n bits
subnet prefix	000...00000

Figure 4-16
Anycast address

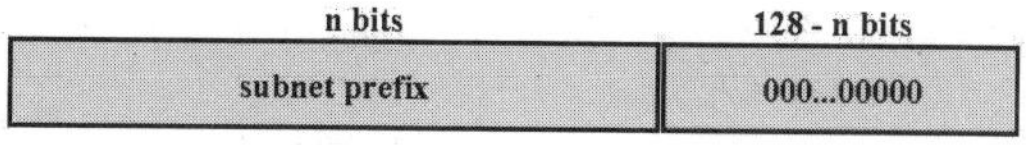

The Subnet router anycast address is useful, for example, either to solve the problem, present in IPv4, of the manual configuration of the default gateway on all hosts, or for a mobile host that needs to communicate with one of the routers on its home network.

4.8   Multicast Addresses

The possibility of implementing multicast transmissions on the Internet was developed in 1988 with the advent of class D IPv4 addresses. This feature is used widely by new multimedia applications that frequently need to transmit from one node to many nodes.

For this purpose, IPv6 specifies an addressing space identified by FP = 1111 1111; this format is illustrated in Figure 4-17.

The *flg* (flag) field is 4 bits long, and its structure is shown in Figure 4-18.

The first 3 bits are reserved for future uses and must be set to zero. The T bit can assume two different values:

- T = 0 indicates a permanently assigned (well-known) multicast address, assigned by the global Internet numbering authority (IANA).

- T = 1 indicates a transient multicast address, not permanently assigned.

The 4-bit *scp* (scope) field is used to limit the scope of the multicast group. Possible values for this field are indicated in Table 4-3.

The 112-bit *group ID* field identifies the multicast group, either permanent or transient, within a given scope. This means, for example, that equal ID groups can be simultaneously used in different parts of the network without interference, if their scopes are separate.

The meaning of a permanently assigned multicast address is independent of the scope value. Let's consider, for example, the *Network Time Protocol* (NTP) [15] servers group, which is the permanent group 43 hexadecimal

Figure 4-17
Multicast address

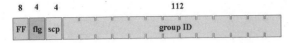

Figure 4-18
The flg field

Table 4-3

Allowed values for scp

scp	Meaning
0	Reserved
1	Node Local scope
2	Link Local scope
3	(Unassigned)
4	(Unassigned)
5	Site Local scope
6	(Unassigned)
7	(Unassigned)
8	Organization Local scope
9	(Unassigned)
A	(Unassigned)
B	(Unassigned)
C	(Unassigned)
D	(Unassigned)
E	Global scope
F	Reserved

assigned by IPv6. All the following four addresses belong to group 43, while having different meanings:

- FF01::43 means all NTP servers on the same node as the sender.
- FF02::43 means all NTP servers on the same link as the sender.
- FF05::43 means all NTP servers on the same site as the sender.
- FF0E::43 means all NTP servers present on the network.

Transient addresses can be associated with different applications in different parts of the network.

Moreover, multicast addresses must not be used as source addresses or appear in any Routing header (see Section 3.2.5).

4.8.1 Predefined Multicast Addresses

RFC 1884 [3] predefines a certain number of multicast addresses. They will be described in the following subsections.

4.8.1.1 RESERVED MULTICAST ADDRESSES   The following multicast addresses are reserved for future uses:

```
FF00:0000:0000:0000:0000:0000:0000:0000
FF01:0000:0000:0000:0000:0000:0000:0000
FF02:0000:0000:0000:0000:0000:0000:0000
FF03:0000:0000:0000:0000:0000:0000:0000
FF04:0000:0000:0000:0000:0000:0000:0000
FF05:0000:0000:0000:0000:0000:0000:0000
FF06:0000:0000:0000:0000:0000:0000:0000
FF07:0000:0000:0000:0000:0000:0000:0000
FF08:0000:0000:0000:0000:0000:0000:0000
FF09:0000:0000:0000:0000:0000:0000:0000
FF0A:0000:0000:0000:0000:0000:0000:0000
FF0B:0000:0000:0000:0000:0000:0000:0000
FF0C:0000:0000:0000:0000:0000:0000:0000
FF0D:0000:0000:0000:0000:0000:0000:0000
FF0E:0000:0000:0000:0000:0000:0000:0000
FF0F:0000:0000:0000:0000:0000:0000:0000
```

4.8.1.2 ALL NODES ADDRESSES   The following multicast addresses identify the group of all IPv6 nodes within the scope 1 (Node Local) and the scope 2 (Link Local):

```
FF01:0000:0000:0000:0000:0000:0000:0001
FF02:0000:0000:0000:0000:0000:0000:0001
```

4.8.1.3 ALL ROUTERS ADDRESSES   The following multicast addresses identify the group of all IPv6 routers within the scope 1 (Node Local), the scope 2 (Link Local), and the scope 5 (Site Local):

```
FF01:0000:0000:0000:0000:0000:0000:0002
```

```
FF02:0000:0000:0000:0000:0000:0000:0002
FF05:0000:0000:0000:0000:0000:0000:0002
```

4.8.1.4 SOLICITED NODE MULTICAST ADDRESS Multicast addresses in the range from

```
FF02:0000:0000:0000:0000:0001:FF00:0000
```

to

```
FF02:0000:0000:0000:0000:0001:FFFF:FFFF
```

are reserved for the Neighbor Discovery protocol (see Chapter 6) within the link. They are formed by taking the low-order 32 bits of the address (unicast or anycast) and appending them to the following prefix:

```
FF02:0000:0000:0000:0000:0001
```

For example, the Aggregatable Global Unicast address

```
2037::01:800:200E:8C6C
```

is associated with the Neighbor Discovery address (*Solicited Node Multicast Address*)

```
FF02::1:FF0E:8C6C
```

4.8.1.5 OTHER MULTICAST ADDRESSES Other multicast addresses currently defined are as follows:

```
FF02:0:0:0:0:0:0:4        DVMRP Routers
FF02:0:0:0:0:0:0:5        OSPFIGP
FF02:0:0:0:0:0:0:6        OSPFIGP Designated Routers
FF02:0:0:0:0:0:0:7        ST Routers
FF02:0:0:0:0:0:0:8        ST Hosts
FF02:0:0:0:0:0:0:9        RIP Routers
FF02:0:0:0:0:0:0:A        EIGRP Routers
FF02:0:0:0:0:0:0:B        Mobile-Agents
FF02:0:0:0:0:0:0:D        All PIM Routers
FF02:0:0:0:0:0:0:E        RSVP-Encapsulation
FF02:0:0:0:0:0:1:1        Link Name
FF02:0:0:0:0:0:1:2        All-dhcp-agents
FF05:0:0:0:0:0:1:3        All-dhcp-servers
FF05:0:0:0:0:0:1:4        All-dhcp-relays
FF05:0:0:0:0:0:1:1000
```

```
to FF05:0:0:0:0:0:1:13FF   Service Location
FF0X:0:0:0:0:0:0:100       VMTP Managers Group
FF0X:0:0:0:0:0:0:101       Network Time Protocol (NTP)
FF0X:0:0:0:0:0:0:102       SGI-Dogfight
FF0X:0:0:0:0:0:0:103       Rwhod
FF0X:0:0:0:0:0:0:104       VNP
FF0X:0:0:0:0:0:0:105       Artificial Horizons
FF0X;0:0:0:0:0:0:106       NSS - Name Service Server
FF0X:0:0:0:0:0:0:107       AUDIONEWS - Audio News
FF0X:0:0:0:0:0:0:108       SUN NIS+ Information Service
FF0X:0:0:0:0:0:0:109       MTP Multicast Transport Protocol
FF0X:0:0:0:0:0:0:10A       IETF-1-LOW-AUDIO
FF0X:0:0:0:0:0:0:10B       IETF-1-AUDIO
FF0X:0:0:0:0:0:0:10C       IETF-1-VIDEO
FF0X:0:0:0:0:0:0:10D       IETF-2-LOW-AUDIO
FF0X:0:0:0:0:0:0:10E       IETF-2-AUDIO
FF0X:0:0:0:0:0:0:10F       IETF-2-VIDEO
FF0X:0:0:0:0:0:0:110       MUSIC-SERVICE
FF0X:0:0:0:0:0:0:111       SEANET-TELEMETRY
FF0X:0:0:0:0:0:0:112       SEANET-IMAGE
FF0X:0:0:0:0:0:0:113       MLOADD
FF0X:0:0:0:0:0:0:114       any private experiment
FF0X:0:0:0:0:0:0:115       DVMRP on MOSPF
FF0X:0:0:0:0:0:0:116       SVRLOC
FF0X:0:0:0:0:0:0:117       XINGTV
FF0X:0:0:0:0:0:0:118       microsoft-ds
FF0X:0:0:0:0:0:0:119       nbc-pro
FF0X:0:0:0:0:0:0:11A       nbc-pfn
FF0X:0:0:0:0:0:0:11B       lmsc-calren-1
FF0X:0:0:0:0:0:0:11C       lmsc-calren-2
FF0X:0:0:0:0:0:0:11D       lmsc-calren-3
FF0X:0:0:0:0:0:0:11E       lmsc-calren-4
FF0X:0:0:0:0:0:0:11F       ampr-info
FF0X:0:0:0:0:0:0:120       mtrace
FF0X:0:0:0:0:0:0:121       RSVP-encap-1
FF0X:0:0:0:0:0:0:122       RSVP-encap-2
FF0X:0:0:0:0:0:0:123       SVRLOC-DA
FF0X:0:0:0:0:0:0:124       rln-server
FF0X:0:0:0:0:0:0:125       proshare-mc
FF0X:0:0:0:0:0:0:126       dantz
FF0X:0:0:0:0:0:0:127       cisco-rp-announce
FF0X:0:0:0:0:0:0:128       cisco-rp-discovery
FF0X:0:0:0:0:0:0:129       gatekeeper
FF0X:0:0:0:0:0:0:12A       iberiagames
FF0X:0:0:0:0:0:0:202       SUN RPC PMAPPROC_CALLIT
FF0X:0:0:0:0:0:2:0000
to FF0X:0:0:0:0:0:2:7FFD   Multimedia Conference Calls
FF0X:0:0:0:0:0:2:7FFE      SAPv1 Announcements
FF0X:0:0:0:0:0:2:8000
to FF0X:0:0:0:0:0:2:FFFF   SAP Dynamic Assignments
```

4.9 Which Addresses for a Node?

A reasonable question at this point is: Which addresses must a node have? The answer comes, once again, from RFC 1884, which lists all addresses that an IPv6 node can have.

4.9.1 Addresses of a Host

A host is required to recognize the following addresses as identifying itself:

- Its Link Local address for each interface
- Unicast addresses assigned to interfaces
- The loopback address
- All-Nodes multicast address
- Neighbor Discovery multicast addresses associated with all unicast and anycast addresses assigned to interfaces
- Multicast Addresses of groups to which the node belongs

4.9.2 Addresses of a Router

A router is required to recognize the following addresses as identifying itself:

- Its Link Local address for each interface
- Unicast addresses assigned to interfaces
- The loopback address
- The Subnet Router anycast address for all links on which it has interfaces
- Other anycast addresses assigned to interfaces
- All-nodes multicast address
- All-routers multicast address
- Neighbor Discovery multicast addresses associated with all unicast and anycast addresses assigned to interfaces
- Multicast addresses of groups to which the node belongs

4.10 The EUI-64 Interface Identifier

The IEEE has introduced a new type of MAC address, 64-bits long, called the EUI-64.

Until now, MAC addresses have been on 48 bits: 24 bits assigned by the IEEE and 24 bits manufacturer selected. The 24 bits assigned by the IEEE are called *Organization Unique Identifier* (OUI). Any company that has received an OUI from the IEEE can use it also for the new EUI-64 identifiers. It is sufficient to use the OUI as the first 24 bits and append them to the 40 manufacturer-selected bits.

Mapping the old 48-bit MAC addresses to a new 64-bit representation is also possible. The mapping process consists of inserting two octets with the value 0xFF and 0xFE between the OUI and the manufacturer-selected bits.

To obtain an IPv6 interface identifier from an EUI-64 address, we must complement the Universal/Local bit—that is, the next-to-last bit of the first octet.

The mapping of Universal MAC addresses to IPv6 interface identifiers is illustrated in Figure 4-19 for 48-bit MAC addresses and in Figure 4-20 for EUI-64.

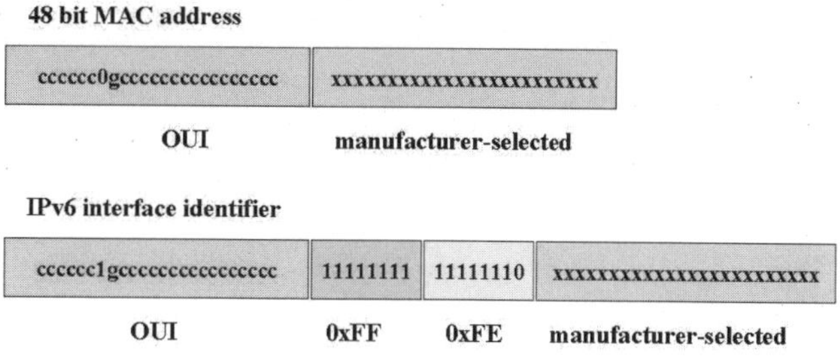

Figure 4-19
Address mapping from 48-bit to IPv6

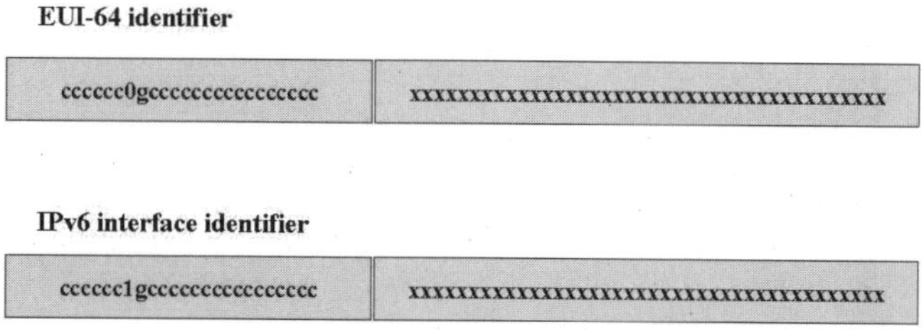

48 bit MAC address

ccccccc0ccccccccccccccccc	xxxxxxxxxxxxxxxxxxxxxxxx
OUI	manufacturer-selected

IPv6 interface identifier

ccccccc1gccccccccccccccccc	11111111	11111110	xxxxxxxxxxxxxxxxxxxxxxxx
OUI	0xFF	0xFE	manufacturer-selected

Figure 4-20
Address mapping from EUI to IPv6

EUI-64 identifier

ccccccc0ccccccccccccccccc	xxxxxxxxxxxxxxxxxxxxxxxxxxxxxxxxxxxxxxxx

IPv6 interface identifier

ccccccc1gccccccccccccccccc	xxxxxxxxxxxxxxxxxxxxxxxxxxxxxxxxxxxxxxxx

REFERENCES

[1]S.O. Bradner, A. Mankin, *IPng: Internet Protocol Next Generation*, Addison-Wesley, 1995.

[2]V. Cerf, *RFC 1607: A View From The 21st Century*, April 1994.

[3]R. Hinden, S. Deering, *RFC 1884: IP Version 6 Addressing Architecture*, December 1995.

[4]J. Bound, B. Carpenter, D. Harrington, J. Houldsworth, A. Lloyd, *RFC 1888: OSI NSAPs and IPv6*, August 1996.

[5]C. Huitema, *IPv6: the new Internet Protocol*, Prentice-Hall, 1996.

[6]IAB & IESG, *RFC 1881: IPv6 Address Allocation Management*, December 1995.

[7]Y. Rekhter, T. Li, *RFC 1518: An Architecture for IP Address Allocation with CIDR*, September 1993.

[8]Y. Rekhter, T. Li, *RFC 1887; An Architecture for IPv6 Unicast Address Allocation*, December 1995.

[9]Y. Rekhter, B. Moskowitz, D. Karrenberg, G. de Groot, *RFC 1597: Address Allocation for Private Internets*, March 1994.

[10]Y. Rekhter, B. Moskowitz, D. Karrenberg, G. J. de Groot, E. Lear, *RFC 1918: Address Allocation for Private Internets*, February 1996.

[11]ISO/IEC 8473, *IS8473: Data communications protocol for providing the connectionless-mode network service*, 1988.

[12]ISO/IEC 8348, *IS8348: Annex A, Network Layer Addressing, and Annex B, Rationale for the material in Annex A*, 1993 (same as CCITT X.213, 1992).

[13]Uyless Black, *ATM: Foundation for Broadband Networks*, Prentice-Hall, 1995.

[14]Matthew Naugle, *Network Protocol Handbook,* McGraw-Hill, 1994.

[15]D.L. Mills, *RFC 1305: Network Time Protocol (Version 3) Specification, Implementation*, March 1992.

[16] R. Hinden, S. Deering, *IP Version 6 Addressing Architecture,* Internet Draft, July 1997.

ICMPv6

The ICMPv6 (Internet Control Message Protocol version 6)[1] is an integral part of the IPv6 architecture[2] and must be completely supported by all IPv6 implementations. ICMPv6 combines functions previously subdivided among different protocols, such as ICMP (Internet Control Message Protocol version 4)[3], IGMP (Internet Group Membership Protocol)[4], and ARP (Address Resolution Protocol)[5], and it introduces some simplifications by eliminating obsolete types of messages no longer in use.

In this chapter, we will analyze the protocol's main characteristics and the packet's format, while a more thorough discussion about Neighbor Discovery problems is deferred until Chapter 6.

5.1 Protocol Overview

ICMPv6 (in the following text called *ICMP* for the sake of brevity) is a multipurpose protocol; for example, it is used for reporting errors encountered in processing packets, performing diagnostics, performing Neighbor Discovery, and reporting multicast memberships. For this reason, ICMP messages are subdivided into two classes: *error messages* and *information messages*.

ICMP messages are transported within an IPv6 packet in which extension headers can also be present (see Section 3.2). An ICMP message is identified by a value of 58 in the Next Header field of the IPv6 header or of the preceding Header (see Table 3-2).

5.2 Packets Format

ICMPv6 packets have the format shown in Figure 5-1.

The 8-bit *Type* field indicates the type of the message. If the high-order bit has value zero (values in the range from 0 to 127), it is an error message; if the high-order bit has value 1 (values in the range from 128 to 255), it is an information message. A list of currently defined message types is shown in Table 5-1.

The 8-bit *Code* field content depends on the message type, and it is used to create an additional level of message granularity.

The *Checksum* field is used to detect errors in the ICMP message and in part of the IPv6 message.

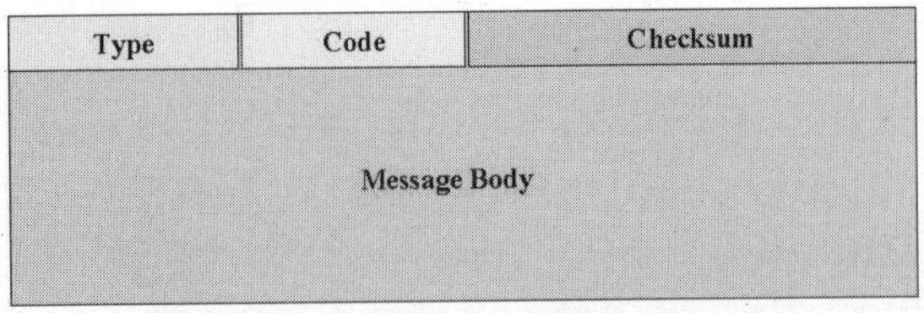

Figure 5-1
Format of an ICMPv6 message

Type	Code	Checksum
Message Body		

Table 5-1

Types of ICMP
messages

Type	Meaning
1	Destination Unreachable
2	Packet Too Big
3	Time Exceeded
4	Parameter Problem
128	Echo Request
129	Echo Reply
130	Group Membership Query
131	Group Membership Report
132	Group Membership Reduction
133	Router Solicitation
134	Router Advertisement
135	Neighbor Solicitation
136	Neighbor Advertisement
137	Redirect

5.3   ICMP Message Transmission

A node that forwards an ICMP message has to determine both the source and
the destination IPv6 addresses for the ICMP message. Particular care must
be put into the choice of the source address. If a node has more than one unicast address, it must choose the source address of the message as follows:

- If the message is a response to a message sent to one of the node unicast
  addresses, the Source Address of the reply must be that same address.

- If the message is a response to a message sent to a multicast or
  anycast group to which the node belongs, the Source Address of
  the reply must be a unicast address belonging to the interface on
  which the multicast or anycast packet was received.

- If the message is a response to a message sent to an address that
  does not belong to the node, the Source Address should be the unicast address belonging to the node that will be the most helpful in

checking the error (for example, the unicast address belonging to the interface on which the packet forwarding failed).

■ In other cases, the node routing tables must be examined (see Section 2.6) to determine which interface will be used to transmit the message to its destination, and the unicast address belonging to that interface must be used as the Source Address of the message.

When an ICMP node receives a packet, it must undertake actions that depend on the type of message. A more detailed discussion is beyond the aim of this book. Refer to Section A.3 in Appendix A for an excerpt from RFC 1885 [1] dealing with this subject.

Moreover, the ICMP protocol must limit the number of error messages sent to the same destination to avoid network overloading. For example, if a node continues to forward erroneous packets, ICMP will signal the error to the first packet and then do so periodically, with a fixed minimum period or with a fixed network maximum load.

An ICMP error message must never be sent in response to another ICMP error message.

5.4   Error Messages

ICMPv6 error messages are similar to ICMPv4 error messages. They belong to four categories: Destination Unreachable, Packet Too Big, Time Exceeded, and Parameter Problems. We will analyze them further in the following subsections.

5.4.1   Destination Unreachable

The *Destination Unreachable* message, which is illustrated in Figure 5-2, is generated when the network must discard an IPv6 packet because the destination is unreachable. The IPv6 destination address of the ICMP packet is therefore the source address of the discarded packet.

The *Type* field value is 1.

The *Code* field can assume values reported in Table 5-2.

The *Unused* field, of course, is not used; it is initialized to zero during the transmission and ignored on reception.

The first part of the IPv6 packet that caused the generation of the ICMP packet follows. Because being able to transmit the ICMP packet on

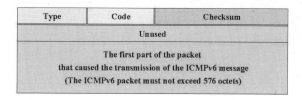

Figure 5-2
Destination Unreach-
able message

any link must be possible (see Section 3.3), the packet must not exceed 576 octets (the IPv6 header and eventual extension headers included).

This type of message can be generated either by a router or by a destination node that cannot deliver the message; the router or node is therefore forced to discard the message. A packet is dropped without generating a message of this type only when the network is congested; generating ICMP messages will make the congestion worse.

The reasons for the failure in delivering a packet are as follow:

- *No route to destination:* A router cannot find a matching entry for the destination address in its routing table, and therefore it doesn't know on which interface to retransmit the packet.

- *Communication with destination administratively prohibited:* The message is dropped by a firewall—that is, by a router that contains a set of rules that forbid some communications.

- *Not a neighbor:* The message contains a Routing header, the next destination address has the Strict / Loose bit equal to Strict, and the next destination address doesn't belong to any of the router links (it is not a neighbor).

- *Address unreachable:* The destination address is unreachable for other reasons—for example, for an interface error or for the inability to compute the link layer address of the destination node.

- *Port unreachable:* The packet reached the destination node, but the layer 4 protocol (for example, UDP) to which the packet should be delivered (the port) is unreachable.

5.4.2   Packet Too Big

The *Packet Too Big* message, which is illustrated in Figure 5-3, is generated when the network must discard an IPv6 packet because its size exceeds the MTU of the outgoing link. The information contained in the ICMP packet is used as part of the Path MTU Discovery procedure. The

Figure 5-3
Packet Too Big message

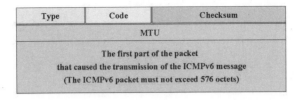

Type	Code	Checksum
MTU		
The first part of the packet that caused the transmission of the ICMPv6 message (The ICMPv6 packet must not exceed 576 octets)		

Table 5-2

Destination
Unreachable: Code

Code	Meaning
0	No route to destination
1	Communication with destination administratively prohibited
2	Not a neighbor
3	Address unreachable
4	Port unreachable

IPv6 destination address of the ICMP packet is therefore the source address of the dropped packet.

The *Type* field has value 2.

The *Code* field always has value zero.

The 32-bit *MTU* field indicates the MTU of the link on which transmitting the packet was impossible.

The first part of the IPv6 packet that caused the ICMP packet follows. Because being able to transmit the ICMP packet on any link must be possible (see Section 3.3), the packet must not exceed 576 octets (the IPv6 header and eventual extension headers included).

5.4.3   Time Exceeded

The *Time Exceeded* message, which is illustrated in Figure 5-4, is generated when a router must discard an IPv6 packet because its Hop Limit field (see Section 3.1.6) is zero or decrements to zero. This message indicates that either a routing loop or an initial Hop Limit value is too small. Another reason is the impossibility to reassemble a fragmented packet within the allowed time limit. The IPv6 destination address of the ICMP packet is therefore the source address of the dropped packet.

The *Type* field has value 3.

The *Code* field can have the values reported in Table 5-3.

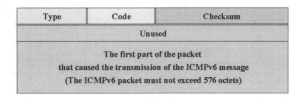

Figure 5-4
Time Exceeded
message

Type	Code	Checksum
Unused		
The first part of the packet that caused the transmission of the ICMPv6 message (The ICMPv6 packet must not exceed 576 octets)		

Table 5-3

Time Exceeded:
Code field values

Code	Meaning
0	Hop limit exceeded in transit
1	Fragment reassembly time exceeded

The *Unused* field is unused for all code values, and it must be initialized to zero by the sender and ignored by the receiver.

The first part of the IPv6 packet that caused the ICMP packet follows. Because being able to transmit the ICMP packet on any link must be possible (see Section 3.3), the packet must not exceed 576 octets (the IPv6 header and eventual extension headers included).

5.4.4   Parameter Problems

The *Parameter Problem* message, which is illustrated in Figure 5-5, is generated when an IPv6 node must discard a packet because it detects problems in a field of the IPv6 header or of an extension header. The IPv6 destination address of the ICMP packet is therefore the source address of the dropped packet.

The *Type* field has value 4.

The *Code* field can have the three values reported in Table 5-4.

The *Pointer* field identifies the octet in the original message where the error was detected.

The first part of the IPv6 packet that caused the ICMP packet follows. Because being able to transmit the ICMP packet on any link must be possible (see Section 3.3), the packet must not exceed 576 octets (the IPv6 header and eventual extension headers included).

The following three errors can be detected:

■ *Erroneous header field:* A field in a header holding an illegal value has been detected.

Figure 5-5
Parameter Problem
message

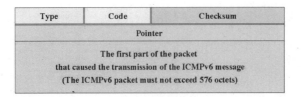

- *Unrecognized Next Header*: A Next Header is unrecognized for the IPv6 implementation present on the node.
- *Unrecognized IPv6 option*: The packet holds an unrecognized option (see Section 3.2.2) for the IPv6 implementation present on the node.

5.5 Informational Messages

A second type of ICMP message is the informational message. These messages are subdivided into three groups: diagnostic messages, messages for the management of multicast groups, and Neighbor Discovery messages.

5.5.1 Echo Request Message

The *Echo Request* message and its corresponding *Echo Reply* message are ICMP diagnostic messages. In particular, these two messages are used to implement the **ping** diagnostic application that allows us to test whether a destination is reachable. The format of these two messages is the same, as illustrated in Figure 5-6. The IPv6 destination address can be any valid IPv6 address.

The *Type* field has value 129.

The *Code* field has value zero.

The *Identifier* field is an identifier used to set a relationship between Echo Request and Echo Reply messages. It can also be set to zero.

The *Sequence Number* field is a sequence number used to set a relationship between Echo Request and Echo Reply messages. It can also be set to zero.

The *Data* field contains zero or more octets of data arbitrarily generated by the diagnostic procedure.

Code	Meaning
0	Erroneous header field
1	Unrecognized Next Header
2	Unrecognized IPv6 option

Table 5-4

Parameter Problem: Code field values

5.5.2 Echo Reply Message

Every IPv6 node must implement an ICMP Echo reply function that receives Echo requests and sends corresponding Echo replies, whose format is illustrated in Figure 5-6. The IPv6 destination address is set equal to the IPv6 source address of the Echo Request message.

The *Type* field has value 129.

The *Code* field has value zero.

The *Identifier* field is copied from the field of the same name in the Echo Request message.

The *Sequence Number* field is copied from the field of the same name in the Echo Request message.

The *Data* field is copied from the field of the same name in the Echo Request message.

An example of this type of packet is shown in Section B.2 in Appendix B.

5.5.3 Group Membership Messages

ICMP Group Membership messages are used to convey information about multicast group membership from nodes to their neighboring routers (connected on the same link). Their format is illustrated in Figure 5-7.

The IPv6 destination address values change in function for the different types of messages:

■ In a *Group Membership Query* message, the destination address is equal to the multicast address of the group being queried or equal to the link local All-Nodes (FF02::1, see Section 4.8.1) multicast address.

■ In a *Group Membership Report* or *Group Membership Reduction* message, the destination address is equal to the multicast address of the group being reported or terminated.

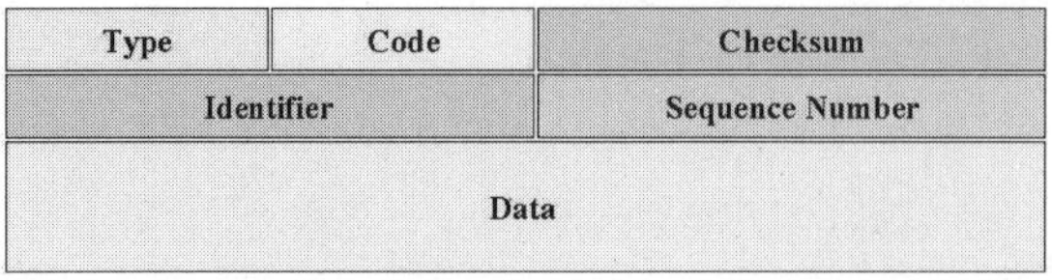

Figure 5-6
Echo Request and
Echo Reply messages

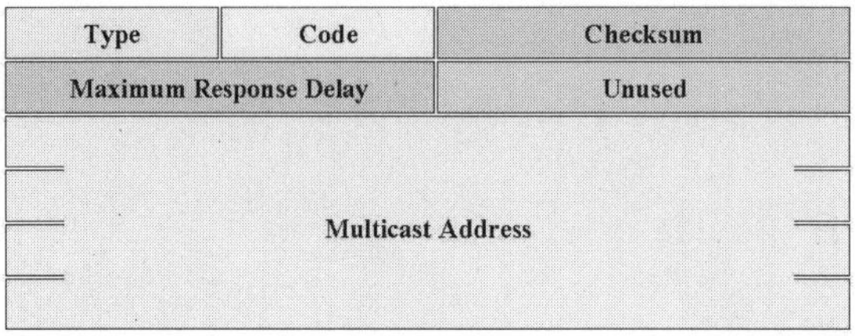

Type	Code	Checksum
Identifier		Sequence Number
Data		

Figure 5-7
Group Membership
message

Type	Code	Checksum
Maximum Response Delay		Unused
Multicast Address		

The IPv6 header *Hop Limit* field is set to 1 (packets are exchanged only between adjacent nodes).

The *Type* field assumes values 130 (Group Membership Query), 131 (Group Membership Report), or 132 (Group Membership Reduction).

The *Code* field has value zero.

The *Maximum Response Delay* field expresses a value in milliseconds. In Group Membership Query messages, this field indicates the maximum time that the responding Report messages can be delayed. In Group Membership Report or Group Membership Reduction messages, this field is initialized to zero by the sender and ignored by the receiver.

The *Unused* field is unused and must be initialized to zero by the sender and ignored by the receiver.

5.5.4 Router Solicitation Message

ICMP messages that will be introduced from this point to the end of the chapter are messages of Neighbor Discovery type (specified by RFC 1970[6]). We discussed the need and use of these types of messages in Section 2.8. In this section, we will analyze formats of different messages in more detail.

IPv6 nodes transmit *Router Solicitation* messages (see Figure 5-8) to prompt routers to generate Router Advertisements immediately.

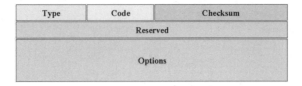

Figure 5-8
Router Solicitation
message format

The source address of a Router Solicitation message is either the unicast address of the interface from which the message is sent or, if this address doesn't exist, the unspecified address. The destination address is typically the All-Router (FF02::2) multicast group.

The *Hop Limit* field of the IPv6 header is set to 255. This setting is a form of protection against attack from hackers. In fact, routers verify that this field has value 255, and if not, they discard the packet. A hacker could never forward a message with the Hop Limit equal to 255 from outside the LAN because the router will decrement it by one. Only packets really generated on the LAN can have a Hop Limit equal to 255.

The *Priority* field of the IPv6 header is set to 15.

The *Type* field is equal to 133.

The *Code* field is equal to zero.

The *Reserved* field is unused; it must be initialized to zero during transmission and ignored on reception.

In the *Options* field can appear the option carrying the layer 2 (link layer) address of the source node, if known (see Section 5.5.10).

An example of this kind of packet is shown in Section B.5 of Appendix B.

5.5.5   Router Advertisement Message

Routers send out Router Advertisement messages periodically or in response to Router Solicitation messages. The format of *Router Advertisement* messages is illustrated in Figure 5-9.

The IPv6 source address is set equal to the link local address of the interface from which the message is sent, and the destination address is equal either to the address of the node that solicited the message or to the All-Node multicast address (FF02::1).

The *Hop Limit* field of the IPv6 header is set to 255 (see Section 5.5.4).

The *Priority* field of the IPv6 header is set to 15.

Figure 5-9
Router Advertisement
message format

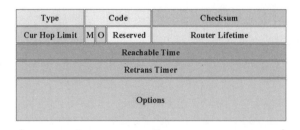

Type		Code		Checksum
Cur Hop Limit	M	O	Reserved	Router Lifetime
Reachable Time				
Retrans Timer				
Options				

The *Type* field is equal to 134.

The *Code* field is equal to zero.

The 8-bit *Cur Hop Limit* field specifies, to nodes that receive the Advertisement, the default value for the Hop Limit field of the IPv6 header to be used during packet transmission. A value of zero means that the sender's router doesn't suggest any default.

The 1-bit *M* (Managed address configuration) field, when set, indicates to nodes that receive the Advertisement that they must use the stateful protocol (see Section 6.7.3) for address autoconfiguration in addition to the stateless address autoconfiguration.

The 1-bit *O* (Other Stateful configuration) field, when set, indicates to nodes that receive the Advertisement that they must use the stateful autoconfiguration protocol for additional information.

The *Reserved* field is unused; it must be initialized to zero by the sender and ignored by the receiver.

The 16-bit *Router Lifetime* field contains the period of time in seconds for which the router can be used as the default router by receiving nodes. If this field is equal to zero, the router cannot be used as the default router.

The 32-bit *Reachable Time* field contains the time, in milliseconds, that a node assumes a neighbor is reachable after having received a reachability confirmation. This parameter is used by the Neighbor Unreachability Detection algorithm (see Section 6.6).

The 32-bit *Retrans Timer* field contains the time, in milliseconds, between retransmitted Neighbor Solicitation messages. It is used by address resolution and Neighbor Unreachability Detection algorithms.

The following options can be present in the *Options* field:

■ The option that specifies the layer 2 (link layer) address of the source node, if known (see Section 5.5.10).

■ The option that specifies the link MTU (see Section 5.5.13).

■ The Prefix Information option that specifies prefixes to be used for the address autoconfiguration (see Section 5.5.11). A router should include all its on-link prefixes (except the link local prefix) so that multihomed hosts will correctly autoconfigure themselves.

An example of this type of packet is shown in Section B.6 of Appendix B.

5.5.6   Neighbor Solicitation Message

IPv6 nodes transmit *Neighbor Solicitation* messages (see Figure 5-10) to request link layer addresses of Target nodes, while also providing the Target with its own link layer address. Neighbor Solicitation messages are sent to multicast addresses (see Section 4.8.1) when a node needs to resolve an address (from IPv6 to link layer) or to unicast addresses when a node seeks to verify the reachability of a neighbor.

The source address of a Neighbor Solicitation message is either the unicast address of the interface that transmits the message or, during the Duplicate Address Detection procedure (see Section 6.7.4), the unspecified address.

The *Hop Limit* field of the IPv6 header is set to 255 (see Section 5.5.4).

The *Priority* field of the IPv6 header is set to 15.

The *Type* field is equal to 135.

The *Code* field is equal to zero.

The *Reserved* field is unused; it must be initialized to zero by the sender and ignored by the receiver.

The 128-bit *Target Address* field specifies the Target node address—that is, the IPv6 address of the node to which the Neighbor Solicitation message is sent.

In the *Options* field can be present the option that specifies the link layer address of the source, if known (see Section 5.5.10).

An example of this type of packet is shown in Section B.7 of Appendix B.

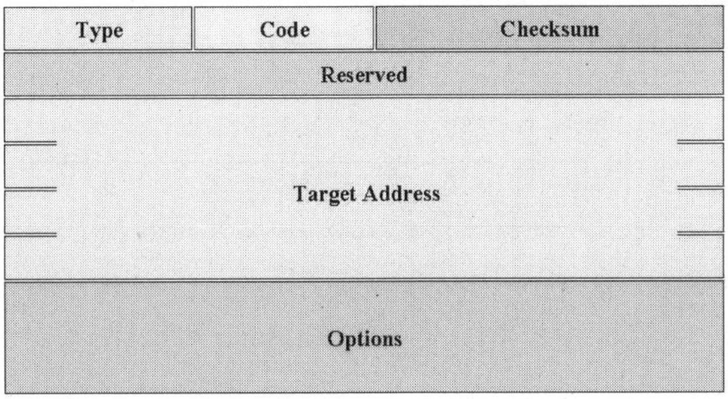

Figure 5-10
Format of the Neighbor Solicitation message

Type	Code	Checksum
Reserved		
Target Address		
Options		

5.5.7 Neighbor Advertisement Message

When the state of a node changes, it forwards a Neighbor Advertisement message (see Figure 5-11) to propagate modifications quickly and in response to a Neighbor Solicitation message.

The source IPv6 address field is set equal to the address of the interface from which the message is sent, and the destination address is equal either to the address of the node that solicited the message or to the All-Node (FF02::1) multicast address.

The *Hop Limit* field of the IPv6 header is set equal to 255 (see Section 5.5.4).

The *Priority* field of the IPv6 header is set equal to 15.

The *Type* field is set equal to 136.

The *Code* field is equal to zero.

The 1-bit *R* (Router flag) field indicates, if set, that the source node is a router.

The 1-bit *S* (Solicited flag) field indicates, if set, that the message has been sent as a reply to a Neighbor Solicitation message.

The 1-bit *O* (Override flag) field indicates, when set, that the message should update the cached link layer address.

The 29-bit *Reserved* field is unused; it must be initialized to zero by the sender and ignored by the receiver.

The 128-bit *Target Address* field specifies, for solicited advertisements, the address of the node that prompted this advertisement. For unsolicited advertisements, this field specifies the IPv6 address whose link layer address has changed.

The *Options* field can contain the option specifying the Target Link Layer Address—that is, the link layer address of the node that sent the Neighbor Advertisement (see Section 5.5.10).

An example of this type of packet is shown in Section B.8 of Appendix B.

5.5.8 Redirect Message

Routers transmit *Redirect* messages to inform other nodes of a better first hop toward a destination. Hosts can be redirected to another router connected to the same link, but more commonly to another neighbor (this can be obtained by setting the Redirect message Target Address field and the

Figure 5-11
Format of the Neighbor Advertisement message

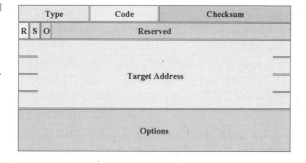

Figure 5-12
Format of the Redirect message

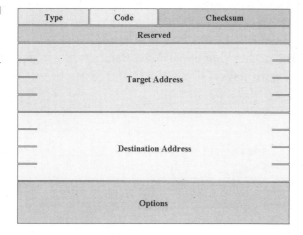

Destination Address field to the same value). The format of the Redirect message is illustrated in Figure 5-12.

The IPv6 source address field is equal to the link local address of the interface from which the message is sent, and the destination address is equal to the source address of the packet that caused the Redirect message.

The *Hop Limit* field of the IPv6 header is set equal to 255 (see Section 5.5.4).

The *Priority* field of the IPv6 header is set equal to 15.

The *Type* field is equal to 137.

The *Code* field is equal to zero.

The *Reserved* field is unused; it must be initialized to zero by the sender and ignored by the receiver.

The 128-bit *Target Address* field contains, for solicited messages, the address of the node that solicited the response. When the Target Address is the endpoint of a communication—that is, the destination is a neighbor—the Target Address field must contain the same value as the Destination Address field. Otherwise, the Target Address is the link local address of a better first hop router toward the destination.

The 128-bit *Destination Address* contains the IPv6 address of the destination that is redirected to the Target Address.

In the *Options* field, the following options can appear:

- The option containing the link layer address of the Target Address, if known (see Section 5.5.10).

- The Redirect header—that is, the option containing the initial part of the packet that caused the Redirect message, truncated so that the ICMP packet doesn't exceed 576 octets (see Section 5.5.12).

5.5.9   Options Format

Neighbor Discovery messages can include zero, one, or more options. Some options can appear multiple times in the same message. All options have the general format illustrated in Figure 5-13.

The 8-bit *Type* field specifies the option type, coded as described in Table 5-5.

The 8-bit *Length* field specifies the option length in units of 8 octets. The value zero is invalid, so nodes that receive a Neighbor Discovery packet that contains an option with length zero must discard it.

5.5.10   Source/Target Link Layer Address Option

Type 1 (*Source Link Layer Address*) and type 2 (*Target Link Layer Address*) options have an identical format; they are illustrated in Figure 5-14.

The link layer address is a layer 2 address with variable length. The minimum length (Length = 1) reserves 48 bits for the link layer address; this length is ideal to transport the MAC address on LANs.

Figure 5-13
Options format

Type	Length	...
...		

Table 5-5

Type field possible values

Type	Option Name
1	Source Link Layer Address
2	Target Link Layer Address
3	Prefix Information
4	Redirect Header
5	MTU

Figure 5-14
Format of Source / Target Link Layer Address option

Type	Length	Link Layer Address
Link Layer Address ...		

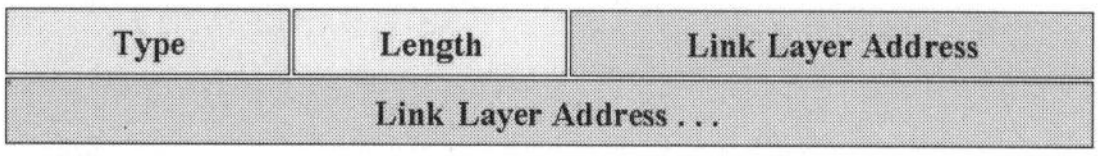

The Source Link Layer Address option contains the link layer address of the sender of the packet. This option is used in Router Solicitation, Router Advertisement, and Neighbor Solicitation messages.

The Target Link Layer Address contains the link layer address of the target. This option is used in Neighbor Advertisement and Redirect messages.

5.5.11   Prefix Information Option

The *Prefix Information* option provide hosts with on-link prefixes for address autoconfiguration. The format of the Prefix Information option is illustrated in Figure 5-15.

The 8-bit *Prefix Length* field contains the prefix length. Valid values range from 0 to 128.

The 1-bit *L* (on-Link flag) field indicates, if set, that the prefix can be used for on-link determination—that is, all addresses belonging to that prefix are on the link. When this field is not set, some addresses can be on-link and others off-link (outside the link).

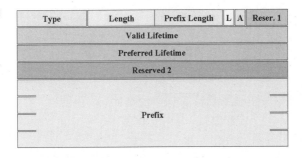

Figure 5-15
Format of the Prefix
Information option

The 1-bit *A* (Autonomous address configuration flag) field indicates, if set, that the prefix can be used for autonomous address configuration.

The 6-bit *Reser. 1* field is unused; it must be initialized to zero by the sender and ignored by the receiver.

The 32-bit *Valid Lifetime* field contains the number of seconds that the address generated from the prefix via stateless autoconfiguration remains valid. The hexadecimal value FFFFFFFF represents infinity.

The 32-bit *Preferred Lifetime* field contains the number of seconds that an address generated from the prefix via stateless autoconfiguration remains preferred. The hexadecimal value FFFFFFFF represents infinity.

The 32-bit *Reserved 2* field is unused; it must be initialized to zero by the sender and ignored by the receiver.

The 128-bit *Prefix* field contains an IPv6 address or a prefix of an IPv6 address. Only first Prefix Length bits are significant, so others must be ignored and initialized to zero.

5.5.12   Redirect Header Option

The *Redirect Header* option is used in ICMP Redirect packets to contain the first part of the message that caused the request of redirection. The Redirect Header option format is shown in Figure 5-16.

The 48-bit *Reserved* field is unused; it must be initialized to zero by the sender and ignored by the receiver.

The *IP header + data* field contains the packet that generated the redirect message. The original packet is truncated to ensure that the size of the redirect message does not exceed 576 octets.

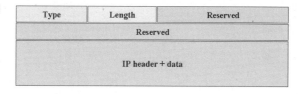

Figure 5-16
Format of the Redirect Header option

Figure 5-17
Format of the MTU option

5.5.13   MTU Option

The *MTU* option is used in Router Advertisement messages to ensure that, on links with variable MTU values, all nodes use the same MTU value. The format of the MTU option is illustrated in Figure 5-17.

The 16-bit *Reserved* field is unused; it must be initialized to zero by the sender and ignored by the receiver.

The 32-bit *Maximum Transmission Unit* (MTU) field contains the recommended MTU for the link.

REFERENCES

[1]A. Conta, S. Deering, RFC 1885: Internet Control Message Protocol (ICMPv6), December 1995.

[2]S. Deering, R. Hinden, RFC 1883: Internet Protocol, Version 6 (IPv6) Specification, December 1995.

[3]J. Postel, *RFC 792: Internet Control Message Protocol*, September 1981.

[4]S.E. Deering, *RFC 1112: Host extensions for IP multicasting*, August 1989.

[5]D.C. Plummer, *RFC 826: Ethernet Address Resolution Protocol: On converting network protocol addresses to 48 bit Ethernet address for transmission on Ethernet hardware*, November 1982.

[6]T. Narten, E. Nordmark, W. Simpson, *RFC 1970: Neighbor Discovery for IP Version 6 (IPv6)*, August 1996.

Neighbor Discovery

Neighbor Discovery is used by IPv6 nodes to implement important functions, among which are the following:

- Locating neighbor routers
- Learning prefixes and configuration parameters related to address configuration
- Autoconfiguring their addresses to establish relationships between link layer addresses and IPv6 addresses
- Determining that a neighbor is no longer reachable
- Discovering duplicated addresses

Problems related to Neighbor Discovery were introduced in Section 2.8, and they are solved by using the ICMPv6 protocol, which was discussed in Chapter 5.

6.1 Terminology

The following definitions are excerpted from the RFC 1970[1]; they are in addition to those reported in Section 2.2:

- *prefix:* The initial part of an IPv6 address, common to all nodes connected to the same link.
- *link layer address:* The layer 2 address of an interface.
- *on-link:* An IPv6 address that is assigned to an interface on a specified link.
- *off-link:* An IPv6 address that is not assigned to any interfaces on the specified link.
- *longest prefix match:* The process of determining which prefix includes a given IPv6 address. When multiple prefixes cover an address, the longest prefix is the one that matches.
- *next hop:* The next node toward which to transmit a packet. The node must be on-link and therefore must be a neighbor.
- *reachability:* Whether the one-way "forward" path to a node is functioning properly.
- *target:* An address searched through a process of address resolution or the address of the first hop obtained through the redirection process.
- *proxy:* A router that responds to Neighbor Discovery query messages on behalf of another node—for example, in the case of mobile nodes.
- *random delay:* A delay introduced before the transmission of a packet to prevent multiple nodes from transmitting at exactly the same time.
- *cache:* A small memory area that contains information stored on a node for a given period of time.
- *global address:* A unique worldwide address.
- *tentative address:* An address whose uniqueness is verified within a link before assigning it to an interface.
- *preferred address:* An address associated with an interface whose use by upper layer protocols is allowed without limitation.
- *deprecated address:* An address associated with an interface whose use by upper layer protocols is discouraged.
- *valid address:* A preferred or a deprecated address.
- *invalid address:* An address not assigned to any interface.

- *preferred lifetime:* The period an address remains preferred—that is, the time before it becomes deprecated.
- *valid lifetime:* The period of validity of an address.
- *interface token:* A link layer interface identifier that is unique (at least) at the link layer; usually derived from the interface MAC address.
- *relay:* A node that acts as an intermediate device in the transmission of a packet between two other nodes—for example, between client and server.
- *agent:* A server or a relay.

6.2 Link Types

Neighbor Discovery problems are strictly related to links belonging to one of the following classes:

- *point-to-point:* A link that connects exactly two interfaces. The Neighbor Discovery protocol deals with these links as a particular case of multicast links.
- *multicast:* A multiple access link that supports a native mechanism for sending packets to all nodes (or to a subset) by a single link layer transmission. The Neighbor Discovery protocol is implemented on this type of link according to the specifications of RFC 1970[1], which is discussed in this chapter.
- *Non Broadcast Multiple Access* (NBMA): A multiple access link that does not support the transmission of a packet to all stations using multicast or broadcast modalities; examples of NBMA links are X.25, Frame Relay, and ATM. This type of link supports only Redirect, Neighbor Unreachability Detection, and next hop identification functions. Other functions are specified by other standards; see, for example, Chapter 9 about IPv6 on ATM networks.
- *shared media:* A type of link that allows direct communication among a number of nodes. Attached nodes are configured without a complete list of prefixes; for this reason, different nodes, connected to the same shared medium, can ignore neighbors. Examples of shared media are SMDS and B-ISDN. The Neighbor

Discovery protocol exploits the extended semantics of the ICMPv6 Redirect message (see Section 6.3.3).

■ *variable MTU:* A type of link that does not have a well-defined MTU. The Neighbor Discovery protocol simplifies its management by standardizing the MTU of all nodes connected to the same link.

■ *asymmetric reachability:* A type of link in which packets from node A reach node B, but packets from node B don't reach node A. At present, the Neighbor Discovery protocol limits itself to identifying asymmetric reachability situations, and IPv6 does not use those links.

Note that all the types of links cited here (also NBMA ones) must provide IPv6 with a multicast service; if they cannot support the service natively, they can emulate it through a server (see Figure 6-1). Moreover, it is not yet clear whether IPv6 will use the emulated multicast service on nonmulticast links or whether it will prefer other alternative solutions to implement the Neighbor Discovery service (see Chapter 9).

6.3   Neighbor Discovery Service

The Neighbor Discovery Service uses five types of ICMPv6 messages: Router Solicitation (see Section 5.5.4), Router Advertisement (see Section 5.5.5), Neighbor Solicitation (see Section 5.5.6), Neighbor Advertisement (see Section 5.5.7), and Redirect (see Section 5.5.8).

6.3.1   Router and Prefix Discovery

The Router Discovery function is used to identify which routers are connected to a given link, and to learn prefixes related to the link and parameters to be used in the node's autoconfiguration procedure described in Section 6.7.

Routers periodically, or in response to a solicitation, send multicast Router Advertisement messages to announce their reachability to the nodes on the link (see Figure 6-2). Each host receives Router Advertisement messages from all routers connected on its links and builds a list of default routers (routers to be used when the path to a destination is unknown). Routers generate Router Advertisement messages frequently enough so that hosts learn of their presence within a few minutes but not so frequently to be used to detect unreachability problems (for example,

Figure 6-1

Emulation of a multicast service through a server

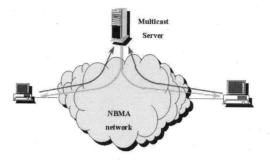

Figure 6-2

Router Advertisement

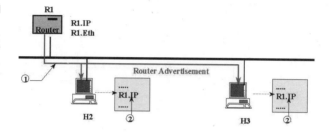

in the case of errors). Unreachability problems are handled by the Neighbor Unreachability Detection procedure, which is discussed in Section 6.6.

Router Advertisement messages contain a list of prefixes used to determine the on-link reachability. Hosts use prefixes extracted from Router Advertisement messages to determine whether a destination is on-link and can therefore be directly reached, or whether it is off-link and can therefore be reached only through a router. Note that a destination can be on-link even if it is not covered by prefixes learned through Router Advertisement messages; in this case, the host considers the destination as off-link, and the router sends a Redirect message to the sender.

Router Advertisement messages contain a set of flags that allow routers to inform hosts how to perform the address's autoconfiguration. For example, routers can specify whether hosts must use a stateful (based on DHCP servers) or a stateless—that is, autonomous—autoconfiguration procedure without resorting to servers. These procedures are described in Section 6.7.

Moreover, Router Advertisement messages contain parameters to facilitate a centralized administration of the network—for example, the default value for the Hop Limit parameter to be used in packets generated by hosts, or the link MTU.

Hosts can request routers to transmit Router Advertisement messages immediately through a Router Solicitation message, speeding up the configuration phase in this way.

6.3.2   The Address Resolution

IPv6 nodes accomplish the resolution of IPv6 addresses into link layer addresses through Neighbor Solicitation and Neighbor Advertisement messages. In IPv4, this problem is separately treated by the ARP protocol[2], which doesn't exist any longer in IPv6 and whose functions are included in ICMPv6.

A node activates the address resolution procedure (see Figure 6-3) by multicasting a Neighbor Solicitation packet that requests the target node to return its link layer address. Neighbor Solicitation messages are multicast to the solicited-node multicast address (see Section 4.8.1) associated with the target address. Starting from this multicast address, IPv6 algorithmically computes a multicast link layer address; this process happens in different ways depending on the type of link (see, for example, Section 6.8.4). The target returns its link layer address in a unicast Neighbor Advertisement message. A pair of messages is sufficient for both the initiator and the target to resolve each other's link layer address. In fact, the initiator node includes its link layer address in the Neighbor Solicitation message.

The Neighbor Solicitation message is also used in the Duplicate Address Detection procedure (see Section 6.7.4) to determine whether the same unicast address has been assigned to more than one node.

Moreover, the Neighbor Solicitation is used in the Neighbor Unreachability Detection procedure (discussed in Section 6.6) to detect whether a node is reachable. This process requires the positive confirmation that packets have been received by the node. This confirmation can be provided from upper layer protocols that confirm that a connection is "progressing" —that is, that transmitted data has been correctly delivered. When positive confirmation is not generated from upper-layer protocols, a node sends Neighbor Solicitation messages to the target node, which has to confirm its reachability through a Neighbor Advertisement message.

Figure 6-3
Redirect function

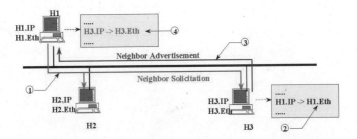

6.3.3   Redirect Function

When a packet must be transmitted to an off-link destination, choosing the router through which the packet will be routed is necessary. The choice cyclically falls on all reachable routers. The chosen router is the next hop to which the message will be transmitted. The chosen next hop is not necessarily the best one. For this reason, the router can generate a Redirect message to inform the source node of the presence of a router that represents a better next hop toward a specific destination.

Let's consider, for example, the network shown in Figure 6-4. Suppose that node A must transmit a packet to node H. Node A examines its Default Router List and randomly chooses the R2 router to which it transmits the packet. R2 routes the packet toward R1 and then on toward R3, which delivers the packet.

Node R2 has, however, retransmitted the packet on the same link on which it received the packet. This process causes the generation of a Redirect message, which R2 sends to A, identifying the router R1 as the best next hop toward H; A uses this information for next packets addressed to H, which are directly sent to R1.

In IPv6, the Redirect message has another use if compared to IPv4; it is similar to the one specified in the XRedirect proposal[4]. When an IPv6 node receives a Redirect message, it always assumes that the next hop is on-link; therefore, it executes a procedure to translate the IPv6 address into a link layer address. This capability allows, for example, hosts belonging to different subnets on the same link to exchange messages directly, passing through the router only for the first packet. This capability is particularly important for shared media links.

6.3.4   Other Functions

The Neighbor Discovery procedure also handles the following situations:

- *Link layer address change:* A node that knows its link layer address has changed can send a few unsolicited Neighbor Advertisement messages to update information quickly in hosts' cache memories. This function is used to improve the network performances because, as time passes, the change will be learned anyhow through the Neighbor Unreachability Detection procedure.

- *Inbound load balancing:* Nodes with multiple interfaces can balance the load among different interfaces on the same link.

Figure 6-4
Example of a
network

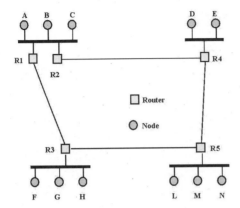

■ *Anycast addresses:* The Neighbor Discovery procedure is ready to receive multiple Neighbor Advertisement messages for the same target because many different nodes can be configured as belonging to the same anycast address on the same link. Neighbor Advertisement messages for anycast addresses are marked as being "nonoverride" advertisements; a procedure specifies the Neighbor Advertisement to be considered valid.

■ *Proxy advertisement:* A router willing to accept packets on behalf of another node that is unable to respond can issue non-Override Neighbor Advertisement messages. At present, the use of proxy advertisements is not standardized, but clearly, this use may have applications—for example, for mobile hosts.

6.4   Data Structures of a Host

One of the principles on which IPv6 design is based is that hosts must correctly work even if they have a very limited vision of the network. In fact, hosts, unlike routers, do not store the routing table (see Section 2.6) and may not have any permanent configuration. This means that, during the bootstrap, they must autoconfigure themselves; then they must learn a minimum set of information only about destinations with which they exchange data. This information is stored in memory in a set of small data structures called *caches*. These data structures are technically arrays of records, and each record will be referred to as an *entry* in the following text. Information stored in each entry has a limited period of validity, and obsolete entries are periodically purged from caches to limit the sizes of caches themselves.

RFC 1970[1] describes a possible implementation based on the four types of caches, specifying that actual implementations can choose different organizations of the cache (for example, by aggregating two or more of them in a unique cache). Caches are partly present also on routers, where, however, the main data structure remains the routing table. In the following subsections, we will analyze the different roles of the four caches, which we already mentioned in Section 2.8.

6.4.1   Neighbor Cache

The Neighbor Cache contains one entry for each neighbor to which the node has recently sent any traffic. Each entry contains an on-link unicast IPv6 address, the associated link layer address, a flag indicating whether the neighbor is a router, and a pointer to packets waiting to be transmitted. Moreover, each entry contains the state information used by the Neighbor Unreachability Detection algorithm (see Section 6.6).

6.4.2   Destination Cache

The Destination Cache contains one entry for each destination to which the node has recently sent some traffic. Entries contain a unicast IPv6 address and a pointer to the entry of Neighbor Caches that contain the address of the node that is the next hop toward the destination. Destination Cache entries are updated by Redirect messages sent by routers. Nodes can store additional information such as the Path MTU.

The main difference between this cache and the one previously described is the fact that the Destination Cache contains one entry for each destination, either on-link or off-link; whereas the Neighbor Cache contains entries only for on-link destinations.

6.4.3   Prefix List

The Prefix List contains one entry for each on-link prefix, and it is used to define whether an address is on-link or off-link. Prefix List entries are created from information received in Router Advertisements. These messages also specify the temporal validity that can be either limited or unlimited. The link local prefix belongs to the Prefix List with an unlimited validity.

6.4.4   Default Router List

The Default Router List contains one entry for each router that can be used as a default router. Default Router List entries contain a pointer to Neighbor Cache entries that contain IPv6 and link layer addresses of default routers and state flags. The algorithm for selecting a default router can favor these entries whose state indicates that the router is known to be reachable. Moreover, Default Router List entries have an invalidation time value extracted from Router Advertisement.

6.4.5   An Example of a Cache

Figure 6-5 shows a simplified example of the content of a host's caches. In particular, with reference to Figure 6-4, host A's caches are shown.

The Default Router List contains two pointers to the Neighbor Cache relevant to the two routers present on LANs R1 and R2.

The Destination Cache contains, for all destinations with which communications are active, the next hop—that is, the pointer to a neighbor. In the case of destination C (on-link), the neighbor is C itself; in the case of other destinations (off-link), the neighbor is R1 or R2. In the case of off-link destinations, Destination Cache pointers have been optimized by Redirect messages.

The Neighbor Cache contains associations between IPv6 addresses and link layer addresses for neighbors toward which communications are active. Note that node B has no association; in fact, even if it is connected to the same LAN as A, B is not exchanging packets with A.

The Prefix List contains prefixes associated with the LAN on which node A is connected. The first prefix is the link local one (see Section 4.6.4); the second one is the site local relevant to subnet 3 (see Section 4.6.5); and the third one is a provider-based address (see Section 4.6.2).

6.4.6   Possible States Associated with Entries

Neighbor Cache entries have associated states that can be one of the following:

■ *Incomplete:* The entry has been created, but the link layer address

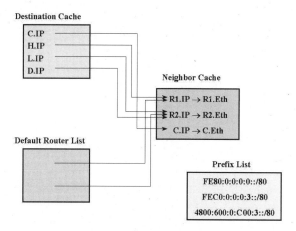

Figure 6-5
Example of a cache

has not yet been determined because the address resolution is in progress.

■ *Reachable:* The entry is known to have been reachable recently.

■ *Stale:* The entry is unknown to have been reachable recently, but until traffic is sent to the neighbor, no attempt should be made to verify its reachability.

■ *Delay:* The entry is unknown to have been reachable recently, and the traffic has been sent to the neighbor. In this state, Neighbor Solicitation packets (called *probes*) are delayed for a short time to give upper layer protocols a chance to provide neighbor reachability confirmation.

■ *Probe:* The neighbor reachability is very uncertain, and probe messages have been sent to verify reachability.

6.5 Transmission Algorithm of a Packet

When a node is sending a packet to a destination, it uses a combination of the Destination Cache, the Prefix List, and the Default Router List to determine the IP address of the appropriate next hop. After this operation, the node consults the Neighbor Cache to determine the link layer address of that neighbor.

The next hop determination for an IPv6 unicast address operates as follows. The sender performs a longest prefix match by using prefixes stored in the Prefix List to determine whether the packet destination is on-link or off-link. If the destination address is on-link, the next hop address is the same as the destination address; otherwise, the sender selects a router from the Default Router List as the next hop. If the Default Router List is empty, the sender assumes that the destination is on-link.

The next hop determination is stored in the Destination Cache and used for next packets. In particular, when a node has a packet to send, it first examines the Destination Cache, and only if no relationship exists in the Destination Cache, it activates the procedure for the next hop determination.

After the IPv6 address of the next hop node is known, the sender examines its Neighbor Cache to determine the link layer information, mainly the link layer address. If no entry exists for the IPv6 address of the next hop, the node does the following:

■ Creates a new entry and sets its state to Incomplete

■ Initiates the address resolution (see Section 6.3.2)

■ Queues packets for transmission

When the address resolution ends, the link layer address is available and can be stored in the Neighbor Cache. At this point, the entry assumes the new Reachable state, and queued packets can be transmitted.

For multicast packets, the next hop is always considered to be on-link. The procedure for determining the link layer address corresponding to a multicast IPv6 address depends on the type of the link; for example, the case of Ethernet networks will be described in Section 6.8.4.

Each time a Neighbor Cache entry is accessed to transmit a unicast packet, the sender checks related reachability information according to the Neighbor Unreachability Detection algorithm presented in Section 6.6. This check might result in the transmission of probes to verify the neighbor reachability.

In case a neighbor becomes unreachable, the next hop determination procedure may be performed again to verify whether another path toward the destination is available. For an off-link destination in a partially meshed network, this is possible. For example, let's consider a case in which the LAN's egress router has an error, but an alternative backup router is present on the LAN. Another example is represented by the possibility of rerouting traffic destined for mobile nodes.

6.6 Neighbor Unreachability Detection

A node can be unreachable for numerous reasons. These reasons range from hardware failure, to the lack of power, to network problems, and so on. If the problem concerns the end nodes of the communication, no recovery is possible, and the communication fails. On the other hand, if the problem concerns the path between two nodes, then an alternative path may exist, and it allows the communication to be continued without upper layers detecting any change. For this reason, all nodes continuously check the reachability of neighbors to which packets are sent by using the Neighbor Unreachability Detection procedure.

This procedure is used between hosts and hosts, between hosts and routers, and between routers and hosts. It can also be used between routers and routers, but it turns out to be useless because protocols to compute routing tables such as RIP[6] and OSPF[7] already perform equivalent functions.

Neighbor Unreachability Detection is also called *black hole* detection because it is used to identify particular nodes on the network that discard packets without signaling it in any way.

We have already seen that the main source of reachability confirmations are upper layer protocols, and in particular the TCP[8] protocol that, being a connection-oriented protocol, is able to probe whether the connection continues to transmit data. However, in many cases, the reachability information cannot come from upper layers. For example, all UDP-based applications[9] cannot provide these confirmations because UDP is a connectionless protocol. Another example is represented by a router sending messages to a host because the router doesn't process upper layer packets.

When the confirmations described in the preceding paragraph are not available, a node must send *probes*, or Neighbor Solicitation packets. Let's suppose that node A has doubts about the reachability of node B. A sends probes to B and waits to receive Neighbor Advertisement packets with the flag S (Solicited) set (see Section 5.5.7). These packets are considered reachability confirmations for node B. Note that possible Neighbor Advertisement messages with the flag S clear received by B indicate only that the transmission from B to A is working properly, but these messages give no information about the transmission from A to B; therefore, they cannot be considered reachability confirmations.

Neighbor Unreachability Detection operates in parallel to packet transmission, and it is activated only in the presence of traffic. When one entry of the Neighbor Cache is Reachable, but 30 seconds have elapsed since the last reachability confirmation, that entry enters the *Stale* state. In the Stale state, at the moment of the transmission of the first packet toward the neighbor associated with the entry, a 5-second period begins (the *Delay* state), at the end of which the entry enters the *Probe* state. In the Probe state, three probe packets are sent, one per second. At the end of the transmission of the probe packets, if the reachability has not been confirmed, the entry is deleted and will be created again by the first packet through the Address Resolution procedure (see Section 6.3.2).

Receipt of a reachability confirmation brings the entry back to the Reachable state. The time periods cited here can be changed; the times reported are default values.

6.7   Address Autoconfiguration

The two types of Address Autoconfiguration procedures are *stateless* and *stateful*. The *stateless* type is the integrating part of IPv6 and is described in RFC 1791[3]. The other type, stateful, is based on the *Dynamic Host Configuration Protocol* (DHCP) and is described in a Draft of the IETF[10]. The purpose of these procedures is to solve two problems, better known by the following expressions:

■ *Dentist's office:* Dentists are supposed to be rich enough to afford the purchase of many computers, but they don't know anything about computer networks. Therefore, they simply take PCs out of their boxes, connect cables, and expect the network to work.

■ *Thousand computers on the dock:* The recurring nightmare of network administrators is that a thousand new PCs are delivered on Friday, and they have to be installed as soon as possible (spoiled weekend!). In this case, the know-how isn't lacking, but to meet the strict deadline, the network must nearly autoconfigure itself.

IPv6 has, among its specifications, the capability to succeed in solving both the situations described here by using the Address Resolution procedures.

6.7.1   Stateless Autoconfiguration

The stateless autoconfiguration procedure has been designed to meet the following requirements:

- Before connecting an IPV6 host to the network, no form of manual configuration must be required. A mechanism must be in place to create a unique address automatically for each interface, starting from the interface token (almost always the interface link layer address).

- Small LANs consisting of some hosts connected to a link must not require the presence of a stateful server (DHCP) or of a router to communicate. They must be able to configure with link local addresses automatically and to use these addresses for communications.

- Big company networks consisting of hosts and routers must not require the presence of stateful servers (DHCP) to communicate. Hosts must be able to derive site local or global addresses from Router Advertisements that must contain lists of prefixes associated with links.

- The stateless configuration procedure must simplify renumbering operations (change of addresses). In fact, renumbering operations will be periodically executed because global addresses are usually provider based (see Section 4.6.2). Transition periods will be required to allow the coexistence of new addresses with old addresses to make the migration painless.

- Network administrators should be allowed to specify if they will use the stateless configuration, the stateful configuration, or both of them.

After we consider these requirements, let's discuss how an interface can autoconfigure itself. First, we must determine that only multicast-capable interfaces (those able to transmit multicast packets) can autoconfigure themselves, and therefore the autoconfiguration is present only on links that support multicast traffic. When an interface is activated (either just turned on or following a reset), the host generates a link local address for the interface (see Section 4.6.4) by deriving it from the interface token. The generated address is not immediately assigned to the interface, but it is set in a *tentative* state, and a Duplicate Address Detection is started (see Section 6.7.4) to check that the link local address is not already in use. If the procedure confirms that the address is unique, the address will be assigned to the interface.

At this point, the interface has a link local address, and the first autoconfiguration step, which is executed both by hosts and by routers, ends. The following steps will be executed only by hosts.

The following step consists of obtaining a Router Advertisement message or of verifying that no routers are available on the network. We have already seen that routers periodically send Router Advertisements (see Section 6.3.1 and Section 5.5.5), but the interval between two Router Advertisements is very long. Therefore, the interface can decide to send one or more Router Solicitations to the All-Router (FF02::2) multicast address.

Router Advertisements contain two flags (see Section 5.5.5) that indicate the type of autoconfiguration to be executed. The flag M (Managed address configuration) indicates whether the host must use the stateful autoconfiguration for addresses. The flag O (Other stateful configuration) indicates whether the host must use the stateful autoconfiguration for other information (except addresses).

Moreover, Router Advertisements contain prefixes to be used for the stateless autoconfiguration of site local and global addresses. Remember that stateless and stateful procedures are not mutually exclusive; they can be used in parallel by a host to autoconfigure both stateless derived addresses and stateful derived addresses.

As Router Advertisements are also periodically generated, a host's addresses are continually updated. New addresses can be added as a consequence of the proliferation of new prefixes, and old addresses can become invalid as they are no longer announced by any router.

6.7.2   Site Renumbering

Site renumbering is an unwelcome operation for network administrators because the process is usually complicated and susceptible to faults. This operation is undoubtedly very simplified in IPv6.

At present, upper layer protocols such as TCP identify connections by also using the IP address; therefore, a change of address cannot be executed without interrupting connections in progress. To understand this point, we must know that addresses are divided into two categories: valid addresses and invalid addresses. Valid addresses are further subdivided into two subcategories: preferred addresses and deprecated addresses.

When upper layer protocols have to open a new connection, they must always use a preferred address. When network administrators start a renumbering procedure, they first insert new prefixes in routers (prefixes that will be used to form new addresses), and then they wait for the DNS to propagate these prefixes in the whole network (an operation that can require several days). At this point, the administrators remove old prefixes (prefixes of addresses that will be used no longer). This operation creates new preferred addresses on all interfaces and transforms some addresses that were previously preferred into deprecated addresses. An address remains in the deprecated state for a reasonable period of time (for example, for several days) to allow all connections that were open when the address was preferred to be closed correctly. Note that a deprecated address is valid anyhow, and it can be used with the only limitation being that new connections cannot be opened by using a deprecated address. Eventually, the deprecated address becomes invalid, and the transition from old addresses to new ones ends. In the transition phase, routers must announce both addresses (see Chapter 7).

6.7.3   DHCPv6 and Stateful Autoconfiguration

At the time this book was written, the stateful autoconfiguration procedure is not yet a standard; however, an Internet Draft on DHCPv6[10] is in an advanced state, and a standard version of DHCP for IPv4 is already available[11].

Dynamic Host Configuration Protocol version 6 (DHCPv6) is designed to provide clients (IPv6 nodes) with configuration information that is stored on a server. In the following text, DHCPv6 will be indicated as *DHCP*, omitting the version number. The information provided by DHCP mainly concerns IPv6 addresses, but other parameters can be provided, too. Therefore, DHCP is based on a client-server paradigm, in which servers manage the addresses and network parameters database and provide them to clients that choose a stateful configuration procedure.

Because, in a complex network, having a server for each link is impossible, DHCP introduces the concept of *relay*—that is, of a node that operates as an intermediary in the transmission of a packet between a client and a server. It also introduces the concept of *agent*, which can be a server or a relay. Moreover, storing the configuration information on many DHCP servers must be possible, in order to increase the reliability and the performance of the network itself.

The DHCP protocol is based on a *User Datagram Protocol* (UDP)[9] transport. In particular, DHCP agents transmit all messages to clients by using the port UDP 546 and receive all messages from the port UDP 547. Messages exchanged by the DHCP protocol are subdivided into the following six types:

■ *DHCP Solicit:* This type is a message sent by the client to the multicast address of all DHCP Server/Relay agents (FF02::C); it is used when a new client doesn't know any DHCP server or it wants to locate a new server.

■ *DHCP Advertise:* This type is a unicast message sent by an agent to a client in response to a DHCP Solicit message.

■ *DHCP Request:* This type is a unicast message from a client to a server to request parameters for the network configuration.

■ *DHCP Reply:* This type is a unicast message sent by a server to a client in response to a DHCP Request message. It contains the indication of resources (for example, addresses and parameters) that the server allocated for the client.

■ *DHCP Release:* This type is a unicast message sent by the client to the server to inform that the client released certain resources (which, therefore, the server can reallocate to other clients).

■ *DHCP Reconfigure:* This type is a unicast message sent by the server to notify the client about some modifications on the network. The client must acquire modifications by sending a DHCP Request message and waiting for the DHCP Reply message.

The types of messages listed here reveal the DHCP protocol to be a Request / Response protocol on an unreliable communication channel like the one supplied by UDP on IPv6. A pair of DHCP Request and DHCP Reply messages is also indicated with the term *transaction.*

When a client decides to use a stateful configuration procedure (for example, because doing so is specified in the Router Advertisement message), it first has to discover the address of a DHCP server (that can be on another link). To discover this address, the client sends a DHCP Solicit multicast message on its link, and a server or a relay responds with a DHCP Advertise message. The DHCP Advertise message contains one or more IPv6 unicast addresses of DHCP servers.

At this point, the server can acquire configuration parameters by sending to the selected DHCP server a DHCP Request message and obtaining in response a DHCP Reply message. Note that, because the communication channel is unreliable, both the request message and the reply message can be lost or can be delivered corrupted. In this case, the client simply retransmits one or more DHCP Request messages until it obtains a valid DHCP Reply message.

If the server must reconfigure the client, it doesn't do so directly, but it requests the client to start a transaction through a DHCP Reconfigure message. In this way, reliability mechanisms supplied by the Request/Response philosophy become valid again.

6.7.4   Duplicate Address Detection

The Duplicate Address Detection procedure is used for all unicast addresses, either written manually or obtained through a stateful or stateless procedure. However, it must never be used for anycast or multicast addresses.

The Duplicate Address Detection procedure uses a Neighbor Solicitation packet sent to the tentative address to check whether the tentative address is already present on the link. In fact, if the address is unique, no response will be made to the Neighbor Solicitation message; whereas, if the address is already being used, the node using the address will respond with a Neighbor Advertisement packet.

In this second case, the tentative address will not be used, and the network administrator will have to resolve the conflict manually, typically by configuring a different interface token on one of the two nodes.

The default configuration sees that only one Neighbor Solicitation packet will be sent and that it will wait for the Neighbor Advertisement for one second. Default values can be different for different types of links.

6.8   IPv6 on Ethernet

In this section, we will analyze some problems related to the transmission of IPv6 packets on Ethernet. This case has been chosen as extremely important based on the current market and because it is already standardized by RFC 1972[5].

6.8.1   Frame Format

The first thing to be standardized, when we want to decide how to transport IPv6 on a certain type of link, is the enveloping of the IPv6 packet within the frame (link layer envelope). In our case, we must standardize how to envelope IPv6 packets in the Ethernet frame. The solution adopted by RFC 1972[12] was presented in Section 2.9 and shown in Figure 2-6(a). As the data field length in an Ethernet envelope must be less than or equal to 1500 octets, the IPv6 MTU on Ethernet is by default equal to 1500, and it can be decremented through manual configurations.

6.8.2   Link Local Addresses

A second point to be standardized is what to use as an interface token—
that is, as a unique identifier of the node (at least) inside the link. In the
case of Ethernet, the choice is obvious: The 48-bit MAC address is used
as the interface token. At this point, the construction of the link local address can be standardized, and it turns out to be

`FE80::XXXX:YYYY:ZZZZ`

where `XXXX:YYYY:ZZZZ` indicates the interface MAC address. This result is based on the description in Section 4.6.4, illustrated by Figure 4-8.

6.8.3   Link Source/Target Addresses

Neighbor Discovery packets need to include link layer addresses (in this
case, MAC addresses) within the Link Source/Target Address option (see
Section 5.5.10).

These addresses are used, for example, in the Neighbor Advertisement
message during address resolution. In this case, the solution is obvious;
it is shown in Figure 6-6. Here Type = 1 indicates a Source Link Layer
Address, and Type = 2 indicates a Target Link Layer Address. The value
of the Length field is 1.

6.8.4   Multicast Addresses

In conclusion, deciding how to map IPv6 multicast addresses and Ethernet addresses is necessary[12]. With this aim, the IETF registered at
IEEE all OUIs beginning with 33-33 (hexadecimal). The mapping is implemented as shown in Figure 6-7, where DST13, DST14, DST15, and
DST16 are the octets 13, 14, 15, and 16, respectively, of the IPv6 destination address.

Note that this type of mapping considerably improves performance as
network boards can filter almost all the multicast traffic that doesn't interest the node, and this process wouldn't be possible if all the multicast
traffic were sent to the same link layer address.

Figure 6-6
Link Source/Target
Address Option

Type	Length	XXXX
YYYY - ZZZZ		

Figure 6-7
IEEE 802 Multicast
address obtained
from an IPv6 address

33	33	DST13	DST14	DST15	DST16

REFERENCES

[1] T. Narten, E. Nordmark, W. Simpson, *RFC 1970: Neighbor Discovery for IP Version 6 (IPv6)*, August 1996.

[2] D.C. Plummer, *RFC 826: Ethernet Address Resolution Protocol: On converting network protocol addresses to 48 bit Ethernet address for transmission on Ethernet hardware*, November 1982.

[3] S. Thomson, T. Narten, *RFC 1971: IPv6 Stateless Address Autoconfiguration*, August 1996.

[4] B. Braden, J. Postel, Y. Rekhter, *RFC 1620: Internet Architecture Extensions for Shared Media*, May 1994.

[5] M. Crawford, *RFC 1972: A Method for the Transmission of IPv6 Packets over Ethernet Networks*, August 1996.

[6] G. Malkin, *RFC 1723: RIP Version 2—Carrying Additional Information*, November 1994.

[7] J. Moy, *RFC 1583: OSPF Version 2*, March 1994.

[8] J. Postel, *RFC 793: Transmission Control Protocol*, September 1981.

[9] J. Postel, *RFC 768: User Datagram Protocol*, August 1980.

[10] IETF Draft, *Dynamic Host Configuration Protocol for IPv6 (DHCPv6)*, August 1996.

[11] S. Alexander, R. Droms, *RFC 1533: DHCP Options and BOOTP Vendor Extensions*, October 1993.

[12] S. Gai, P.L. Montessoro, P. Nicoletti, *Reti Locali: dal Cablaggio all'Internetworking*, SSGRR (Scuola Superiore G. Reiss Romoli), 1995.

The Routing in IPv6

This chapter will deal with problems related to the routing of packets in IPv6. The chapter analyzes the IPv6 network architecture, the main algorithms used to compute routing tables, and routing protocols used with IPv6, and it closes with an analysis of relationships between addressing and routing.

7.1   Terminology

The following terms are used in this chapter:

- *routing:* Determination of the path that an IP packet must follow to reach its destination.

- *path:* An ordered set of links that connect a source with a destination.

- *subnet:* A subset of nodes identified by addresses with a common prefix; these nodes are connected to the same physical link.

- *Autonomous System (AS):* A set of routing domains managed by a unique administrative authority.

- *routing domain:* A hierarchical partitioning of the network that contains a set of hosts and routers; routers share the same routing information, compute tables using the same IGP, and are managed by a common administrative authority.

- *exterior router:* A router that handles connections between different ASs.

- *border router:* A synonym for *exterior router.*

- *interior router:* A router that handles connections only within an AS.

- *Interior Gateway Protocol (IGP):* Generic term applied to each protocol used to advertise reachability and routing information within an AS. The term *gateway,* which is obsolete, is replaced by *router.*

- *Exterior Gateway Protocol (EGP):* Generic term applied to each protocol used to advertise reachability and routing information between different ASs. The term *gateway,* which is obsolete, is replaced by *router.*

- *static routing:* Technique in which routing tables are statistically determined during the network configuration.

- *dynamic routing:* Technique used to compute and update routing tables dynamically, taking into account the topology and the state of the network.

- *distributed routing:* Dynamic routing technique in which routing tables are computed through processes distributed on routers.

- *distance vector:* Distributed routing algorithm that computes routing tables based on an iterative exchange of routing tables between adjacent routers.

- *link state:* Distributed routing algorithm to compute routing tables in which a router communicates to all other routers in the network the state of the links directly connected to it through an LSP.

- *Link State Packet* (LSP): Packet generated by a link state protocol for the computation of routing tables; it contains the list of adjacent nodes.

- *hop:* The crossing of a link.

- *cost:* Metric associated with a link or to a path.

- *load splitting:* Balancing the load on several parallel paths.

- *static route:* One entry in a routing table, written manually by the network administrator.

- *End Routing Domain (ERD):* A routing domain in which routes are computed primarily to provide intra-domain routing services.

- *Transit Routing Domain (TRD):* A routing domain in which routes are computed primarily to carry transit—that is, inter-domain—traffic.

- *Routing Domain Confederation:* A set of routing domains seen as a unique entity and identified by a unique IPv6 prefix.

- *Internet Service Provider* (ISP): A public or a private organization that provides Internet services. Often simply called *provider.*

- *core router:* TRD's routers.

- *multihomed:* A network belonging to two or more routing domains.

- *Intranet:* A private network based on the Internet model.

7.2   Network Model

In Section 6.3.2, we saw that in IP packet routing a first level of hierarchy is represented by *subnets*. In fact, nodes, before transmitting packets, make a test to determine whether the destination is on-link or off-link. In the first case, the nodes send the packet directly to the final destination; in the second case, they use a router that, by consulting routing tables, determines which is the best path toward a given destination. If we take into account that IP addresses are associated with interfaces, not with nodes, the resulting model of the network is as illustrated in Figure 7-1.

Subnets are grouped into *Autonomous Systems (AS)*—that is, into sets of subnets controlled and administered by a unique authority[1]. Routers routing messages within the same ASs are called *interior routers,* and those routing messages between different ASs are called *exterior routers.*

An example of interconnection between two ASs (indicated by letters A and B) is shown in Figure 7-2.

Interior routers exchange routing information through an *Interior Gateway Protocol* (IGP), whereas exterior routers use an *Exterior Gateway Protocol* (EGP). The same IGP is normally used on all routers within an AS.

Figure 7-1
Model of an IP network

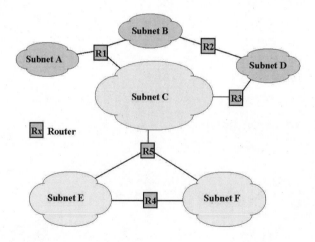

Figure 7-2
Example of interconnection of two ASs

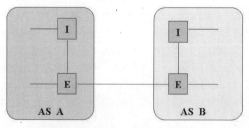

E: Exterior router
I: Interior router

7.3 Routing Algorithms

Routers, no matter whether they are interior or exterior, base their operation on routing tables (see Section 2.6). Routing tables can be written manually by the network administrator (*static routing*) or automatically computed through an appropriate algorithm (*dynamic routing*)[2]. These algorithms operate through an exchange of information between routers, relative to the topology and to the state of the network.

Today, the most-used dynamic routing algorithms are the *distributed routing* algorithms, which don't have a central point where tables are computed, but each router computes its tables by interacting with other routers. Among these types of algorithms, the two main families are *distance vector* algorithms and *link state* algorithms.

Both static routing and dynamic routing exist in different regions of the network for various reasons, as shown in Figure 7-3. In fact, even if having dynamic routing algorithms is necessary in order to take advantage of meshed networks, static routing can be more simple and may not present drawbacks in the most peripheral regions of the network with tree topology, regions in which only a path interconnects them to the rest of the network.

Note that, because IP subnets are associated with physical networks, each entry of the routing tables, independently from the type of routing used, specifies the reachability of a subnet or of a set of subnets (when the subnets belonging to the set can be aggregated).

7.3.1 Static Routing

Static routing requires the network administrator to write the routing tables manually. The administrator has total control of traffic flow on the

Figure 7-3
Dynamic and static routing

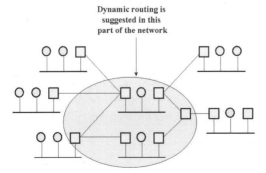

Dynamic routing is suggested in this part of the network

network, but manual intervention is required to reroute this flow in case of an error. This approach is frequently used in IP in the regions of the network that are not meshed; in these regions, no alternative routing paths are available, and tables can be simplified by using an entry that indicates a default path for all unknown destinations. A static entry within a routing table is called *static route*.

In large networks, the manual management of routing tables can be very complex.

An entry in the routing table can be manually created by a command of the type

```
route add 4800:600:0:C00:5/80 4800:600:0:C00:7:800:2B3C:
    4D5E
```

that specifies that all addresses beginning with the prefix on 80 bits `4800:600:0:C00:5` can be reached through the router connected on the same link (and therefore a neighbor), whose interface address is

```
4800:600:0:C00:7:800:2B3C :4D5E
```

The default entry can be manually created by a command of the type

```
route add default 4800:600:0:C00:9:800:2B3C:1234
```

that specifies that all addresses without a matching entry in the routing table can be reached through the router whose interface address is

```
4800:600:0:C00:9:800:2B3C:1234
```

Note that specifying default entries on hosts for the default router is not necessary. (This operation is necessary in IPv4, however.) In IPv6, routers present on links are automatically learned through the Neighbor Discovery process (see Section 6.3.1).

7.3.2   Metrics

To implement dynamic routing algorithms, introducing metrics is essential. Using metrics, we can measure a path's characteristics. This process is necessary for choosing, for example, the best among several alternative paths.

The only two metric parameters universally accepted are the following:

- The number of *hops*—that is, the number of routers along a path
- The *cost*—that is, the sum of the costs of all links that compose the path

Both of these parameters state a negative metric because the cost of a line is assigned in a way inversely proportional to the speed of the line itself, and the hop count indicates the number of routers to be traversed and therefore a potential increase of the delay.

Taking into consideration the load of the network, metrics are more difficult to deploy because they easily lead to routing instability. The most modern techniques allow us to implement *load splitting* between parallel paths. This may also imply the activation of switched circuits like those provided by *Integrated Service Digital Network* (ISDN), either to manage an overloaded link or in the case of an error (backup function of a point-to-point WAN link).

7.3.3 Distance Vector

The distance vector algorithm is the first distributed routing algorithm to be implemented. Each router, besides the routing table, maintains a data structure, called a *distance vector*, for each line. The distance vector contains an entry for each destination, and each entry contains the destination address and the associated metrics. The distance vector contains information extracted from the routing table of the router connected on the other end of the line. Routing tables are computed, merging all the distance vectors associated with the router active lines. Each router periodically sends its routing table to other adjacent routers (neighbor routers) in the form of distance vectors.

When a router receives a distance vector from an adjacent router, it adds the received line metrics to those of the distance vector; it stores the results in its local data structure; it checks whether any change occurred in comparison with the distance vector previously stored, and if so, it recomputes routing tables by merging all distance vectors of active lines. The same recomputation operation occurs when a line goes from the ON state to the OFF state, or vice versa.

The merging is based on a criterion of lowest metrics: For each destination, the chosen path is the one with the lowest metrics among all possible paths.

If the routing table turns out to be changed in comparison with the previous one, the relevant distance vector is sent to adjacent routers. Some implementations of distance vector protocols periodically send distance vectors, too; for example, the RIP (see Section 7.4.1) sends the distance vector every 30 seconds.

The benefit of this class of algorithms is the extreme ease of implementation. Its drawbacks are as follows:

- The high complexity, exponential in the worst case and normally in the range between $O(n^2)$ and $O(n^3)$, where n is the number of entries. This makes the use of this algorithm not suitable for routing tables with more than 1000 entries.

- The slow convergence toward steady routing. The algorithm converges at a speed proportional to that of the slowest link and of the slowest router on the network.

- The difficulty to understand and to foresee its behavior on large networks because no node has the map of the network.

This algorithm is used to compute routing tables in RIP (see Section 7.4.1) and IGRP (see Section 7.4.4).

7.3.4   Path Vector

Path vector algorithms are similar to distance vector algorithms, but instead of metrics, they advertise the list of ASs to be traversed to reach each destination. Using the AS list is a simple way to discover possible loops on the network and to implement routing policies that prefer certain routings, in function of ASs to be traversed.

Path vector algorithms are used in EGP protocols (see Section 7.4.3).

7.3.5   Link State

Link state algorithms have been recently adopted. They are based on the idea that each router, interacting with other ones, builds a complete map of the network on which it computes optimal routings by using Dijkstra's algorithm[3] or *Shortest Path First* (SPF).

Routers interact by exchanging *Link State Packets* (LSPs). Through LSPs, each router communicates to other routers which subnets it is directly connected to. Each router contains a database called an *LSP database* in which it stores the most recent LSP generated by each other router. The LSP database is a representation of the graph of the network given as a matrix of adjacent neighbors (see **2** and **3**). Note that the LSP database is, by definition, exactly identical on all routers of the network.

Moreover, the previous approach presents a duality: Distance vector routers send information concerning all subnets only to neighbor routers; link state routers send information concerning only subnets to which they are directly connected to all routers on the network.

The LSP database, representing the map of the network with associated metrics, provides necessary and sufficient information for a router to compute its routing table.

Again, note the difference with the distance vector: In that case, routers directly cooperate to compute routing tables; whereas here routers cooperate to maintain the updated map of the network, and then each router autonomously computes its own routing table.

The computation of the link state algorithm is equal to $O(L \bullet log(N))$, where L is the number of links and N is the number of nodes. Because metrics are small integers, sophisticated data structures, which make the complexity algorithm tend to $O(N)$, can be implemented.

The link state algorithm can administer very large networks (10,000 entries in the routing table). It quickly converges; it rarely generates loops; and in any case, it can easily detect and interrupt them. Also, it can be easily understood and predicted because each node contains the whole map of the network.

Link state algorithms have been used in the OSI IS-IS (Intermediate System to Intermediate System) ISO 10589[4] standard, in the OSPF protocol (see Section 7.4.2), and in the Dual IS-IS (see Section 7.4.4) protocol.

7.3.6   Redistribution

Though the definition of AS clearly indicates that, within an AS, all interior routers must use the same IGP, in practice this rule is frequently violated. Many ASs use different IGPs at the same time because the software available on routers allows them to do so. Therefore, there is the need to allow an IGP #1 to redistribute reachability information learned from an IGP #2, and vice versa. This operation implies an accurate correspondence of metrics used by the two IGPs. This can be quite easily implemented in parts of the network with a star topology (for example, redistributing the reachability information learned from static routes is fairly common), but it presents considerable problems in the presence of meshes partly managed by IGP #1 and partly by IGP #2. This configuration is highly discouraged because it can easily create loops not easy to detect.

7.3.7   Multi-Protocol Routing

Real networks rarely are mono-protocol—that is, networks using only one layer 3 (Network) protocol. Usually, LANs simultaneously transport many protocols by marking frames with different Protocol Types (see Section 2.9) —for example, 0800 hexadecimal for IPv4 and 86DD hexadecimal for IPv6. Network administrators also sometimes need to transport many protocols at the same time on the geographic part of the network; for this purpose, *multi-protocol routers* are used. These routers must compute routing tables for many protocols, and this process can be performed through the use of two different approaches: *integrated* or *ships in the night*.

In the integrated approach, only one protocol is used to compute all routing tables. This result is achieved by enabling the protocol to transport the reachability information of several protocols at the same time.

In the "ships in the night" approach, each routing table is computed by a specific protocol, and the different protocols travel in parallel, ignoring each other like ships that pass in the night.

The integrated approach is undoubtedly very elegant, but its implementation is very complex and less flexible. The author of this book takes the liberty, after many years spent working on networks, to suggest that all readers use the "ships in the night" approach.

7.4   Routing in IPv6

The three main protocols for the computation of routing tables that will be used with IPv6 are RIPv6 (see Section 7.4.1), OSPFv6 (see Section 7.4.2), IDRPv2 (see Section 7.4.3), and probably EIGRP and Dual IS-IS (see Section 7.4.4).

None of the algorithms previously used for IPv4 can be used without modifications because they are unable to transport IPv6 addresses on 128 bits.

7.4.1   RIPv6

The *Routing Information Protocol* (RIP) is an IGP originally designed by Xerox for its XNS network. It was introduced in the TCP/IP architecture in 1982 at the University of California at Berkeley with the name *routed* (route daemon), defined in RFC 1058 in 1988[5] and updated by RFC 1388 in 1993[6]. RIP is widely adopted, mainly in implementations of personal computer networks, and many other routing protocols are based on it, such as AppleTalk, Novell, 3Com, Banyan, and so on.

RIP is a distance vector protocol in which each router sends its distance vector to adjacent routers, every 30 seconds (see Section 7.3.3). Routing tables store only the best next hop toward each destination. The main limit of RIP is that it allows a maximum of 15 hops; each destination more distant than 15 hops is considered unreachable.

Moreover, RIP ignores lines' speeds, not allowing the definition of costs or other metrics, but it bases the routing only on the minimization of the number of hops. In case of modifications of the network topology, RIP is slow to converge. For these reasons, RIP can be used only on small networks.

RIPv6[7] is the version of RIP that can be used with IPv6. This update of RIP allows it to bear the new 128-bit addresses and relevant prefix lengths without adding any new features and without eliminating the limits cited previously. The reason for this choice is based on the need to maintain RIPv6 simplicity so that it can also be implemented on very simple devices on which the implementation of OSPFv6 would be problematic.

RIPv6 has only two types of messages—Request and Response—that are transported in the UDP (User Datagram Protocol)[8]. In RIPv6, a limited number of destinations per each packet is allowed so that the resulting IPv6 packet doesn't exceed the link-MTU.

7.4.2 OSPFv6

The *Open Shortest Path First* (OSPF) is an IGP purposely developed for IP. In 1988, an IETF working group was appointed to implement a *link state* protocol (see Section 7.3.5) for IP. OSPF was defined by RFC 1247 in 1991[9] and redefined by RFC 1583 in 1994[10].

OSPF is based on the concept of hierarchy. The root of the hierarchy is the AS that can be subdivided into areas, each one containing a group of interconnected networks. The routing within an area is called *intra-area;* the routing between different areas is called *inter-area.* Each AS has a *backbone* area that can also be not contiguous; in this case, configuring *virtual links* is necessary to guarantee its cohesion. All other areas are connected to the backbone area.

OSPF routers are classified into four categories, not mutually exclusive:

- *Internal router:* A router connecting subnets all belonging to the same area. These routers use only one instance of the OSPF algorithm. Routers having interfaces only on the backbone belong to this category.

■ *Area border router:* A router connecting the backbone area to one or more areas. These routers use many instances of the OSPF algorithm: one instance for each directly connected area and one instance for the backbone. Area border routers collect the reachability information from areas to which they are connected and redistribute it on the backbone. The backbone redistributes this information to other areas.

■ *Backbone router:* A router with an interface on the backbone. This category includes all routers connected to more than one area (area border router). Backbone routers with all interfaces on the backbone are considered internal routers.

■ *AS boundary router:* A router exchanging router information with routers belonging to other ASs. This classification is orthogonal to the previous ones; an AS boundary router can be an internal or an area border router.

Figure 7-4 shows an example of AS subdivided into three OSPF areas and connected to another AS.

OSPFv6[11] is the version of OSPF that can be used with IPv6; it is also the IGP protocol suggested for IPv6. As the standard implemented by all router manufacturers, it is suited for large networks.

OSPFv6, which is an update of OSPF, allows transportation of the new 128-bit addresses and the associated prefix lengths. In OSPFv6, areas are identified by 128-bit addresses.

No new functions have been added because OSPF represents the "state of the art" of IGP protocols. OSPF for IPv4 and OSPF for IPv6 operate in parallel, following the "ships in the night" approach (see Section 7.3.7).

Figure 7-4
Example of use of OSPF

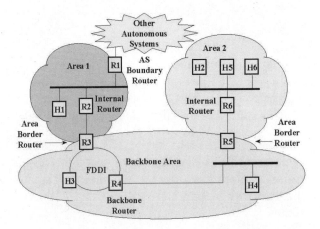

OSPFv6 is layered directly on IPv6, and the OSPFv6 header is identified by the value 89 in the Next Header field of the preceding header (see Table 3-2 and Section 3.1.5).

7.4.3 IDRPv2

The *Inter-Domain Routing Protocol* (IDRP)[12] is an EGP protocol to be used with IPv6. The IDRP is a path vector protocol (see Section 7.3.4), designed to be used in the OSI architecture for the CLNP ISO 8473 protocol and derived from the BGP-4 (Border Gateway Protocol version 4, RFC 1711[13]) used as EGP on the Internet. The IDRP version suitable for operating with IPv6 is version 2 (IDRPv2[14]).

IDRPv2 uses the term *routing domain* instead of the term *autonomous system*. A routing domain is identified by an IPv6 prefix (128-bit address); this identification simplifies the IANA's work (see Section 4.5) because explicitly assigning the AS's identifiers, which in IPv4 are on 16 bits, is no longer necessary.

Routing domains can be grouped into a *Routing Domain Confederation*. Confederate routing domains are seen as unique entities, and they are identified by IPv6 prefixes, too. Confederate routing domains can be confederated by introducing an arbitrary number of hierarchy levels.

IDRP subdivides routing domains into two types:

■ *End Routing Domain (ERD)*: A routing domain in which routes are computed primarily to provide intra-domain routing services.

■ *Transit Routing Domain (TRD)*: A routing domain in which routes are computed primarily to carry transit (that is, inter-domain) traffic.

The IDRPv2 has been chosen to replace the BGP because of the following reasons:

■ Although defined in the OSI architecture, it doesn't present any specific dependence on the OSI architecture itself.

■ It has been conceived from the beginning for the multi-protocol routing, allowing several types of addresses.

■ It includes all BGP-4 functions, and it is based on the same path vector philosophy (it advertises the routing domain or routing domain confederation sequence to be traversed to reach a given destination).

Each router computes its preferred routing toward a given destination and transmits it to IDRP-adjacent routers through a path vector. The policy to make this computation is configurable on each IDRP router.

IDRP is layered on IPv6, and the IDRP header is identified by the value 45 in the Next Header field of the preceding header (see Table 3-2 and Section 3.2.5).

7.4.4 Other Routing Protocols

Other protocols to compute routing tables have been used in IPv4, and some of them will probably be used in IPv6 as well. Among them, the most important are IGRP and Dual IS-IS.

7.4.4.1 IGRP The *Interior Gateway Routing Protocol* (IGRP)[15] is an IGP developed by Cisco Systems, Inc., in the mid '80s to overcome RIP's limits. It is a distance vector protocol, but it features a very sophisticated metric. IGRP chooses the best path by combining metric vectors containing delay, bandwidth, reliability, maximum length of the packet, and load. Moreover, IGRP allows *multi-path routing*—that is, the subdivision of traffic among parallel lines. The traffic is subdivided on the basis of metrics associated with lines.

Extended IGRP (EIGRP), which is an improved version of IGRP, allows multi-protocol routing and the management of the variable subnetting and of the *Classless Inter-Domain Routing* (CIDR)[16]. Cisco will probably introduce support for IPv6 in future versions of EIGRP.

7.4.4.2 DUAL IS-IS The *integrated IS-IS*, also called *dual IS-IS*[17], is a version of the IS-IS (ISO 10589) protocol[4] that also can compute routing information for protocols different from OSI CLNP (ISO 8473).

RFC 1195[17] standardizes operation of the dual IS-IS in a mixed OSI CLNP and IPv4 environment. The IETF will probably introduce support for IPv6 in future versions of the dual IS-IS.

7.5 Relationships between Addressing and Routing

So far, we have analyzed routing problems (in this chapter) and addressing problems (in Chapter 4) separately. Now we can further analyze existing relationships between addressing and routing. Topics reported in the following subsections are discussed in more depth in RFC 1887[18].

7.5.1 Internet Structure

The Internet is organized into routing domains that exchange information on the reachability of networks on which they are composed. These routing domains do not have equal importance, and we have already seen that IDRP makes a distinction between Transit Routing Domain (TRD) and End Routing Domain (ERD). An example of interconnection between ERDs and TRDs is illustrated in Figure 7-5.

ERDs are associated with the network's end users—that is, to organizations connected to the Internet that usually have connections with only one TRD. Sometimes an ERD can have connections with many TRDs; in this case, the ERD is called *multihomed* (for example, in Figure 7-5, the ERD B). It, however, maintains its ERD nature—that is, it doesn't operate as a transit domain—and it therefore remains a leaf (see Section 7.5.5).

Another possibility is that two ERDs have a private link (see Section 7.5.7) because they have to exchange large volumes of traffic, without passing through the Internet. This is the case of ERDs F and G in Figure 7-5.

TRDs are usually associated with *Internet Service Providers* (ISPs); in the following text, we will simply call them *providers*. These providers can be subdivided into the following categories:

■ *Direct Service Providers*: These providers connect end users and connect themselves to international backbones. Examples of Direct Service Providers are America Online and NSFnet regional.

Figure 7-5
Interconnection between ERDs and TRDs

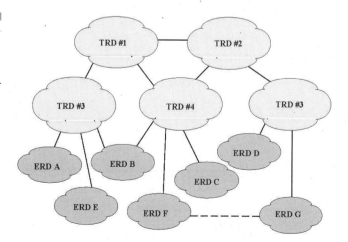

■ *Indirect Service Providers*: These providers administer large international backbones, the highest level in the hierarchy. They connect only Direct Service Providers and big users.

7.5.2   IPv4 Problems

In IPv4, no relationship exists between addresses and topology. In fact, addresses are directly assigned to end users and, even if an effort is made to assign addresses by nations or continents, this use poses no particular benefits for routing. The Internet, by its nature, doesn't respect nations' political borders. For example, Italian organizations can connect to Italian providers and these to European providers, but they can also connect to American providers. As a result, Italian networks are announced partly in Europe and partly in the United States. This situation is likely to become more and more complicated with the coming of a telecommunications free market.

In this situation, ERD routers don't present any particular drawbacks; in fact, it is sufficient that they maintain in their routing table one entry for each network within the ERD and one default network for all other networks. The default entry points to the TRD of the provider to which the ERD is connected.

The case of TRD routers (also called *core routers*) is more complex. In fact, they must maintain in their routing tables one entry for each network connected to the Internet (this is undoubtedly true for Indirect Service Provider routers). Therefore, the routing tables tend to explode with the dizzying growth of the Internet.

To limit the growth of routing tables, the *Classless Inter-Domain Routing* (CIDR)[16] was introduced with BGP-4. The CIDR allows grouping of announcements of many networks whose addresses are contiguous in only one entry (see Section 1.2.1). Nevertheless, the CIDR cannot bring important benefits due to the assignment philosophy of IPv4 addresses. In fact, it is not sure that contiguous addresses are assigned to users connected to the same TRD and that the TRD can therefore group them.

7.5.3   The IPv6 Solution

To solve the problems cited in the preceding subsection, IPv6 migrates from a scheme based on the assignment of addresses to end users (like that of IPv4) to a provider-based scheme (see Section 4.6.2). In this new scheme, each Direct Service Provider is assigned a set of addresses that it divides into smaller sets to be assigned to its users. Because the IPv6 address is much longer than the IPv4 address, it can easily contain this new hierarchy level. Sets of addresses assigned to the users can be grouped by definition by the provider because they are the result of a partition.

For ERDs' routers, the situation remains unchanged. They continue to have one entry for each network within the ERD, one default entry toward the TRD, and they announce their set of addresses to the TRD with only one entry.

For Indirect Service Providers' TRD routers, the situation is completely different. In fact, now each Direct Service Provider announces all its networks with only one entry; therefore, the size of routing tables is proportional to the number of providers, not to the number of networks.

For the Direct Service Provider's TRD routers, the situation can change significantly if many connections are made with other providers (either Direct or Indirect). In fact, all networks associated with a provider are announced with a single entry in routing tables in this case.

Other possible aggregation schemes have been proposed. For example, providers can be aggregated on a continental basis, or Indirect Service Providers can be assigned address sets to be subdivided by assigning the addresses to Direct Service Providers, and the Direct Service Providers, in their turn, can assign the addresses to end users. The usefulness of these schemes is questionable.

What is not questionable, however, is that the providers' assignment of addresses to end users brings about a significant containment of routing tables (that we can estimate in two orders of magnitude). IPv6 will therefore follow this approach.

7.5.4   Drawbacks for Users

The main drawback for users happens when they decide to change providers—that is, to buy Internet services from another ISP. In fact, users have to renumber their networks. As we already explained in Section 6.7.2, this operation is simplified by IPv6 Neighbor Discovery mechanisms, but it still can cause some inefficiency.

Nevertheless, a user can operate with addresses from provider A while still being connected to provider B. In this case, provider B must explicitly announce addresses assigned to the user by provider A. All Internet routers should have one additional entry to indicate that the user, though having addresses from provider A, can still be reached through provider

B. This situation can occur for a limited period of time during a transition to allow the user to renumber networks without service interruptions; however, this situation cannot continue indefinitely because it will rapidly recreate the unacceptable growth of routing tables, as in the previously analyzed IPv4 case.

7.5.5   Multihomed Routing Domains

The previously discussed theories apply to ERDs that are connected to only one TRD. However, what happens when we want an ERD to be multihomed—that is, to be connected to many TRDs—without becoming a TRD, but remaining a leaf routing domain?

Examples of multihomed ERDs are routing domains in a big organization covering the whole nation that decides to connect to the Internet in many points through different providers, or even that of an international organization that decides to connect its network to the Internet in the nations where its main subsidiaries are located.

There are several reasons to have an ERD multihomed. The two main reasons are the larger availability of bandwidth, and the possibility of having alternative paths in case of errors and, therefore, a more reliable network.

In IPv6, an entire domain can be multihomed, but also a single subnet or a single host can be. A multihomed host can, in turn, be multihomed because it has many IPv6 addresses assigned to different interfaces (this case is common in reliable hosts) or because it has many addresses associated with the same interface (for example, a LAN with many prefixes associated with different providers). This topic is still the subject of debate in the Internet community, and at the time this chapter was written, only an Internet Draft[18] on this topic is available.

RFC 1887[19] provides four possible solutions for connecting an ERD to many TRDs. C. Huitema[20], who highlights the existing implications between multihoming and upper layer protocols, proposes a fifth solution.

7.5.5.1   SOLUTION #1   A multihomed organization obtains a prefix independently of the providers to which it is connected. This solution causes an additional entry in all core routers, and it is acceptable only for a few very large organizations. This solution does not scale to all organizations that will connect to the Internet in the future and that want to be multihomed because many hundreds of thousands of organizations could want this capability.

7.5.5.2 SOLUTION #2 The organization is assigned as many different prefixes as there are providers it will be connected to. In each part of the network, the organization will use a prefix chosen on the basis of the distance of that part of the network to a particular provider. For example, let's suppose that an organization has a network covering Italy, France, and Spain, and that it wants to be connected to the Internet in these three nations. For the Italian part of the network, it will use addresses derived from the set it has been assigned by an Italian provider; for the French part, addresses from a French provider; and for the Spanish part, addresses from a Spanish provider.

For this solution, core routers don't need to maintain any additional information for the organization because it will be reached as three separate organizations that are part of three different providers. Routers within the organization can be efficiently configured by using private links (see Section 7.5.7), without upgrading the ERD to a TRD.

The main disadvantage of this solution is the lack of backup mechanisms in case one of the three connections with the providers fails. The part of the network configured with addresses of that provider simply becomes unreachable because those addresses are not announced by the other two providers. Announcing them would be possible, but doing so would be much more expensive than in the preceding case because core routers should maintain three entries for the organization, one for each prefix used on the network. Moreover, if a provider is changed, all addresses associated with that provider should be changed, too.

Also, note that, with the previous approach, packets enter the organization via the point that is closest to the source node (which tends to maximize the load on the internal network); with this second solution, packets enter the organization via the point that is closest to the destination node (which tends to maximize the load on the Internet).

7.5.5.3 SOLUTION #3 Now suppose that a second organization uses provider A's prefix as the prefix for its networks because provider A is meant to be used as the default to the Internet. Other TRDs to which this organization is connected will advertise A's prefix only in restricted and controlled areas. For example, let's suppose that this organization also belongs to the Italian Public Administration network, administered by provider B. Provider B will advertise, within the public administration network, that this organization can be reached by a set of addresses from provider A. This capability entails that routers of the TRD of B have an explicit entry in routing tables for the organization, but it doesn't introduce any additional entry on core routers.

7.5.5.4 SOLUTION #4 The fourth solution can be used when two or more providers have many customers in common. This solution is hypothetical and will become fairly common when the use of IPv6 on public networks is more widespread. In this case, the two providers request a third set of addresses (in addition to the two they already have) to be assigned to customers they have in common and interconnect their TRDs. There is no penalty at the core router level because all users in common between the two providers are advertised with only one entry in the routing tables.

7.5.5.5 SOLUTION #5 For the fifth solution, each station is assigned as many addresses as there are providers. This situation is illustrated in Figure 7-6, where station X has two addresses: A::X derived from provider A and B::X derived from provider B.

This solution is not perfect. Suppose that X establishes a Telnet session with Y by using its address A::X. If, during the session, provider A becomes overloaded or it cannot reach X through A, the session cannot be rerouted using provider B. This operation will entail the use of address B::X in the IPv6 packet instead of the A::X address, but this use is not possible. In fact, the Telnet application lays on the *Transmission Control Protocol* (TCP), which also uses the IPv6 address as the connection identifier; according to RFC 793[21], this address cannot be modified during the connection itself.

A less pragmatic solution is to close the Telnet session and to open another one, this time using the address B::X.

A second solution, currently under discussion, is to modify the TCP protocol allowing IPv6 addresses to change during the connection.

A third possibility is that Y inserts a Routing Header (see Section 3.2.5) to force the routing to pass through B::X. In this way, the destination ad-

Figure 7-6
Example of multi-homing

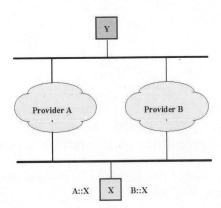

dress in the IPv6 packet remains A::X, but the packet is delivered to B::X, which routes it within itself to A::X—that is, to itself. The only drawback to this solution is represented by the routing header overhead (24 octets in the case of a single intermediate address).

7.5.6   Tunnel

In the solutions described in the preceding subsections are frequent references to the possibility that a multihomed host decides which address to use among many source addresses. Frequently, this is not possible because hosts don't have enough information to decide correctly or because network administrators don't want this situation to occur.

Network administrators typically want to base their decisions about which provider to use on the borders of the network—that is, on border routers. A possibility is represented by the creation of tunnels, which means transporting IP packets inside other IP packets.

This possibility, at the time this chapter was written, is described by an Internet Draft[22], and it corresponds to creating "virtual links" between two IPv6 nodes that see the tunnel as a communication channel at data link level—that is, as a link. The two nodes have two specific tasks: A node encapsulates the original packet and transmits it on the tunnel; and the other one receives the packet from the tunnel, eliminates the encapsulation, and transmits it to its destination.

Tunnels are unidirectional mechanisms; a bidirectional tunnel can be implemented by using two unidirectional tunnels.

Tunnels have at least three important applications:

- Bypassing providers' routing policies
- Interconnecting Intranets through the Internet network (see Section 7.7)
- Implementing 6-Bone—that is, a first core of the Internet using IPv6

Tunnels can be simple or routed (see Figure 7-7).

In the case of simple tunnels, an IP packet is transported inside an IP packet with an overhead equal to the size of the IP header (in the case of IPv6, 40 octets). In the example shown in Figure 7-7, the simple tunnel allows the packet originating in the routing domain B to reach Y by traversing routing domain C.

In the case of routed tunnels, a Routing Header is inserted to specify other routing domains that must be traversed on the path toward the des-

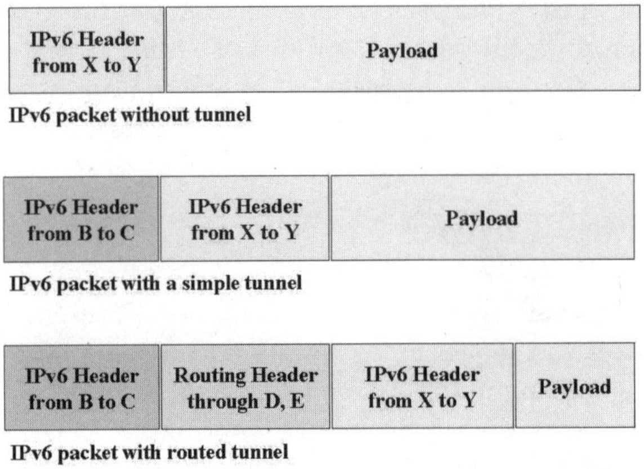

Figure 7-7
Examples of tunnels

IPv6 Header from X to Y	Payload

IPv6 packet without tunnel

IPv6 Header from B to C	IPv6 Header from X to Y	Payload

IPv6 packet with a simple tunnel

IPv6 Header from B to C	Routing Header through D, E	IPv6 Header from X to Y	Payload

IPv6 packet with routed tunnel

tination. In the example shown in Figure 7-7, the routed tunnel allows the packet originating in routing domain B to reach Y by traversing the routing domains D, E, and C.

7.5.7 Private Links

Suppose that two organizations X and Y have two ERDs and decide to improve their interconnection performance by acquiring a point-to-point link between the two ERDs. This approach doesn't raise any particular routing concerns on the Internet; it is a local agreement that is ignored by core routers. To create this link, adding one entry relevant to Y in routing tables of the ERD of X is sufficient, and vice versa. If Y connects other ERDs of other organizations with which it has an intense exchange of information to its ERD, accessing these organizations from X through a private link is also possible, by adding the necessary entries in routing tables.

7.6 Multicast Routing

The term *multicast routing* refers to routing of packets whose destination address is a multicast address—that is, the address of a group of stations. In Section 4.8, we saw that some of these multicast addresses are associated with predefined groups and have meaning only with regard to the node or to the link; whereas other multicast groups can have members in various parts of the Internet network, and therefore packets addressed to these multicast groups must be routed by routers.

The problem of multicast routing in IPv6 is similar to that in IPv4, with the following main differences:

- In IPv4, members of groups are administered with a specific protocol called *Internet Group Membership Protocol* (IGMP)[23], which in IPv6 became an integrated part of ICMPv6 (see Section 5.6.3) while maintaining the same functions.

- In IPv4, multicast packets are routed by two alternative protocols: the *Distance Vector Multicast Routing Protocol* (DVMRP) standardized in RFC 1075[24], or the *Multicast OSPF* (MOSPF) consisting of extensions to the protocol OSPF standardized in RFC 1584[25] to deal with multicast packets. In IPv6, the MOSPF extension became an integrated part of OSPFv6[11].

In summary, to route multicast packets, we must create a distribution tree (*multicast tree*) to reach all members of the group. The tree is clearly dynamic because new members can join the group, and existing members can leave it at any moment. The addition of members typically induces growth of the tree; whereas members leaving the group potentially "prunes" the tree.

Therefore, the multicast routing problem turns out to be an integrated part of IPv6 and, in particular, of ICMPv6 and OSPFv6 protocols.

7.7 Intranet

Many organizations, while deciding to implement networks based on the IP protocol, don't want to be interconnected to the Internet or want to have extremely controlled access to the Internet. These organizations implement Intranets, which are private networks based on the Internet model (see RFC 1918[26], even if relevant to IPv4). The configuration of Intranet networks is hugely simplified in IPv6, from the addressing point of view, because assigning site local addresses to the private part of a network is sufficient (see Section 4.6.5). The public part has, on the other hand, provider-based global addresses.

Figure 7-8 shows an example of Internet/Intranet configuration. To communicate between the public and the private part, a consolidated technical solution is used; it provides the installation of application gateways (for example, for the electronic mail) and proxy servers (for example, for WWW, FTP, and Telnet) on public hosts.

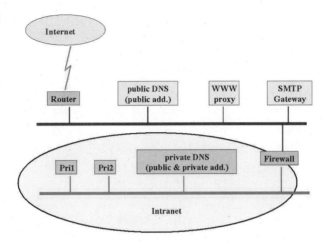

Figure 7-8

Connection scheme between an Intranet and the Internet

Between public and private networks, either a router, with appropriate access filters, or a real firewall is inserted to avoid propagating information about the private network on the Internet. Moreover, if a company implements many Intranets—for example, one for each subsidiary—it can interconnect these Intranets by implementing "tunnels" on the Internet between the firewalls of the different subsidiaries. The term *tunnel* (see Section 7.5.6) indicates an encapsulation of an IP packet in another IP packet: The IP packet of the Intranet is encapsulated in an IP packet of the Internet.

A public DNS server, connected to worldwide DNS systems, must be available; it is used to define the addresses of public hosts. A second private DNS server contains both public hosts' addresses and private hosts' addresses, and uses the public DNS as the sender toward the Internet. All hosts (either public or private) use the private DNS.

Another practical method to increase the security is to adopt a separate cabling for the public part (Internet) and the private part (Intranet) of the network. The term *separate cabling* here means a physical organization of the cabling in which, even if a hacker succeeds in loading a program for the capture of the network packets on a host that can be reached on the Internet, this program cannot see the Intranet packets because they travel on other cables.

REFERENCES

[1]G. Bennett, *Designing TCP/IP Internetworks*, Van Nostrand Reinhold, 1995.

[2]S. Gai, P.L. Montessoro, P. Nicoletti, *Reti Locali: dal Cablaggio all'Internetworking*, SSGRR (Scuola Superiore G. Reiss Romoli), 1995.

[3]J. V. Aho, J. E. Hopcroft, J. D. Ullman, *Data Structures and Algorithms*, Addison-Wesley, 1983.

[4]ISO 10589, *Intermediate system to Intermediate system Intra-Domain routing information exchange protocol for use in conjunction with the Protocol for providing the connectionless-mode network service.*

[5]C.L. Hedrick, *RFC 1058: Routing Information Protocol*, June 1988.

[6]G. Malkin, *RFC 1388: RIP Version 2 Carrying Additional Information*, January 1993.

[7]G. Malkin, R. Minnear, *RIPng for IPv6*, August 1996.

[8]J. Postel, *RFC 768: User Datagram Protocol*, August 1980.

[9]J. Moy, *RFC 1247: OSPF Version 2*, July 1991.

[10]J. Moy, *RFC 1583: OSPF Version 2*, March 1994.

[11]R. Coltun, D. Ferguson, J. Moy, *OSPF for IPv6*, June 1996.

[12]ISO 10747, *Protocol for Exchange of Inter-Domain Routing Information among Intermediate Systems to Support Forwarding of ISO 8473 PDUs.*

[13]Y. Rekhter, T. Li, *RFC 1771: A Border Gateway Protocol 4 (BGP-4)*, March 1995.

[14]Yakov Rekhter, Paul Traina, *Inter-Domain Routing Protocol, Version 2*, June 1996.

[15]Cisco Systems, *Router Products Configuration and Reference*, Cisco Systems DOC-R9.1, Menlo Park, CA, September 1992.

[16]V. Fuller, T. Li, J. Yu, K. Varadhan, *RFC 1519: Classless Inter-Domain Routing (CIDR): an Address Assignment and Aggregation Strategy*, September 1993.

[17]R.W. Callon, *RFC 1195: Use of OSI IS-IS for routing in TCP/IP and dual environments*, December 1990.

[18]M. Shand, M. Thomas, *Multi-homed Host Support in IPv6*, June 1996.

[19]Y. Rekhter, T. Li, *RFC 1887; An Architecture for IPv6 Unicast Address Allocation*, December 1995.

[20]C. Huitema, *IPv6: the new Internet Protocol*, Prentice-Hall, 1996.

[21]J. Postel, *RFC 793: Transmission Control Protocol*, September 1981.

[22]A. Conta, S. Deering, *Generic Packet Tunneling in IPv6 Specification*, June 1996.

[23]S.E. Deering, *RFC 1112: Host extensions for IP multicasting*, August 1989.

[24]D. Waitzman, C. Partridge, S.E. Deering, *RFC 1075: Distance Vector Multicast Routing Protocol*, November 1988.

[25]J. Moy, *RFC 1584: Multicast Extensions to OSPF*, March 1994.

[26]Y. Rekhter, B. Moskowitz, D. Karrenberg, G.J. de Groot, E. Lear, *RFC 1918: Address Allocation for Private Internets*, February 1996.

CHAPTER 8

Security Features of IPv6[1]

TCP/IP networks based on IPv4 are plagued with security problems because they are designed to work in a friendly environment and with physically secure connections. When these assumptions are no longer valid—as they are nowadays—the many security weaknesses of IPv4 become manifest and can be easily exploited.

In general, IP communications are exposed to several types of attack:

[1]This chapter was written by Antonio Lioy, professor at Politecnico di Torino, who, besides being one of the greatest Italian experts in the security field, is a good friend of mine. I sincerely thank him for his important contribution to my book.

■ *packet sniffing:* Due to network topology, IP packets sent from a source to a specific destination can also be read by other nodes, which can then get hold of the payload (for example, passwords or other private information).

■ *IP spoofing:* IP addresses can be very easily spoofed both to attack those services whose authentication is based on the sender's address (as the `rlogin` service or several WWW servers) and to supply wrong information to subvert the logical organization of the network (for example, by forging false ICMP messages of the type "destination unreachable" or "redirect").

■ *connection hijacking:* Whole IP packets can be forged to appear as legal packets coming from one of the two communicating partners, to insert wrong data in an existing channel.

Solutions to these and other attacks are not always available. When countermeasures do exist, they are usually placed at the application level. As a consequence, solutions are usually not interoperable, and several functions are duplicated inside different applications. The development of a new version of the IP protocol has offered a chance to insert some basic security mechanisms at the network level so that they can be available to all the layered applications. The security techniques adopted in IPv6 have been designed to be easily inserted also in IPv4, as detailed in RFC 1825[1], which introduces IPSEC, the new generic security architecture at the IP level. However, because the IPv4 protocol also suffers from other problems, it is unlikely that current network stacks and applications will be modified only to implement IPSEC. On the contrary, it is very likely—and probably will even be required for standard's compliance—that the IPSEC security features be implemented in IPv6.

We might question whether locating the security functions at the IP level is appropriate. Obviously, no definitive answer exists because, generally, the security of a system is not based on a single element; rather it is the result of a combination of several elements. The IP level is surely the right one to block many low-level attacks, as those mentioned at the beginning of this section, which account for a large percentage of all the network attacks due to their simple implementation. On the other hand, IPSEC is not a complete solution when the applications to be protected are user-oriented (as in the case of electronic mail) rather than network-oriented. Last but not least, the IPv6 security features are implemented by extension headers (see Section 3.2) so that they can be easily turned off when security aspects are not relevant and network throughput is of paramount importance.

8.1   Security Features

Security features in IPv6 have been introduced mainly by way of two dedicated extension headers: the *Authentication Header* (AH) and the *Encrypted Security Payload* (ESP), with complementary capabilities.

The AH header was designed to ensure authenticity and integrity of the IP packet. Its presence guards against two threats: illegal modification of the fixed fields and packet spoofing. On the other hand, the ESP header provides data encapsulation with encryption to ensure that only the destination node can read the payload conveyed by the IP packet. The two headers can be used together to provide all the security features simultaneously.

Both the AH and the ESP headers exploit the concept of security association (SA) to agree on the security algorithms and parameters between the sender and the receiver. In general, each IPv6 node manages a set of SAs, one for each secure communication currently active. The *Security Parameters Index* (SPI) is a parameter contained in both the AH and ESP headers to specify which SA is to be used in decrypting and/or authenticating the packet.

In unicast transmissions, the SPI is normally chosen by the destination node and sent back to the sender when the communication is set up. In multicast transmissions, the SPI must be common to all the members of the multicast group. Each node must be able to identify the right SA correctly by combining the SPI with the multicast address.

The negotiation of an SA (and the related SPI) is an integral part of the protocol for the exchange of security keys.

8.1.1   Authentication Header (AH)

The Authentication Header[2] is one of the general extension headers defined for IPv6; it is identified by the value 51 in the Next Header field (see Table 3-2) of the previous header. Normally, it is inserted between the IPv6 header and the upper level payload, as shown in Figure 8-1.

The format of the AH header (depicted in Figure 8-2) is simple; it is composed of a 64-bit fixed part followed by a variable number of 32-bit blocks. The fixed part contains the following:

■ The value of the next type of payload in the daisy chain of headers (8 bits)

■ The Payload Length—that is, the total length of the authentication data expressed as a multiple of 32-bit words (8 bits)

■ A reserved field (16 bits)

■ The SPI used by this header (32 bits)

The variable part of the AH header is composed of a variable number of 32-bit blocks, which contain the actual authentication data. Because the Payload Length is expressed as an 8-bit number, a maximum of 255 32-bit blocks can be used—that is, 1020 bytes. As a consequence, the exact length of this header depends on the selected authentication algorithm.

When the destination node receives a packet with an AH header, the packet's authenticity and integrity can be checked by using the procedure illustrated in Figure 8-3. For the preliminary step, care should be taken in normalizing the received packet, to eliminate all the variable parts and correctly compute the authentication value only on the fixed parts. Figure 8-4 illustrates the procedure to normalize the packet and to compute the authentication value.

8.1.2 Authentication Techniques

Data integrity in telecommunication systems is normally ensured by computing and checking the value of a suitable function of the data, often named *Message Digest* (MD). Among the most frequently used algo-

Figure 8-1
Examples of use of the AH header

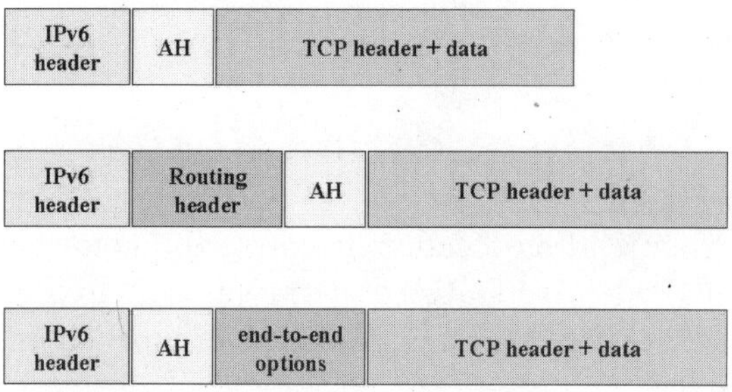

Figure 8-2
Structure of the AH header

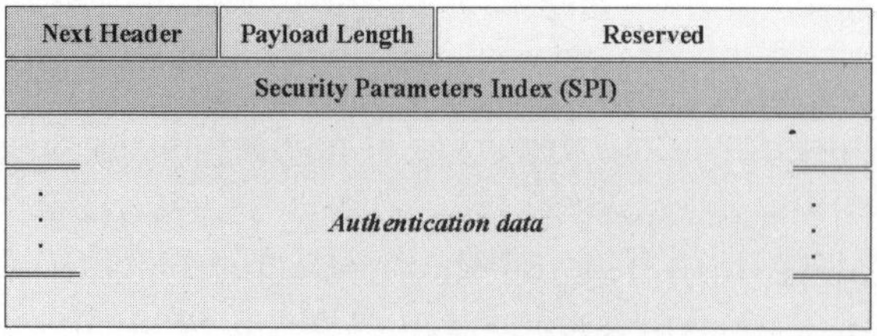

Figure 8-3
Procedure to verify
the authenticity of a
packet protected by
the AH header

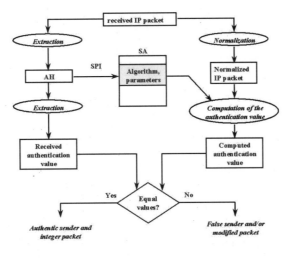

Figure 8-4
Procedure for packet
normalization to
compute the
authentication value

1. Clear the Hop Count field.

2. If the packet contains a Routing Header, then do the following:

   2.1. Set the Destination Address field to the address of the final destination.

   2.2. Set the Routing Header field to the value that it will have at the final destination.

   2.3. Set the Address Index field to the value that it will have at the final destination.

3. Clear all the options that have the C bit (change en route) active.

rithms are CRC-16 and CRC-32 (see *Applied Cryptography* [3]).

These functions effectively perform their tasks when data modifications are caused by random errors, but they are completely inadequate to protect the packets against deliberate modifications. In this case, a reasonable degree of protection can be ensured only by better digest algorithms, such as MD5[4] or SHA[5].

We should note that data integrity without origin authentication is completely useless. Therefore, digest algorithms are normally applied in a way to include some parameters that can be used to provide proof of the sender's identity simultaneously. Often this result is achieved by using public key encryption algorithms; unfortunately, they are computationally much heavier than digest algorithms. Because speed is a premium in computer networks, the default authentication technique chosen for IPSEC is a simpler one, named *keyed MD5*[6]. Briefly, the technique calls for computing the MD5 digest on the data to be protected, preceded and followed by a *key* (a secret string of bits). The exact sequence of operations to compute this type of digest is shown in Figure 8-5.

The keyed-MD5 algorithm must be provided by any standard implementation of IPv6. However, the MD5 algorithm has been recently shown to be attackable, so it is highly likely that in the near future other authentication techniques will be standardized for use in IPv6. For example, the *keyed-SHA* technique has been proposed in RFC 1852[7]. It is based on the SHA[5] message digest algorithm, which exhibits better security properties than MD5 because it produces a 160-bit digest rather than a 128-bit digest.

8.1.3 Encrypted Security Payload (ESP)

The Encrypted Security Payload[8], which is one of the general extension headers defined in IPv6, is identified by the value 52 in the Next Header field (see Table 3-2) of the preceding header. When used, this block must always be the last one in the header chain because it completely hides both the upper level payload and all the next headers (see Figure 8-6).

Even the ESP header itself is only partly in the clear (see Figure 8-7); it consists of an integer number of 32-bit blocks, with the first one containing the SPI to select the SA to be used in decrypting all other blocks in the packet.

The exact format of the encrypted part depends on the encryption algorithm used. The default encryption technique in IPv6 is DES-CBC[9], which is the DES algorithm applied in *Cipher Block Chaining* (CBC) mode. DES is a private key encryption algorithm that is normally applied to 64-bit data blocks with a 56-bit key (extended to 64 bits by adding one parity bit for each 7 bits of the key). Various techniques have been proposed to apply the DES transformation to blocks bigger than 64 bits. The CBC mode divides the data stream into a sequence of 64-bit blocks, and

---

Figure 8-5

Algorithm to generate a keyed MD5 digest

---

1. Given a message M to protect, normalize it (M′).

2. Pad the message M′ by adding as many zero bytes as necessary to align the message to a multiple of 128 bits (message M'_p).

3. Pad the key K by adding as many zero bytes as necessary to align the key to a multiple of 128 bits (message K_p).

4. Compute the authentication value as the result of the MD5 function applied to the argument given by the concatenation K_p, M'_p, K_p.

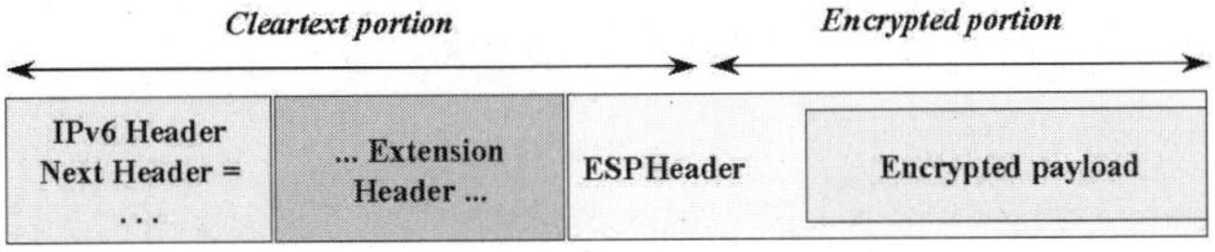

Figure 8-6

IPv6 packet with an
ESP header

Figure 8-7

Structure of the ESP
header

each block is EX-ORed with the result of the previous encryption before being encrypted itself. Let $E(d,k)$ be the encryption operation applied to the data block d with key k; then the CBC mode can be described by the following transform to generate the i-th encrypted block:

$$c_i = E\ (d_i \oplus c_{i-1},\ k)$$

Obviously, the encryption of the first data block d^1 requires an initial value c^0, commonly called the *Initialization Vector* (IV). The initialization vector must not be null and must be carefully chosen to insert a random factor in the encryption process. This is needed to avoid cryptographic attacks based on partial knowledge of the data being encrypted, such as the *known-plaintext* attacks that can be led against the fixed header of some common files (for example, the data files of various office automation tools). Normally, the IV value is either a 64-bit number generated by a pseudo-random number generator, or the value is a 32-bit number generated in a similar way and is then extended to 64 bits by concatenating it to its complement.

In the DES-CBC mode, the encrypted portion of the ESP header (see Figure 8-8) begins with an initialization vector composed of an integer number of 32-bit words. In general, the exact length of the IV depends on the security association being used; however, RFC 1829[9] provides specification only for vectors of 32 or 64 bits.

The IV is followed by the encrypted payload that is padded with blocks to ensure that the total dimension of the ESP header is a multiple of 64 bits. The next-to-last byte in the ESP header contains the padding length (expressed in bytes), whereas the last byte contains the payload type. The minimum length of the padding varies between 0 and 7 bytes, but using a longer padding (up to 255 bytes) to hide the real length of the encrypted data is legal.

Figure 8-8
Structure of the ESP
header in the DES-
CBC case

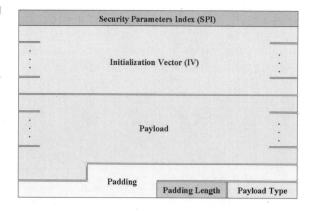

The DES-CBC algorithm must be available in all IPv6 standard implementations. Because the DES algorithm can be regarded at best as a moderately difficult algorithm to be broken, it is very likely that in the near future other algorithms will be standardized for use in IPv6. For example, the 3DES-CBC algorithm is proposed in RFC 1851[10]. This technique is based on the repeated application of the DES transformation to the same data block with three different keys, and it is cryptographically stronger than plain DES because it is equivalent to an encryption algorithm that uses a 112-bit key (rather than the 56-bit key used by DES).

8.2 Key Management

Correct application of the AH and ESP headers requires that all the communicating parties agree on a common key to be used in forming and checking the security headers. IPv6 allows for key management to occur either out-of-band or with specifically crafted protocols. However, no general agreement has yet been reached on this subject within the Internet community, with different groups stressing different needs: fast key exchange, strong authentication, lightweight protocols, and others. Key management is the area that is still mostly unsettled within the whole IPSEC architecture.

8.2.1 Manual Key Management

IPv6 requires every implementation to allow for manual setting of the security keys, in case no in-line key management technique is adopted or human-based security is desired. Obviously, manual keying is possible only if the security operators have separately agreed out-of-band on the keys to be used—for example, at a reserved meeting.

This solution exhibits high personnel costs and does not scale well because it requires personal action of an operator on each network device taking part in the secure channel. Additionally, it can generate a false sense of security. Remember that human intervention does not automatically ensure a higher level of security, due to untrusted operators and residual problems related to hardware and software integrity of the device where the key is set.

However, in spite of these disadvantages, manual key management finds application in restricted environments, with a small number of devices physically secured that, according to the security policy, can operate only when explicitly enabled by human intervention.

8.2.2   Automatic Key Management

Within the IPSEC, key management is surely the area that is less settled and the area in which much work has yet to be done before arriving at a set of protocols that completely meet the security needs at the IP level. The only decision that has already been made is that, for sake of generality, the key management protocol (IKMP, Internet Key Management Protocol) will be placed at the application layer, and it will be independent of the protocols at the lower layers.

A first proposal is to base IKMP on the coupling of the ISAKMP[11] and Oakley[12] protocols, as described in the IEFT Draft, *The Resolution of ISAKMP with Oakley*[13].

Internet Security Association and Key Management Protocol (ISAKMP) defines a generic architecture for authenticated SA setup and key exchange, without specifying the actual algorithms to be used. In this way, it can be used with different key exchange techniques.

Oakley is a key-exchange protocol, based on a modified version of the Diffie-Hellman algorithm (see[3]). Therefore, it is one of the natural partners for ISAKMP.

However, in addition to the ISAKMP-Oakley couple, different solutions are being proposed. Currently, the major competitor is *Simple Key-management for Internet Protocols* (SKIP)[14], which bases its operations on the Diffie-Hellman algorithm. SKIP is simple and addresses several problems of key management in high-speed networks, such as zero-message key setup and updates that permit fast dynamic rekeying (that is, frequent in-line change of the security keys to avoid analytic attacks based on accumulation of cyphertext encrypted with the same key). Moreover, although SKIP is not yet standardized, it already features many commercial-level implementations, both for UNIX workstations and personal computers.

So the war of the key-management protocols is raging, and the likely outcome is that more than one protocol will attain RFC status because these protocols exhibit different merits that are valuable in different application environments.

8.3   Application of IPv6 Security Features

The AH and ESP headers can be used in different ways to protect IP communications. In the following subsections, we will briefly review some of the most interesting applications, with references to the corresponding weaknesses in IPv4.

8.3.1   Private Virtual Networks

Nowadays, technical and economical reasons are pushing implementation of corporate wide area networks to migrate from dedicated links and proprietary network technologies to solutions based on public shared links and open network architectures. This migration creates several advantages but currently exhibits a serious drawback: There is a drastic reduction in intrinsic system security, due to the use of shared channels and devices.

To regain the same previous level of network security while maintaining the economic advantages offered by public networks, an organization has to succeed in separating and protecting its own data packets within the crowd of packets traveling across the public links. Usually, this result is achieved by establishing a *Virtual Private Network* (VPN). In IPv4, this is done by using the *IP tunneling* technique: IP packets to be protected are wrapped in a security envelope and encapsulated inside normal IP packets that are used just to transport the original packets across the public network to their final destination. Often, the endpoints of an IP tunnel are not the hosts wanting to exchange the data; rather they are two *firewalls* that protect the LANs from external attacks. This setup is shown in Figure 8-9.

In IPv6, creating a VPN is easier and more standard than in IPv4, thanks to the AH and ESP headers. As an example, with reference to Figure 8-9, let's suppose that a TCP channel between host H1 in network N1 and host H2 in network N2 has to be protected only against data manipulation and origin falsification, while data privacy is not required. In this case, the AH header can be exploited in the following way. The FW1 firewall gets the IP packet shown in Figure 8-10 and modifies it by adding an AH header before sending it to its partner, FW2, as shown in Figure 8-11.

When this packet is received from the FW2 firewall, the firewall checks the packet for integrity and origin authentication by using the data in the AH header. If the check is successful, then the IP header and the AH header are removed, and the remaining data (that is, the original packet) are sent to the final destination, as shown in Figure 8-12.

If the VPN is implemented by using only the AH header, then attackers can neither alter the transmitted packets nor insert forged packets in the channel. However, they can still read the content of the packets. To prevent disclosure of the payload, the ESP header has to be used, too. Even the use of AH in conjunction with ESP does not completely protect the traffic; packets

Figure 8-9

Example of a tunnel between two firewalls

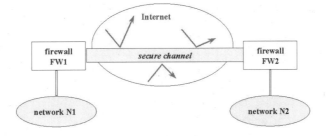

Figure 8-10

IPv6 packet sent from H1 to FW1

| IPv6 header (src=H1, dest=H2, Next Header=TCP) |
| TCP payload |

Figure 8-11

IPv6 packet sent from FW1 to FW2

| IPv6 header (src=FW1, dest=FW2, Next Header=AH) |
| AH header (Next Header=IPv6) |
| IPv6 header (src=H1, dest=H2, Next Header=TCP) |
| TCP payload |

can be deleted by intermediate nodes or recorded and later replayed. These attacks cannot be easily contrasted at the IP level; appropriate defenses (such as the use of unique packet identifiers and the generation of heartbeat packets) are usually placed at some upper level in the network stack. A partial solution at the IP level is likely to be offered by the new format and algorithms that are going to replace the current ones in the AH header.

Comparing this method of creating a VPN with the one usually adopted in IPv4 by many firewall suppliers that also offer secure tunnels is interesting. The basic architecture is the same as that used in IPv6 (refer to Figure 8-9), but, because IPv4 does not allow for multiple headers, the tunnel has to be implemented by some form of encapsulation, such as IP in IP[15]. Obviously, this solution raises problems of compatibility between the firewalls of different vendors as well as fragmentation problems. If the packet to be transmitted already has the maximum dimension allowed for an IP packet, then encapsulating it inside another IP packet is not possible; fragmentation and reassembling must take place at the two endpoints of the tunnel. As a consequence, the performance of the virtual channel can degrade down to 50 percent of the normal throughput. The worst case takes place for larger packets, which are typically used in transferring large data sets that, by contrast, would need no fragmentation to achieve maximum speed. On the other hand, the best case occurs for small packets, such as those used in interactive applications that, ironically, would better accept even a larger performance penalty, as long as the total throughput remains compatible with the reaction time of the human operator.

In IPv6, the situation is completely inverted; because the overhead is fixed in size (the dimension of AH, or that of AH plus ESP) and independent of the dimension of the original packet, the applications that suffer the highest overhead are the interactive ones, which are the applications with better resistance properties.

Anyway, in both cases, the performance penalty is definitely lower for the VPN implemented in IPv6 compared to those built in IPv4.

Last but not least, it is interesting to realize that this VPN technique can be adopted even between a firewall and a single external host (see Figure 8-13). Obviously, this case is of particular relevance to guaranteed security when a mobile host is used outside the protected network perimeter, and it is a perfect complement to the mobility support features of IPv6 (see Chapter 10). The firewall will act as home agent for H_M in the Neigh-

Figure 8-12

IPv6 packet sent from FW2 to H2

IPv6 header (src=H1, dest=H2, Next Header=TCP)
TCP payload

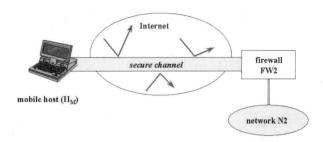

Figure 8-13
Tunnel between a
firewall and a single
host

bor Discovery procedure. H_M will be assigned two different IP addresses: one when it is connected inside the security perimeter and the other one when it is outside the perimeter. In this last case, the firewall will also act as a relay, by redirecting packets coming from inside the corporate network to the external address, after adding the required headers (AH only, or AH plus ESP).

8.3.2   Application-Level Security

Networked applications executing on top of an IPv6 stack may choose to require the use of a communication channel with specific features. To avoid duplication of functionality (and hence performance degradation), being able to specify, at the transport layer, the security attributes of the channel being created is useful. In the first BSD-UNIX implementations of IPv6, this effect can be obtained by properly using the `setsocketoption()` system call.

Anyway, this solution is not complete for application-level security because only partial protection is obtained. AH provides host-based authentication only; whereas applications usually require user-based authentication. Moreover, AH and ESP protect the data only during their transmission along the channel. After the data have been received, they are no longer protected in any way. This fact may not be relevant if the receiving host is a secure one, but there is the additional implication that origin authentication and data integrity properties are lost as well, so formal nonrepudiation cannot occur after the data have been extracted from the secure channel.

We can therefore draw the conclusion that the security features of IPv6 do not eliminate the need for other security mechanisms, which will probably be better placed at the application level.

8.3.3 Routing Security

Because IP addresses in IPv6 are quite often dynamically assigned, it is of the utmost importance that this process be done in a secure fashion. Moreover, as different security properties are available through a proper combination of AH and ESP headers, it is highly desirable that they be applied to the messages exchanged by routers to prevent attacks aiming to subvert the logical architecture of the network.

The following types of communications should be protected:

- The routing advertisement messages, to ensure that they are originated by an authorized router
- The neighbor advertisement messages, to ensure that they come from authorized hosts and to avoid the risk of somebody attaching a new host to the network without proper authorization
- The ICMP messages related to an unreachable host or network (*destination unreachable*) or to a better route (*redirect*), to ensure that these messages come from hosts or routers that were on the original path of the packets

Securing these types of messages is surely not trivial. For example, the routing advertisements are sent to a multicast group; therefore, all the routers in the group must know the (common) secret key to be used to verify and/or decrypt the messages. In turn, this fact implies that they can forge messages and impersonate any router in the group!

Protection of the neighbor advertisements poses a serious problem; these messages can be protected only after an SA has been created between the host and the address distribution center. On the other hand, this SA can be created only after an address has been assigned to the host, so we can conclude that this is the typical "chicken-and-egg" problem, which has no correct solution. To break the loop, partial solutions are possible. For example, priority can be given to the address assignment phase, and SA setup can be permitted only subsequently, but in this way the address assignment phase is not protected. Alternatively, public key authentication can be used. Each host is assigned a key pair (private and public key) and has to be preconfigured with the public key of the authority that signs the certificates of the routers and the address distribution centers. The last alternative is to configure routers so that they do not advertise local prefixes; in this way, each host is forced to contact a router first.

Protection against false ICMP messages requires that they be protected by an AH header, but this approach has the drawback of requiring the establishment of an SA with each router and host on the path between the source and the destination of the packets.

With respect to the security of the messages used by the various routing protocols, they should always be exchanged only within the frame of an SA and be protected by AH. For the sake of generality, this solution is highly preferable to using authentication mechanisms specific for each routing protocol.

Based on the preceding analyses, we can conclude that routing security is apparently still a problem in IPv6, but chances of solving the problem are higher than in IPv4.

8.4   Future Directions

Security is one of the fastest moving areas in computer networks because protecting data and computer resources is vital, as is enabling economic exploitation through electronic commerce. IPv6 security is not the exception to the rule; although this area is new, it is already undergoing a redesign to better achieve its objectives.

Currently, AH and ESP headers are being modified along the following guidelines:

- The AH format is substantially changing to accommodate new and stronger authentication algorithms (HMAC[16]) that support prevention of packet replay and cancellation. (RFC 2085[17] describes this format when used with the MD5 digest algorithm.)

- The ESP specification is only marginally changing to achieve a better orthogonality with algorithms, to simplify application of different encryption algorithms.

The net benefit of these changes will be that more security will be available at the network level; hence, applications will be able to concentrate on different security aspects, such as authorizations and nonrepudiation.

REFERENCES

[1]R. Atkinson, *RFC 1825: Security Architecture for the Internet Protocol*, August 1995.

[2]R. Atkinson, *RFC 1826: IP Authentication Header*, August 1995.

[3]B. Schneier, *Applied Cryptography*, John Wiley & Sons, New York, 1996.

[4]R. Rivest, *RFC 1321: The MD5 Message-Digest Algorithm*, April 1992.

[5]*Secure Hash Standard*, Document FIPS-180-1, National Institute of

Standards and Technology, U.S. Department of Commerce, April 1995.

[6]P. Metzger and W. Simpson, *RFC 1828: IP Authentication using Keyed MD5*, August 1995.

[7]P. Metzger and W. Simpson, *RFC 1852: IP Authentication using Keyed SHA*, September 1995.

[8]R. Atkinson, *RFC 1827: IP Encapsulating Security Payload (ESP)*, August 1995.

[9]P. Karn, P. Metzger, and W. Simpson, *RFC 1829: The ESP DES-CBC Transform*, August 1995.

[10]P. Karn, P. Metzger, and W. Simpson, *RFC 1851: The ESP Triple DES Transform*, September 1995.

[11]D. Maughhan, M. Schertler, M. Schneider, and J. Turner, *Internet Security Association and Key Management Protocol (ISAKMP)*, IEFT Draft (`draft-ietf-ipsec-isakmp-*.txt`).

[12]H. Orman, *The Oakley Key Determination Protocol*, IEFT Draft (`draft-ietf-ipsec-oakley-*.txt`).

[13]D. Harkins and D. Carrel, *The Resolution of ISAKMP with Oakley*, IEFT Draft (`draft-ietf-ipsec-isakmp-oakley-*.txt`).

[14]A. Aziz, T. Markson, and H. Prafullchandra, *Simple Key-Management For Internet Protocols (SKIP)*, IEFT Draft (`draft-aziz-skip-*.txt`).

[15]W. Simpson, *RFC 1853: IP in IP Tunnelling*, October 1995.

[16]H. Krawczyk, M. Bellare, and R. Canetti, *RFC 2104: HMAC: Keyed-Hashing for Message Authentication*, February 1997.

[17] M. Oehler and R. Glenn, *RFC 2085: HMAC-MD5 IP Authentication with Replay Prevention*, February 1997.

IPv6 over ATM

ATM networks[1], for their connection-oriented nature, don't provide an ideal environment for connectionless network protocols such as IPv4, IPv6, IPX, Decnet, and so on. A possible solution for a layer 3 protocol to be supported by an ATM network cannot even be foreseen with acceptable performance. On the one hand, it is true that in the near future, many intranets will probably continue to be multi-protocol and therefore need to transmit and to receive, besides IP packets, other protocols (such as Decnet, IPX, OSI); on the other hand, it is equally true that the only protocol that is worth modifying further to suit ATM is IP (both version 4 and version 6) for the major role it will have in the future of networks. Originally, a classification of IP over ATM approaches was tried, by differentiating them on the basis of their geographic extension (LAN, MAN, and WAN).

This classification was discontinued as improper; in ATM networks, the distance increases the propagation delay and reduces performance, but it doesn't substantially change the network organization and packet routing problems.

The use of an ATM network to transport IPv6 packets can be relatively simple or very complex, depending on how the ATM network itself is used. Many commercial proposals for ATM WANs (wide area networks) offer a service based on *PVCs* (Permanent Virtual Connections) and an internetworking between local networks and the wide area network implemented through routers. This method of using ATM doesn't present particular problems because routers see PVCs as point-to-point channels. This approach is frequently chosen when

- Internetworking sizes are significant
- Heterogeneous transmission media are used, making the use of a unique network technology impossible
- Reliability reasons impose a partially meshed technology, also with heterogeneous transmission media

The only decision to make is how to segment IP packets into ATM cells, but standard solutions are already available for this problem.

The situation is different if we want to use *SVCs* (Switched Virtual Connections), which are activated through UNI (*User to Network Interface*)[2] signaling procedures. SVCs make ATM a multi-access network—that is, a network in which all other users of the network can be reached from any connection point.

Also, LANs are multi-access networks, which are different from ATM for their connectionless nature and because they offer a native support to the broadcast traffic. The lack of a mechanism to transmit the broadcast traffic classifies ATM as an *NBMA (Non Broadcast Multiple Access)* network technology. Other NBMA network technologies have been available for many years—for example, those based on X.25 and Frame Relay protocols—but the transport of IP packets on NBMA networks acquires a particular relevance only with ATM. In fact, market analysis agrees that, in the near future, both ATM and IPv6 will be widespread technologies, and therefore we must find efficient ways to use them jointly.

The use of SVC requires mechanisms in which the IPv6 protocol activates UNI signaling procedures to create and terminate SVCs, mechanisms that are in contrast with the connectionless nature of the IP protocol.

Moreover, the lack of a native support for the broadcast is particularly important for the Neighbor Discovery protocol (see Chapter 6), which is based on the assumption that the link level underlying IPv6 can support multicast transmissions.

Looking to the future of networks and of internetworking, we will see an ever-growing number of ATM networks interconnected at the ATM level—that is, through connections between switches. This structure creates the possibility of setting SVCs between whichever couples of nodes can pass IP subnet limits; however, doing so violates the classic IP model in which distinct IP subnets can communicate between them only through routers.

Problems relevant to IP over ATM internetworking can be better understood by analyzing Figure 9-1, in which IP subnets are identified by the acronym *LLG* (*Logical Link Group*), according with the terminology proposed for IPv6 on ATM.

From the analysis of Figure 9-1, we can understand how much the problem of routing IP over ATM is complicated by the possibility of setting SVCs between two stations directly connected to ATM even if belonging to different LLGs (for example, H1 and H5), implementing a process called *cut-through routing*. Another problem that needs an efficient solution is the identification of the best exit router (*egress router*) toward a station not connected to ATM (for example, the router R2 for the communication between H2 and H7).

Of course, having cut-through routing schemes to use IPv6 on ATM is not necessary; we can still use the classical IP routing approach and cross routers following IP routing rules (in Figure 9-1, for going from H1 to H5, the classical IP routing can occur along the path H1 - R1 - R3 - H5). Cut-

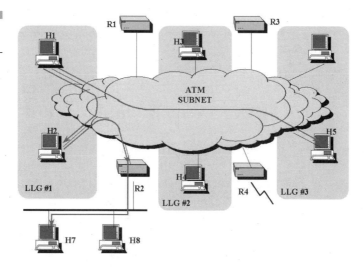

Figure 9-1
IPv6 over ATM

through routing becomes necessary with the growth of network sizes because the number of routers to be traversed can become high, penalizing the performance greatly.

In the following text, we will see how the solution to some problems is already consolidated, based on solutions standardized for IPv4 on ATM; whereas the solution to other problems is currently the subject of further discussion. For this reason, the remaining part of the chapter is subdivided into Section 9.1, which describes the more consolidated aspects, and into Section 9.2, which describes those not yet completely defined. In Section 9.3, we will discuss alternative approaches that don't use UNI and P-NNI signaling procedures.

9.1   Defined Aspects

Defined aspects deal with packet encapsulation, the identification of VC (Virtual Connection) endpoints, and modalities to transport IPv6 packets in ATM cells.

Solutions to these problems are common to all proposals of IPv6 on ATM and are independent of topology or routing considerations and of the use of PVCs or SVCs.

An example of interconnection of two hosts and an IPv6 router through an ATM network (ATM subnet) is shown in Figure 9-2.

The problem of the encapsulation and of the identification of VC endpoints is treated by RFC 1483[3], which provides a multi-protocol solution, valid also for IPv6. RFC 1483 provides two possible solutions: LLC/SNAP encapsulation and VC multiplexing.

The problem of transporting IPv6 packets in ATM cells is solved by adopting the AAL5 (ATM Adaptation Layer 5).

9.1.1   LLC/SNAP Encapsulation

RFC 1483[3] proposes *LLC/SNAP* encapsulation as the default solution. This approach is an adaptation to ATM of the solution developed in project IEEE 802[4]. It allows the transportation of an arbitrary number of protocols within a single VC, identifying them by means of an LLC/SNAP header (see Figure 9-3).

Figure 9-4 shows an example of several Ethernet-derived protocols (OUI = 00-00-00H) that share the same VC and that are differentiated by the value of the PID (*Protocol IDentifier*) field.

The LLC/SNAP encapsulation is used both for IPv6 unicast packets, for multicast packets, and also for the interaction between IPv6 stations and the MARS (*Multicast Address Resolution Server*)[5], described in Section 9.2.4.

In the case of IPv6 unicast packets, the encapsulation used is exactly the one shown in Figure 9-3. In contrast, IPv6 packets sent to the MARS are enveloped by using the OUI 0x00-00-5E registered by the IANA. In the case of control messages, the PID 0x00-03 is used, as shown in Figure 9-5.

A more complex description is needed for multicast IPv6 packets (possibly relayed through an MCS, see Section 9.2.4) that must be encapsulated as shown in Figure 9-6. The presence of the field pkt$cmi (*CMI: Cluster Member ID*) within these packets allows a station to recognize, among received multicast messages, those it transmitted; therefore, it will not to process them. The field pkt$pro (packet protocol) indicates the protocol that generated the encapsulated PDU (IPv6 in the case of Figure 9-6).

Figure 9-2

Interconnection of IP hosts through ATM

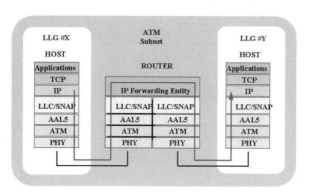

Figure 9-3

LLC/SNAP encapsulation

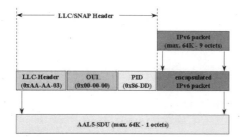

9.1.2 VC Multiplexing

The UNI[2] standard provides that the endpoint of a VC is set during the call setup phase. A simple approach is to use the *VC multiplexing* or *null encapsulation* that provides for termination of a VC through an AAL5 instance directly on a layer 3 protocol (see Figure 9-7). When the VC multiplexing is used in IPv6, the end of the VC is the IPv6 protocol itself; that is, the IPv6 packet is directly placed inside the AAL5-SDU.

This approach is restrictive in multi-protocol environments in which each protocol requires the creation of a separate VC; it causes a considerable load on ATM switches for the signaling associated with the opening and closing of VCs. Moreover, the number of VCs is very high, and it can exceed the maximum number of VCs admitted by switches.

Figure 9-4
Sharing a VC through LLC/SNAP

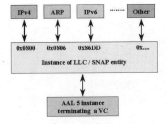

Figure 9-5
Encapsulation of a MARS control message

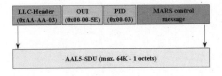

Figure 9-6
LLC/SNAP encapsulation for multicast packets

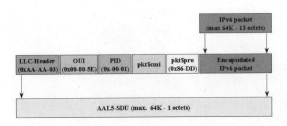

9.1.3 AAL Type 5

Both the preceding solutions assume that the packet is segmented using AAL5 (see **1** and **3**). This AAL has been standardized by the ATM Forum, starting from a proposal to simplify AAL3/4, called SEAL (Simple and Efficient Adaptation Layer). AAL5 is designed to offer only a connectionless service. Today AAL5 has been adopted worldwide to make data transmission very simple and efficient. The simplification is drastic, both for what relates to the CS sublayer (Convergence Sublayer), which has been emptied in practice, and for what relates to the SAR (Segmentation And Reassembly) sublayer.

In preceding sections, we saw how an IPv6 packet is enveloped in an AAL5-SDU. The AAL5 adds a PAD field to the AAL5-SDU to normalize the length of the AAL5-PDU to a multiple of 48 octets, a control field also containing the length of the AAL5-PDU, and a CRC on 32 bits computed on the PDU itself.

The AAL5-PDU is subdivided into a sequence of 48-octet segments (SAR-PDU) that are neither numbered nor identified in any way (see Figure 9-8).

The SAR-PDU, shown in Figure 9-9, is 48 octets long and coincides with the payload of the ATM cell. The last segment is marked by the setting of a bit in the PT (*Payload Type*) field of the header of the ATM cell transporting it.

When a cell, whose bit is set in the PT, is received by the SAR sublayer of the AAL 5, the SAR sublayer assembles all the received SAR-PDUs rebuilding the AAL5-PDU, and it verifies the length and the CRC (refer to Figure 9-8). If the AAL5-PDU is valid, the AAL5-SDU is extracted from it; and from this, the IPv6 packet. In case of errors, the AAL5-PDU is discarded without any other action, like happens at the MAC level in the case of an erroneous Ethernet frame.

Figure 9-7
Multiprotocol networks through VC multiplexing

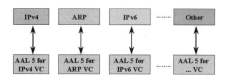

Figure 9-8
Process of AAL5 segmentation and re-assembling

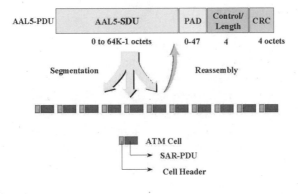

Figure 9-9
Format of the AAL5 SAR-PDU

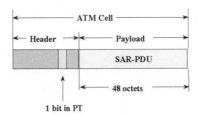

9.2   Work in Progress

Most of the techniques described in the following subsections will certainly be part of the solution or solutions that will be standardized for IPv6 on ATM. Some of these techniques are already included in some RFCs; others have been widely discussed by IETF working groups. Currently, what is not already clear is how different techniques will combine to provide the standard solution or solutions.

9.2.1   Neighbor Discovery

The Neighbor Discovery (ND) protocol, described in Chapter 6, is not easily adaptable to ATM networks because it assumes that the underlying link level supports multicast transmissions and differentiates on-link and off-link stations, and also because it doesn't explicitly deal with cut-through routing problems[6].

The need for cut-through routing derives from the inadequacy of the concepts of on-link and off-link when large ATM networks are deployed. The concept of link is replaced by the concept of LLG (*Logical Link*

Group), a set of stations that share the same IPv6 address prefix and that are therefore neighbors. Many LLGs can or must be configured on the same ATM network for technical and administrative reasons. Given two IPv6 nodes, we can have the following three cases:

■ *On LLG Neighbor:* Two nodes connected to the same ATM network and belonging to the same LLG. This case is the simplest one because it follows the normal way of operating for IPv6. An example is the connection between hosts H1 and H2 in Figure 9-1.

■ *Off LLG Neighbor:* Two nodes connected to the same ATM network but not belonging to the same LLG. When two nodes are Off LLG Neighbor, the cut-through routing can be performed between them. An example of this situation is the connection between hosts H1 and H5 in Figure 9-1.

■ *Off LLG not Neighbor:* Two nodes that are not connected to the same ATM network and that therefore cannot belong to the same LLG. When two nodes are Off LLG not Neighbor, a direct VC cannot be activated between them, but the best egress router can be determined and a cut-through toward it can be activated. An example of this situation is a connection between hosts H2 and H7 in Figure 9-1.

A simplified solution to ND problems is to use a MARS service (see Section 9.2.4) to emulate generalized multicast support and therefore allow the ND to operate like on a LAN. Note that this solution is a further use of MARS; in fact, MARS has mainly been developed to manage layer 3 multicast addresses (see Section 4.8) like those used by multimedia applications.

The use of MARS solves the problem only for the On LLG Neighbor case, but it doesn't allow cut-through routing. To overcome this limit, a more advanced version[7] has been proposed to provide the creation of an ND server's hierarchy (basically MARS servers devoted to ND problems) in which each server can provide direct answers to the On LLG Neighbor case, while exploiting the hierarchical interconnection with other servers for Off LLG cases.

An alternative proposal[8] is to solve ND problems by reusing the huge amount of work already done to allow the cut-through routing in IPv4, using the NHRP protocol (see Section 9.2.5). This proposal also poses a solution to the problem of the autoconfiguration of IPv6 addresses associated with ATM interfaces (see Section 9.2.2).

A third proposal[9] suggests the use of MARS/MCS within the LLG and

NHRP for the cut-through routing. This proposal introduces the concept of *Transient Neighbors*—that is, temporary neighbors created through ICMP Redirect messages (see Section 9.2.5).

9.2.2 Address Autoconfiguration

The autoconfiguration problem of IPv6 addresses associated with ATM interfaces is complicated by the lack of a multicast native mechanism that allows use of the Duplicate Address Detection procedure (see Section 6.7.4), but also by the presence of the concept of logic interface in ATM. In fact, on an ATM network board, many ATM logical interfaces can be configured, obviously having different addresses (*interface tokens*, according to the IPv6 terminology). The Link Local address autoconfiguration therefore becomes more complex than in the case of LANs where 48-bit MAC addresses are used as interface tokens. This issue raises both the problem of using a number of bits sufficient to univocally identify the interface to avoid duplicated addresses and the problem of using a number of bits sufficient for the network prefix.

This problem does not have a general solution so far. A proposal limited to the NHRP case is described in the IETF Internet Draft *IPv6 over NBMA Networks*[8].

9.2.3 ICMP Redirect

The ICMP Redirect message, which is provided by RFC 1885[10], must be correctly supported by all IPv6 nodes (see Section 5.5.8). Its semantic is extended if compared to the IPv4 one because it allows creation of *Transient Neighbors*—that is, nodes that are temporarily considered neighbors. This capability can be useful in the Off LLG Neighbor case because the ICMP Redirect message can transport the Link Source/Target Address option (see Section 5.5.10). This option can be used to carry the ATM address (on 20 octets) of the target node and therefore to allow the source node to open a dedicated VC with the target node through UNI signaling, by implementing the cut-through routing.

9.2.4 MARS (Multicast Address Resolution Server)

In the introduction, we pointed out the lack of native support for broadcast traffic in ATM because ATM is an NBMA network. The IETF working group "IP over NBMA networks" (formerly "IP over ATM") released RFC 2022[5] suggesting that the support for the multicast traffic be built by using point-to-multipoint VCs and a MARS (*Multicast Address Resolution Server*).

The MARS is an extension of the ATMARP server standardized for IPv4 in RFC 1577[11]. It implements a recording entity in which layer 3 multicast addresses are associated with ATM interfaces belonging to the multicast group. MARS messages allow the distribution of information about the composition of multicast groups as well as the addition or the cancellation of a node to or from a multicast group. A MARS server administers a point-to-multipoint VC with all nodes that want to receive a multicast support.

A MARS server only keeps track of the composition of multicast groups; it doesn't attend to the distribution of data packets. Distribution can be made either through an MCS (MultiCast Server) or through a set of point-to-multipoint VCs. In fact, if multicast group A is served by an MCS, the MARS provides the ATM address of the MCS to all the stations that request the resolution of the IPv6 address identifying multicast group A (in Figure 9-10, the address FF15::77). The MCS opens a point-to-multipoint VC with all the stations belonging to the group, and it uses this VC to redistribute multicast data packets.

If the multicast group is not associated with an MCS, the MARS server provides all stations that try to solve the IPv6 multicast address with the list of all ATM addresses associated with the group, and the station creates a dedicated point-to-multipoint VC (see Figure 9-11).

9.2.5 NHRP (Next Hop Resolution Protocol)

A large ATM network is typically subdivided into several independent IP subnets called *LISs* (Logical IP Subnets) in IPv4 and *LLGs* (Logical Link Groups) in IPv6. In IPv4, the ATMARP protocol allows the resolution of the IP address of a destination (host or router) into the corresponding ATM address only if this address belongs to the source LIS. To overcome this limit, the IETF working group called ROLC (Routing Over Large Clouds, which lately joined the group "IP over NBMA networks") devel-

Figure 9-10
Figure 9-10
MultiCast Server associated with a multicast group

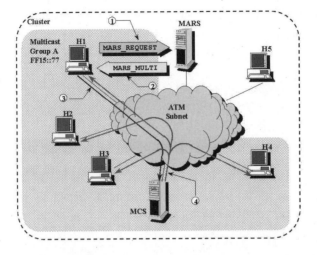

Figure 9-11
A multicast group without MultiCast Server

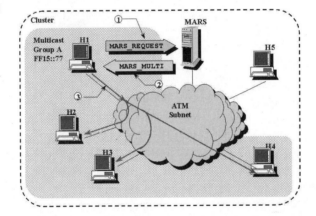

oped the *NBMA Next Hop Resolution Protocol* (NHRP)[12], a routing and address resolution protocol suitable for all NBMA networking technologies that, like ATM, do not support broadcast transmissions.

NHRP allows a source station (host or router), wanting to communicate over an ATM network, to determine IP and ATM addresses of the *next hop* toward the destination station, given the IP address of the destination station. If the destination is part of the source ATM network, the next hop address returned by NHRP will be the ATM address of the destination itself; otherwise, it will be the address of the router located on the shortest possible path (in terms of layer 3 hops) between source and destination. After the next hop ATM address is known, the source station can open an SVC with it and start the transmission of IP packets. For example, with reference to Figure 9-1, by means of NHRP, H1 can learn the

ATM address of H5 and therefore open an SVC with it instead of sending packets along the multi-hop path H1 - R1 - R3 - H5. Moreover, H2 is informed that the "best" egress router to reach H7 is R2, not the default router R1.

The NHRP protocol, by eliminating from end-to-end paths all unnecessary hops, optimizes remarkably the forwarding process of IP packets within an ATM network.

The NHRP protocol requires the installation, within an ATM network, of one or more entities called *Next Hop Servers* (NHSs). Each NHS serves a determined set of hosts and routers (*clients*). NHSs, besides collaborating among themselves for the resolution of a next hop within their ATM networks, can participate with routing protocols to learn the topology of interconnections.

Each NHS administers a relationship table between IP addresses and ATM addresses of the clients it serves. This table, called the *next hop resolution cache,* can be manually configured or built and dynamically updated in the following ways:

- Through a recording process carried out by clients by sending to their own NHS an NHRP_Register message
- By extracting the information from resolution requests received from clients through the NHRP_Request message
- By extracting the information from replies coming from other network NHSs through the NHRP_Reply message

Let's suppose that station S should determine the ATM address of the next hop toward station D. S addresses its own NHS by sending an NHRP_Request message. The NHRP_Request message is encapsulated in an IP packet and transmitted to the NHS through a VC created at the time of the registration or specifically created for transmitting the request.

In the meanwhile, waiting for the reply from the NHS, S can proceed as follows:

- To drop the packet to be transmitted to D
- To retain the packet until the reply from the NHS arrives
- To forward the packet to its default router

The choice depends on local policies of the LLG to which S belongs. The third solution is recommended as the default choice because it allows the packet to reach D in any case, without forcing S to wait. Obviously, the resolution process is not performed for each packet transmitted to a given destination because clients have a local cache at their disposal.

When the NHS receives the NHRP_Request message from S, it checks whether an entry containing the ATM address of the next hop toward D is present in its cache. If not, the NHS forwards the same request to another NHS. The request passes from NHS to NHS until one of the following conditions occurs:

- The request reaches the NHS serving D. This NHS can reply to the request by generating an NHRP_Reply message containing IP and ATM addresses of the next hop toward D. Obviously, if D is not connected to the ATM network, this next hop is the ATM address of the router toward the network where D is located.

- No NHS can resolve the next hop toward D. In this case, the last visited NHS generates a negative NHRP_Reply message.

In both cases, the NHRP_Reply message is sent to S along the same path made by the NHRP_Request so that all NHSs traversed by the reply can insert in their caches the information the reply contains. This capability allows the NHSs to reply to subsequent requests for the same next hop with *nonauthoritative* replies—that is, replies not arriving from the NHS where the client is registered. If a communication attempt based on a nonauthoritative reply fails (probably because some variations on the network occurred), the source station can send a new NHRP_Request requesting an authoritative reply.

An example of the preceding approach is illustrated in Figure 9-12. Host H1 wants to forward a packet to host H5, but H1 doesn't know H5's ATM address. It therefore forwards an NHRP_Request to NHS1, which, nevertheless, doesn't have this information. The request is forwarded to NHS2, which, because the NHS is serving H5, can generate an NHRP_Reply with the requested ATM address. This reply, returning toward H1, traverses NHS1, allowing it to copy this address in its cache for a future use as a nonauthoritative reply. The reply eventually reaches H1, which then can open a VC with H5.

Moreover, NHRP allows the association of the ATM address of a next hop with an entire IP subnet. For example, if router X is the next hop between station S and station D, this means that X is the egress router to be used to reach all other stations belonging to the same IP subnet of D.

Figure 9-12
Example of ATM ad-
dress resolution with
NHRP

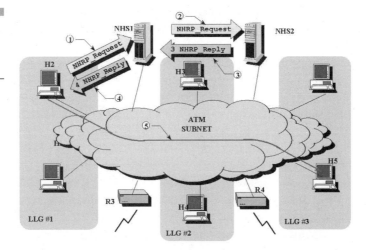

Figure 9-12
Example of ATM ad-
dress resolution with
NHRP

9.3   Alternative Approaches

The approaches described in the preceding sections are based on the principle that the interaction between IPv6 and the underlying ATM network
is implemented by using ATM standard signaling primitives—that is, first
of all the UNI 3.0/3.1[2]. Some manufacturers, following the IETF proposals for CSRs (*Cell Switching Routers*)[13], decided not to follow this
approach and to create alternative signaling protocols that allow more
direct interaction between switches and routers. These approaches use
only the physical part of the UNI specification but completely avoid signaling procedures. Moreover, they don't use the P-NNI. The control of the
network and of the routing remains with routers that use classic IP protocols such as OSPF and BGP for this purpose.

9.3.1   IP Switching

With the term *IP switching,* we usually refer to an approach introduced
by Ipsilon Networks (**www.ipsilon.com**)[14] based on two key principles:

- IP routing functions can be added to an ATM switch if an external
  router is allowed to directly control the ATM switch.
- IP packets can be considered as belonging to flows—that is, to
  have some characteristics in common. This is particularly true for
  IPv6 packets having the Flow Label inside them (see Section
  3.1.3).

By combining these two ideas, the Ipsilon approach proposes to route IP packets by using routers in a hop-by-hop method, or to create ATM VCs dedicated to them, according to traffic characteristics of flows. For example, packets containing queries and DNS replies benefit from hop-by-hop routing implemented through routers because a DNS flow is short and creating a dedicated VC would have an average cost that is too high, although creating a dedicated VC on ATM switches for routing packets generated by a file transfer is undoubtedly useful.

In general, the traffic can be classified according to two types: *flow-oriented* and *short-lived* (see Table 9-1). For packets belonging to the first type, allocating a dedicated VC on ATM switches is convenient; for those belonging to the second type, allowing hop-by-hop routing through a router is convenient.

The IP switching architecture can be better understood by analyzing Figure 9-13. It consists of ATM switches that are always coupled with an IP router and of *IP gateways* that allow the connection of traditional LANs. IP routers control the routing of IP packets using common routing protocols, such as OSPF and BGP, to compute routing tables. Routers provide for directly routing the short-lived traffic, whereas they order switches to create dedicated VCs for the flow-oriented traffic (for this reason, they are also called *switch controllers*).

The interaction between the different elements of the architecture is provided by two protocols: the GSMP and the IFMP.

The GSMP (*General Switch Management Protocol*), which is described by RFC 1987[15], is used by the router to control the switch. In particular, the router can configure the lookup tables of the switch through the GSMP and therefore control the routing of ATM cells. The IFMP (*Ipsilon Flow Management Protocol*), described in RFC 1953[16], is associated with each link and is used by the destination to communicate to the source the VPI/VCI of the VC on which the IP flow must be forwarded. Note that the determination of the VPI/VCI is always made by the receiver and that,

Table 9-1

Types of IP traffic

Flow-Oriented Traffic	Short-Lived Traffic
File Transfer (FTP)	Names Resolution (DNS)
File Sharing (NFS)	Electronic Mail (SMTP)
Web Access (HTTP)	Network Timing Protocol (NTP)
Virtual Terminal (TELNET)	Post Office Protocol (POP)
Multimedia Voice/Video	Network Management (SNMP)

when a flow is not classified, IP packets are forwarded on the default VC (VPI = 0 e VCI = 15), which, at switch level, is always routed toward the router.

Figure 9-14 shows the architecture of an IP switch—that is, the coupling of an ATM switch and a router (called *IP switch controller*) with the additional modules for the management of IFMP and GSMP protocols and for flow classification.

The short-lived traffic is routed on the default VC; it is conveyed by the ATM switch to the switch controller that, operating like a router, determines the next hop by consulting its IP routing tables, computed by protocols such as OSPF and BGP.

A different approach should be followed for the flow-oriented traffic. It is initially routed on the default VC, but flow-classifier modules that are

Figure 9-13
IP switching architecture

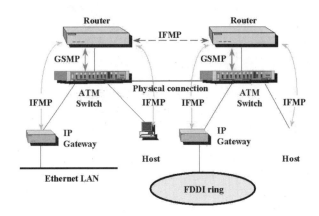

Figure 9-14
IP switch architecture

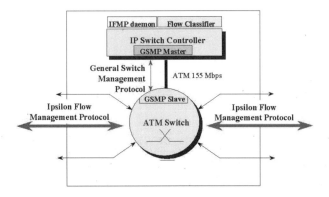

present both on switch controllers and on stations recognize the flow-oriented nature of this traffic and request the creation of a dedicated VC. This VC is created with a series of steps that can be better understood by analyzing the example shown in Figure 9-15.

At the beginning, in phase (1), the traffic is routed on the default VC through the switch controller that rebuilds IP packets starting from ATM cells, consults routing tables, segments packets again, and forwards them to the destination always using the default VC.

When the flow-classifier module of the switch controller recognizes flow-oriented traffic, it requests the switch, through the GSMP protocol, to create a new VC; then it signals to the upstream node through the IFMP protocol to use it (2). The upstream node begins to forward IP packets on the new VC (3), but packets continue to reach the switch controller. Also, the downstream node recognizes the flow-oriented nature of the traffic and requests the switch controller to use a new VC (4). The switch controller begins to use the new VC (5). Eventually, the switch controller realizes that the two dedicated VCs can be interconnected at the switch level; therefore, it programs the switch through the GSMP to directly route cells arriving on the VPI/VCI = 0/X on the VPI/VCI = 0/Y (6). At this point, the cut-through routing is implemented.

In IPv6, the task to classify flows is particularly easy because of the Flow Label field present on IPv6 packets. In fact, the source station itself can indicate whether the traffic is short-lived (Flow Label = 0) or flow-oriented (Flow Label ≠ 0).

9.3.2   Tag Switching

Cisco Systems (www.cisco.com) proposes an alternative to IP switching with its technique called *tag switching*. Tag switching is designed to sim-

Figure 9-15
Example of the creation of a dedicated VC

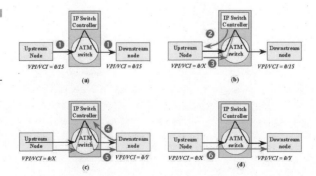

plify and to speed routing operations also on non-ATM networks through the subdivision of routing and control functions[17].

The basic idea is to insert in each packet transmitted on the network an identification, called a *tag*, by which *tag switches* (internetworking devices located between the source and the destination) can implement fast routing (see Figure 9-16). The information contained in tags and that maintained by each tag switch is used to implement the routing; the control, on the other side, is the component of the protocol that is responsible for tables updating within tag switches, and it uses, for this purpose, the TDP (*Tag Distribution Protocol*)[18].

The routing adopted in the tag switching is mainly based on the *label swapping* paradigm. When a packet labeled with a determinate tag is received by a tag switch, this switch uses the tag to examine its TIB (*Tag Information Base*). The TIB is a table in which each entry is formed by an entry tag field and by one or more fields to be used for routing the egress packet. These fields can contain, for example, the tag to be placed on the egress packet, the interface of the switch on which the packet should be transmitted, or further information useful to the layer 2 protocol (for example, the MAC address of the following node).

This routing procedure is extremely simple, and it can be implemented in hardware. Moreover, it is suitable for the management of the multicast at IP level because the same entry tag can be associated with many entries in the TIB.

The main difference between tag switching and IP switching is that in IP switching the presence of IP packets activates the creation of ATM VCs, whereas in tag switching TIBs are created by the existence of an IP

Figure 9-16

Example of network with tag switching

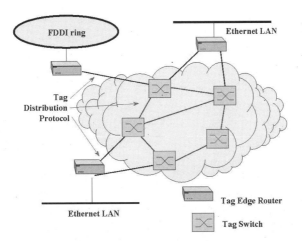

rate independently from the presence of traffic, and therefore all the traffic is treated the same way by the tag switching.

The three possibilities for creating and managing TIBs starting from routing tables are as follow:

■ Downstream allocation

■ Downstream on-demand allocation

■ Upstream allocation

In all three cases, each switch allocates tags by creating the corresponding entries in its TIB for each destination (IP prefix) present within its routing table (*FIB,* or Forwarding Information Base) and creates a connection between FIB and TIB. This connection also allows the association of tags to packets that were originally lacking them.

In the *downstream* allocation scheme, tags are generated and associated with an IP prefix by the node that, on a given link, is located downstream —that is, by the node receiving the traffic. The *downstream on-demand* allocation works in a similar way, but the upstream node requests the downstream node to allocate a tag for a specific IP prefix. In the *upstream* allocation, each upstream node directly allocates tags for each IP prefix known in its FIB.

In all three cases, after an association between a tag and a prefix is created, it is transmitted to the node at the other end of the link.

The mechanism for the diffusion of information for the updating of TIBs can either exploit packets commonly exchanged for the management of routing protocols at the network level (for example, *piggybacking* on BGP) or use the TDP protocol.

The tag can be transported in a packet in the following three ways, and the choice of the most suitable way depends on the network architecture in which the tag switching is inserted:

■ In a proper header between the layer 2 envelope and the layer 3 envelope

■ As part of the header of the layer 2 envelope (ATM)

■ As part of the header of the layer 3 envelope (IPv6)

In particular, in the IPv6 case, Cisco Systems proposes to transport the tag inside the Flow Label field[19], by partly modifying its meaning, as shown in Figure 9-17.

This proposal introduces a bit G, which discriminates between the original semantic of the Flow Label as proposed in IPv6 (end-to-end) and the semantic necessary for the tag switching (hop-by-hop).

Figure 9-17
Proposal to modify
the Flow Label

- G=1: hop-by-hop Flow Label
- G=0: end-to-end Flow Label

Moreover, the tag switching allows each packet to carry many tags, in order to obtain a hierarchical routing. These characteristics can be used, for example, to separate the IGP routing information from the EGP routing information.

We can then see that the tag switching of IPv6 packets can be simply implemented on ATM networks. Both techniques are based on tag switching, and a biunivocal or an identity relationship can be established between the couple VPI/VCI and the tag. Tag allocation is implemented by using the downstream on-demand modality.

To allow an ATM classical switch to work like a tag switch, we need to implement classical routing protocols (such as OSPF and BGP), the FIB, the TIB, the TDP, and control modules of the tag switching itself within the switch.

Problems and protocols associated with tag switching and those associated with the traditional ATM signaling (for example, UNI and P-NNI) are independent. We need to create conditions of coexistence between these two schemes and therefore to define a set of VPIs/VCIs to be used with the tag switching and a separate set to be used with the traditional ATM signaling.

A mechanism similar to IP tunneling has been established to eliminate the disadvantage of crossing classical ATM networks, in which intermediate switches unable to manipulate packets marked with tags exist. In this case, two routers that support the tag switching may be interconnected by a Virtual Path and therefore use the VCI like a tag (VP tunneling).

9.3.3 Other Approaches

The great interest aroused by the approaches described in the preceding subsections, added to the lack of precise standards, also urged other companies to propose solutions in this field. Among them, we must mention the following:

- *Cell Switch Router:* This proposal by Toshiba (www.toshiba.com) represents the evolution of the work on CSRs[13] originally carried on in Japan. Like tag switching, this proposal is not limited to ATM, but it can operate on other NBMA networks as well and in general on all connection-oriented networks. Like IP switching, it is based on the classification of IP flows and on the creation of by-pass pipes. It uses a signaling protocol called FANP (*Flow Attribute Notification Protocol*)[20].

▨ ARIS: This proposal by IBM (**www.ibm.com**) is not limited to ATM, which can operate on other NBMA networks as well and in general on all connection-oriented networks. It uses a signaling protocol called ARIS (Aggregate Route-based IP Switching)[21], which is based on the concept of egress identifiers. ARIS opens some VCs toward each egress identifier, and because thousands of IP destinations can be mapped on a single egress identifier, ARIS minimizes the number of necessary VCs. Each egress router starts the setup of VCs toward its upstream neighbors and these neighbors toward their upstream neighbors using a technique similar to the Reverse Path Multicast. Each router checks the presence of loops on the VC. The VC toward an egress router assumes the form of a tree.

▨ *SITA (Switching IP Through ATM):* This proposal by Telecom Finland (**www.tele.fi**) is for ATM networks with two tag levels. It doesn't need a signaling protocol.

REFERENCES ▨ ▨ ▨ ▨ ▨ ▨ ▨ ▨ ▨

[1]Uyless Black, *ATM: Foundation for Broadband Networks*, Prentice-Hall, 1995.

[2]ATM Forum, *ATM User-Network Interface Specification*, Prentice-Hall, September 1993.

[3]J. Heinanen, *RFC 1483: Multiprotocol Encapsulation over ATM Adaptation Layer 5*, July 1993.

[4]S. Gai, P.L. Montessoro, P. Nicoletti, *Reti Locali: dal Cablaggio all'Internetworking*, SSGRR (Scuola Superiore G. Reiss Romoli), 1995.

[5]G. Armitage, *RFC 2022: Support for Multicast over UNI 3.0/3.1 based ATM Networks*, November 1996.

[6]G. Armitage, *IPv6 and Neighbor Discovery over ATM*, IETF Internet Draft, June 1996.

[7]P. Schulter, *A Framework for IPv6 over ATM*, Internet Draft, February 1996.

[8]R. Atkinson, D. Haskin, J. Luciani, *IPv6 over NBMA Networks*, IETF

Internet Draft, June 1996.

[9]G. Armitage, *Transient Neighbors for IPv6 over ATM*, Internet Draft, June 1996.

[10]A. Conta, S. Deering, *RFC 1885: Internet Control Message Protocol (ICMPv6)*, December 1995.

[11]M. Laubach, *RFC 1577: Classical IP and ARP over ATM*, January 1994.

[12]J. Luciani, D. Katz, D. Piscitello, B. Cole, *NBMA Next Hop Resolution Protocol (NHRP)*, IETF Internet Draft, July 1996.

[13]H. Esaki, M. Ohta, K. Nagami, *High Speed Datagram Delivery over Internet using ATM Technology*, IEEE TRANS. Communications, Vol. E78-B, No. 8, August 1995.

[14]P. Newman, T. Lyon, G. Minshall, *Flow labelled IP: A connectionless approach to ATM*, Proc. IEEE Infocom, San Francisco, March 1996, pp. 1251-1260.

[15]P. Newman, W. Edwards, R. Hinden, E. Hoffman, F. Ching Liaw, T. Lyon, G. Minshall, *RFC 1987: Ipsilon's General Switch Management Protocol Specification Version 1.1*, August 1996.

[16]P. Newman, W. Edwards, R. Hinden, E. Hoffman, F. Ching Liaw, T. Lyon, G. Minshall, *RFC 1853: Ipsilon Flow Management Protocol Specification for IPv4 Version 1.0*, May 1996.

[17]Y. Rekhter, et al., *Tag Switching Architecture Overview*, Internet Draft, September 1996.

[18]P. Doolan, et al., *Tag Distribution Protocol*, Internet Draft, September 1996.

[19]F. Baker, et al., *Use of Flow Label for Tag Switching*, Internet Draft, August 1996.

[20]Y. Katsube, K. Nagami, H. Esaki, *Router Architecture Extensions for ATM: Overview*, Internet Draft, November 1996.

[21]R. Woundy, A. Viswanathan, N. Feldman, R. Boivie, *ARIS: Aggregate Route-Based IP Switching*, Internet Draft, November 1996.

10

User Mobility in IPv6

The "mobile computing" challenge is undoubtedly one of the most intriguing and complex that networks have to face. In fact, although stating the requirement that mobile computing must meet is "access to information, communications and services always and everywhere" is easy, finding satisfactory technical solutions is not equally easy. In fact, mobile computing requires the creation of communication infrastructures and the modification of computer networks, operating systems, and application programs.

IPv6 represents a real turning point for mobile computing. In fact, because IPv6 has been completely redesigned, since its conception it has foreseen the need to effectively support mobile computing and has not been bound, in the choice of solutions, by requirements of compatibility with past versions.

As we mentioned in Chapter 1, a growing number of Internet users don't work at their office desks anymore but work while traveling. The following cases occur more frequently: First, when users are employees of a company with several workstations and they want to be able to work in the same way at all workstations, by connecting their portable PCs to wired networks of the company's different workstations or to the telephone network (in this case, ISDN) at their stations; the second case happens when nomadic users (from which the term *nomadic computing* is derived) travel and work only seldomly at their offices, supposing they even have offices.

This second type of mobile user, who is usually equipped with a mobile PC and with a PCMCIA board for a mobile telephone, connects to the Internet through a public mobile radio network.

Clearly, the requirement to provide support for mobility in IPv6 is a matter of primary importance. In Northern America, estimates indicate that there will be from 20 to 40 million mobile users in 2007. Also, this requirement is clearly one of the more complex to be met because it has to deal with a multitude of problems that range from those related to radio transmission (reliability, roaming, hand-off) to IP protocols (identification, addressing, configuration, routing) to equally important security problems.

10.1   Mobility Problems

IPv6 addressing and routing schemes, already analyzed in Chapters 2 and 4, entail that a host address depends from the point where the host is connected to the network. This is exactly the opposite of what is needed for mobility, because a mobile host frequently changes its connection point to the network and therefore must change its address with equal rapidity.

A first solution consists of handling the mobility by operating at DNS (Domain Name Service) level. In Section 2.3, we saw that, in IPv6, hosts are identified by names, addresses are variable in time and not mnemonic, and names are translated into addresses by the DNS. This approach is not feasible because the DNS has been designed to minimize information search times but not updating times. It is therefore impossible to think that, when a host moves, it propagates its new address through the DNS, because updating could take many days, whereas the host should be allowed to move up to once per second.

In general, it is not possible to think that an IP host changes its address when it moves. In fact, the TCP/IP network architecture has an imperfect layered structure, in which the TCP uses not only the source and destination TCP ports but also the source and destination IP addresses as the connection identifier. This means that if the IP address of a host is changed, then all sessions of upper layer protocols related to this host will be terminated. This problem was examined in Section 6.7.2, where we saw that the process of changing addresses usually requires several days while new and old addresses coexist.

The preceding situation is a result of the fact that IP addresses, in the TCP/IP network architecture, have two different purposes: to identify connections endpoints and to determine the packet's routing. The fact that IP addresses identify connection endpoints means that they must remain stable and that a mobile host must therefore always be identified by the same address that is associated with the DNS name. Because the address is used also for routing purposes, a mobile host must acquire one or more addresses from the network to which it is connected (*foreign network*) to be used for routing packets.

The host permanent address, called the *home address,* is the address of the host when it is connected to its default network, called the *home network*. Addresses that the mobile host acquires when it is connected to a foreign network are called *care-of addresses*. The care-of address is acquired by the mobile host when it connects to a foreign network through a stateless autoconfiguration procedure (see Section 6.7.1) or a stateful procedure through DHCP (see Section 6.7.3).

Problems of mobility management in IPv6 are therefore problems of management of relationships between home addresses and care-of addresses, and problems of the use of the appropriate type of address in relation to the context. Moreover, when the mobile host is connected to a foreign network, it must delegate a router of its home network to "represent" it when it is absent. This router assumes the name of *home agent*.

A home agent usually serves all mobile hosts of a home network by forwarding messages addressed to them. To do so, the home agent traces all movements, and in particular, it records in memory, called a *binding cache*, the mapping between home addresses and care-of addresses.

From this scenario, we can see that IPv6 is suitable for providing support for the mobility on heterogeneous networks and that it can be used both for moving from an Ethernet network to another and for moving from an Ethernet network to a wireless network. Moreover, note that IPv6 has been conceived to support the "macro" mobility and that it is less suitable for the "micro" mobility, in which, for example, a host moves between two cells of a wireless LAN. In the latter case, the mobility can be more efficiently implemented by using link layer mechanisms (layer 2 of the OSI model).

10.2 Operation of a Mobile Host in IPv6

When a mobile host is connected to a foreign network, it decides to acquire a care-of address through a stateful or a stateless procedure on the basis of Router Advertisement messages received and, more specifically, of M and O bits received (see Section 5.5.5).

Each time a mobile host changes its connection point at the link layer from an IPv6 subnet to another IPv6 subnet, it must acquire a new care-of address, which becomes its *primary care-of address*. Other care-of addresses previously acquired can be maintained to allow the host to continue to receive packets addressed to previous care-of addresses. This procedure can be useful in using radio networks in which a host can decide to configure itself on the cell from which it receives the highest power signal but to continue to receive signals also from other cells that previously served it.

The mapping between the home address and the primary care-of address is called *binding*. Every time the mobile host configures a new primary care-of address, and therefore a new binding, it must communicate the address to its home agent through a *Binding Update* message (see Section 10.4.1). The Binding Update message must also be sent to all nodes with which the mobile host had an exchange of packets and which could have obsolete information in their binding caches. For this reason, the mobile host maintains a data structure, called a *Binding Update List*, that contains addresses of all nodes to which it sent Binding Update messages and the relative remaining temporal validity.

A mobile host, in whatever instant, can be reached by sending a message to its home address. If the mobile host is not connected to its home network, all packets forwarded to it will be intercepted by the home agent, which will transmit them to the mobile host through a tunnel (see Section 7.5.6) by using its primary care-of address.

When a packet arrives at the mobile host through a tunnel, the mobile host realizes that it has been forwarded by the home agent and sends a Binding Update message to the source node. When the source node receives this message, it creates in its binding cache an entry that contains the home address and the care-of address. This information allows the source node to directly forward the following packets to the care-of address through a Routing Header (see Section 3.2.5) instead of through a tunnel (a technique used only by the home agent).

Therefore, only the first packet of a sequence of packets exchanged between a source node and a mobile host passes through the home agent, whereas all other packets are directly transmitted by the source to the mobile host through the Routing Header. This process is fundamental in obtaining a scalable and reliable solution and in minimizing the network load.

When the mobile host moves (changes its primary care-of address), it forwards a Binding Update message to all nodes listed in the Binding Update List.

The Binding Update message must include an Authentication Header (see Chapter 8) to avoid a situation in which potential hackers could redirect someone else's traffic toward themselves by a fraudulent use of these messages.

10.3   Examples of Operation of a Mobile Host in IPv6

To better understand the topics presented in the preceding section, let's consider the example shown in Figure 10-1.

The host Z is usually connected to subnet A, which is its home network, and Z acquires from A the address A::1, which is its home address. (Note that the syntax for this address is not formally correct, but only an example.) This address A::1 is put into a relationship with the name Z at the DNS level. In the same way, W is connected to the subnet C, and from C, it acquires the address C::5.

Figure 10-1
Example of mobility

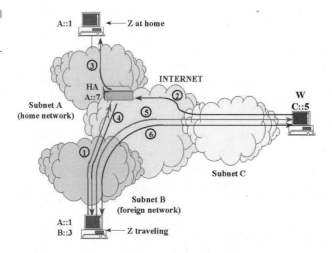

When W wants to forward packets to Z, it asks the DNS and obtains the address A::1. Then W generates IPv6 packets whose destination address is A::1 and source address is C::5 (2). These packets are routed by IPv6 routing and reach the destination subnet A.

At this point, three situations are possible:

- Node Z is connected to its home network. Packets are delivered to Z by using classical IPv6 routing procedures (3).

- Node Z is connected to subnet B, which acts as a foreign network. Z acquires from B its primary care-of address B::3, which is communicated through a Binding Update (1) message to its home agent (HA). Packets received by the home agent are forwarded to Z through a tunnel from A::7 to B::3 (4). When B::3 extracts packets from the tunnel, it checks whether they are addressed to A::1—that is, to itself. At this point, Z sends a Binding Update message to W (5), and W stores the message in its binding cache. From this moment on, W communicates with Z without passing through the home agent, but forwards packets to Z through a Routing Header that forces a source routing on B::3 (6).

- The third possible situation is that Z is not connected in any place. The router connected to the subnet A tries to reach Z at the address A::1, and because it fails, it communicates this failure to the source node by using an ICMP message.

If Z moves from subnet B to subnet D, it acquires a new address belonging to subnet D (for example, D::11) that becomes its new primary care-of address. This new address is communicated through a Binding Update message both to its home agent and to W.

10.4 Options Format

The information necessary to support an IPv6 host's mobility is exchanged through four options implemented in a Destination Option extension header (see Section 3.2.8). Because a Destination Option extension header can be part of any IPv6 packet, options for the mobility can be associated with the following:

- Normal IPv6 packets containing payloads such as TCP or UDP.
- Independent packets, containing only options. In this second case, the Next Header field of the Destination Option Header must be set equal to value 59 to indicate the lack of more headers (see Section 3.2.5).

Options are codified according to the TLV (Type, Length, Value) format (see Section 3.2.2).

10.4.1 Binding Update Option

The Binding Update option (see Figure 10-2) is used by the mobile node to communicate to its home agent, or to the corresponding nodes, its present binding.

The 8-bit *Option Type* field has value 192.

The 8-bit *Option Length* field contains the length in octets of the option, Option Type and Option Length field not included. This field has a minimum value of 6 if both the Care-of Address (C = 0) and the Home Link Local Address (L = 0) are not present. Its maximum value is 38 if both the addresses (C = 1, L = 1) are present.

The 1-bit *A* (Acknowledge) field is set by the source node to request the node that receives the Binding Update option to send a Binding Acknowledgment message.

The 1-bit *H* (Home Registration) field is set by the source node to request the node that receives the Binding Update option to perform as its home agent. The IPv6 packet destination address containing this option must be that of a router interface whose prefix is the same of the mobile node's home address.

Figure 10-2
The Binding
Update option

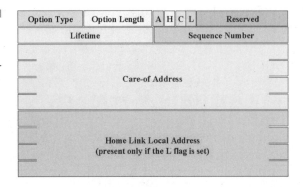

The 1-bit *C* (Care-of Address Present) field is set by the source node to indicate the presence of the care-of address in the Binding Update option.

The 1-bit *L* (Home Link Local Address Present) field is set by the source node to indicate the presence of the Home Link Local Address in the Binding Update option. This bit is set by the source node to request the destination node to perform like a proxy—that is, to participate in the Neighbor Discovery process in place of the mobile host. When this bit is set, the bit H also must be set.

The 12-bit *Reserved* field is reserved for future use. It must be initialized to zero during transmission and ignored on reception.

The 16-bit *Lifetime* field contains the validity interval of the binding information in seconds—that is, how long the binding information must be considered valid in the binding cache. The value zero indicates that the binding information must be deleted from the binding cache; the value 0xffff indicates that the binding information must be indefinitely maintained.

The 16-bit *Sequence Number* field is used to set the mapping between Binding Update messages and Binding Acknowledgment messages. Each Binding Update sent by a mobile node must use a sequence number greater than the sequence number value sent in the previous Binding Update (if any) to the same destination address (modulo 2^{16}).

The 128-bit *Care-of Address* field contains the IPv6 address acquired from the mobile node on the foreign network. IPv6 address codification was analyzed in Chapter 4 of this book. When the care-of address is set equal to the home address, the Binding Update option indicates that it is necessary to cancel existing associations from binding caches for the mobile node and that no new association must be created by the message.

The 128-bit *Home Link Local Address* field contains the IPv6 link local address used by the mobile node during its last connection to the home network. This field, which is optional, is present only if the field L has value 1.

Like in the case of other IPv6 options, the three most significant bits of the Option Type field have a particular meaning (see Section 3.2.2). Because the field has value 192, the bits have value 110. This particular value specifies the following:

- In the case of the two most significant bits (11) that, if a node doesn't recognize the option, it must discard the packet and communicate this fact to the source node through an ICMP Parameter Problem message, only if the destination address is not multicast
- In the case of the third bit (0) that the option cannot be modified en route

Also, optional fields, not currently defined, can be added after the Binding Update option; the presence of these fields can be detected from the value of the Option Length field.

10.4.2   The Binding Acknowledgment Option

The Binding Acknowledgment option is used to confirm the receipt of a Binding Update option. It is generated only if the mobile node explicitly requests it by setting the bit A in the Binding Update option. The format of the Binding Acknowledgment option is shown in Figure 10-3.

The 8-bit *Option Type* field has value 193.

The 8-bit *Option Length* field contains the option's length in octets, Option Type and Option Length fields not included. This field has value 9.

The 8-bit *Status* field can assume the values listed in Table 10-1. Values smaller than 128 indicate that the Binding Update option has been accepted; values greater than or equal to 128 indicate that it has been rejected.

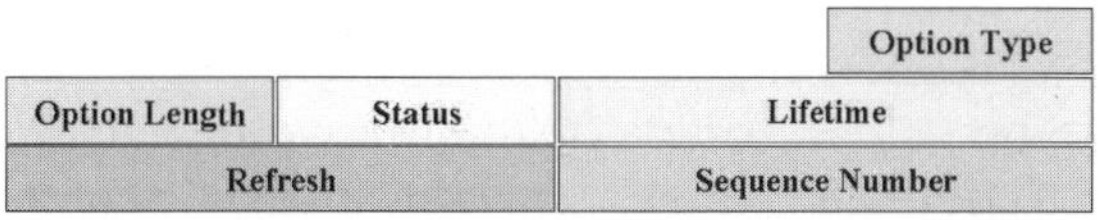

Figure 10-3
ICMP Message
of Binding
Acknowledgment

			Option Type
Option Length	Status	Lifetime	
Refresh		Sequence Number	

Table 10-1

Possible values for
the Status field

Value	Meaning
0	Option accepted
128	Option rejected: unspecified reason
129	Option rejected: poorly formed binding update
130	Option rejected: operation administratively prohibited
131	Option rejected: insufficient resources
132	Option rejected: home registration not supported
133	Option rejected: the network is not the home network
134	Option rejected: Sequence Number field value too small
135	Option rejected: dynamic home agent address discovery response

The *Lifetime* field contains the time the node maintains the information stored in its binding cache.

The *Refresh* field contains the period of time after which the mobile node must send a Binding Update message to update the information in the binding cache.

The 16-bit *Sequence Number* field is used to set the mapping between Binding Update messages and Binding Acknowledgment messages.

Also, optional fields, not currently defined, can be added after the Binding Acknowledgment option; the presence of these fields can be detected from the value of the Option Length field.

10.4.3   The Binding Request Option

The Binding Request option is used to request the mobile node to send a Binding Update. This option is used by a node with one entry in the binding cache, whose temporal validity is going to expire, to obtain updated information. The format of the Binding Request option is shown in Figure 10-4.

The 8-bit *Option Type* field has value 194.

The 8-bit *Option Length* field contains the length of the option in octets, Option Type field and Option Length field not included. This field has value zero.

Also, optional fields, not currently defined, can be added after the Binding Request option; the presence of these fields can be detected from the value of the Option Length field.

10.4.4   The Home Address Option

The Home Address destination option is used in a packet sent by a mobile node to inform the destination of the packet of the mobile node Home Address. If we include this option in the packet, the receiving node can substitute the mobile node's home address for this care-of address, thus making the use of the care-of address transparent to the receiving node. The format of the Home Address option is shown in Figure 10-5.

The 8-bit *Option Type* field has value 195.

The 8-bit Option Length field contains the length of the option in octets, Option Type field and Option Length field not included. This field has value 8.

The 128-bit *Home Address* field contains the IPv6 home address of the mobile node sending the packet.

Also, optional fields, not currently defined, can be added after the Home Address option; the presence of these fields can be detected from the value of the Option Length field.

Figure 10-4
The Binding Request option

Option Type	Option Length

Figure 10-5
The Home Address option

		Option Type	Option Length
		Home Address	

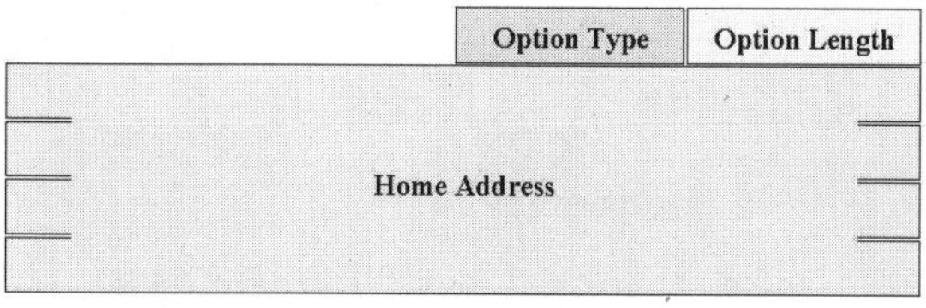

10.5   Characteristics of Nodes

The mobility creates some new requirements on the architecture and on functions of IPv6 nodes. In particular, some of these requirements must be met by all the nodes, whereas others are typical of routers or of mobile nodes.

10.5.1   General Requirements

All IPv6 nodes must meet the following requirements:

▪ To receive a Binding Update option and to generate a Binding Acknowledgment message, if requested.

▪ To administer a binding cache in which the information received from Binding Update messages must be stored.

▪ To administer a Security Association to be jointly used with an IPv6 Authentication Header (see Section 8.1.1). In fact, when an IPv6 node receives a Binding Update option, it must check the identity of the source node through the Authentication Header and, only if the check is positive, store the received information in the binding cache.

10.5.2   Router Requirements

Because an IPv6 router can contain information about a mobile host in its binding cache, all IPv6 routers must meet the following requirement:

▪ Each IPv6 router must be able to use its binding cache for routing packets. This means that, if a router has in its binding cache an entry relevant to the destination address of the packet it is routing, it should encapsulate the packet in a tunnel and send it to the care-of address.

Moreover, to allow a mobile node to leave its home, at least a router of its home network must be able to operate as a home agent. Routers able to operate as home agents must meet the following additional requirements:

▪ To administer a list of nodes for which they operate as home agents

■ To intercept packets addressed to mobile hosts on the local network, for example, by replacing mobile hosts in the Neighbor Discovery procedure

■ To retransmit intercepted packets by creating a tunnel toward mobile hosts' care-of addresses

10.5.3 Mobile Node Requirements

Mobile nodes must meet the following requirements:

■ To receive packets through a tunnel

■ To send Binding Updates and to receive Binding Acknowledgments

■ To administer a Binding Update List in which to store all nodes that have been sent Binding Update messages whose temporal validity has not yet expired

10.6   Transmission of Packets to a Mobile Node

We have already seen that the first packet toward a mobile host connected to a foreign network is routed toward the home network; here it is captured by the home agent and retransmitted in a tunnel to the care-of address. The receipt of the packet by the mobile host produces the transmission of a Binding Update message to the source node, whose information is stored in the binding cache.

At this point, the source node, having valid information for the destination node in its binding cache, should directly send packets using a Routing Header.

For example, in the case it doesn't need to use the Routing Header for other purposes, the source node generates a packet with the care-of address as the IPv6 destination address and with the Routing Header shown in Figure 10-6 (see also Section A.2 in Appendix A).

The Routing Header in Figure 10-5 indicates the existence of only one address to be processed (Segment Left = 1), and this address is the home address. The IPv6 packet is routed to the destination node using the IPv6 destination address—that is, the care-of address. When the packet reaches the destination node, the node processes the Routing Header and

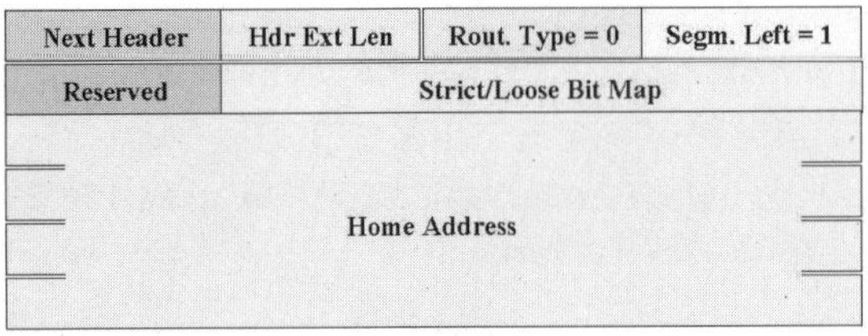

Figure 10-6
Example of Routing
Header

Next Header	Hdr Ext Len	Rout. Type = 0	Segm. Left = 1
Reserved	Strict/Loose Bit Map		

Home Address

determines that the packet must be routed toward the home address—that is, toward itself.

This process allows the upper layer protocols to see the home address as a destination address and therefore not to perceive the mobility.

10.7 Other Functions of Mobile Nodes

Besides the functions just described, a mobile host must also be able to detect its mobility, to transmit, to receive multicast packets, and to return home.

10.7.1 Mobility Detection

A mobile host can use all mechanisms at its disposal to detect its mobility. The main mechanism is the Neighbor Discovery, described in Chapter 6. In fact, mobile hosts must use the Neighbor Discovery to locate the presence of new routers and new network prefixes. Moreover, the mobile host must use the Neighbor Unreachability Detection procedure (see Section 6.6) to check the reachability of its default router because the possibility of it becoming unreachable is much higher than usual.

10.7.2 Multicast Traffic Handling

The mobile node must belong to a multicast group to receive multicast traffic. This traffic handling can be implemented in the following two ways:

■ The mobile host can ask the multicast router present on the foreign network to belong to the multicast group.

■ The mobile host can ask the multicast router present on its home network to belong to the multicast group through a bi-directional tunnel with its home agent.

Likewise, a mobile host willing to transmit multicast packets offers two possibilities: to transmit them directly on the foreign network or to transmit them to its home agent through a tunnel. Because multicast routing depends on the IPv6 source address, in the first case, the mobile host will use its primary care-of address; whereas in the second case, it will use its home address. Note that the second solution treats the home agent also as a multicast router.

10.7.3   Home Again

A mobile host detects its return home when it receives the prefix of its home network through Neighbor Discovery messages. At this point, the mobile host transmits to its home agent a Binding Update message in which the care-of address is equal to its home address to request its home agent not to intercept packets addressed to it anymore because the mobile host is home again. The Binding Update message must be transmitted with the bit A = 1 and repeated until the home agent sends a Binding Acknowledgment message.

The mobile host must also send a Neighbor Advertisement message with the Override flag set (see Section 5.5.7), to request all hosts on the home network to update the neighbor information in their caches. This operation must be repeated a limited number of times both for the home address and for the link local address.

REFERENCES ■ ■ ■ ■ ■ ■ ■ ■ ■

[1]Several authors, *Issues in Mobile Computing Systems*, IEEE Personal Communications, Vol. 2, No. 6, December 1995.

[2]P. Bhagwat, C. Perkins, S. Tripathi, *Network Layer Mobility: An Architecture and Survey*, IEEE Personal Communications, Vol. 3, No. 3, June 1996, pp. 54-64.

[3]D. B. Johnson, C. Perkins, *Mobility Support in IPv6*, July 1997.

IPv6 and Multimedia Traffic

The transportation of multimedia traffic on IP networks is a topical subject because multimedia is becoming cheaper and cheaper and therefore used more and more. All workstations and personal computers available today are equipped with sound boards for recording and reproducing sounds and with video boards for viewing MPEG images[1]. Some of them are now equipped with video input and with small video cameras.

Problems with bearing multimedia flows on IP networks are mainly related to the bandwidth they require and to the strict maximum delay requirements that must be met. This second point is particularly important when multimedia applications have to provide users with real-time interaction.

In the past few years, many experiments have been made to develop a network layered on the Internet for multimedia applications; this network is called Mbone[2]. These experiments have highlighted the intrinsic multicast nature of multimedia traffic (from a source toward many destinations) and therefore the need to improve the routing of multicast packets on IP networks.

Some characteristics of IPv6 will improve the support of multimedia applications (in the following, also called *real-time applications*), such as the availability of the Priority field and of the Flow Label field on the IPv6 header (see Sections 3.1.2 and 3.1.3) and the availability of a large addressing space reserved for multicast addresses (see Section 4.8).

Moreover, other protocols of the stack introduce significant rationalizations in this field. ICMPv6 includes functions for the management of multicast groups (see Section 5.5.3), and OSPFv6 provides the treatment of multicast trees, formerly supported by DVMRP and MOSPF (see Section 7.4.2).

All the innovations cited here aren't enough to solve the problems of using multimedia on networks. IPv6 is part of a more ambitious project called IS (*Integrated Service*) Internet, which is discussed in RFC 1633[3]; it aims to extend the Internet architecture to allow the bearing of either best-effort or real-time traffic, as well as to control the use of transmission links (controlled link sharing).

The *best-effort* traffic is the only type of traffic that has been used on the Internet till now. It is based on the idea that the network's task is to do everything possible to deliver each IP packet, without guaranteeing the packet is delivered or the delivery time.

Multimedia applications frequently generate *real-time* traffic—that is, a type of traffic sensitive to queuing delays and to losses due, for example, to network overloading. Moreover, this type of traffic frequently needs a guaranteed minimum bandwidth.

The possibility of reserving a minimum bandwidth on links for particular classes of users, or protocol stacks, is in general a requirement understood by network administrators, also independently from multimedia applications.

Clearly, typical real-time applications—like the transmission of remote video images, multimedia conferences, and virtual reality—require the extension of IP by introducing the concept of *Quality of Service* (QoS). The extension must in some way allow limited packet delays and must be designed, from the beginning, for IP multicast because most of the multimedia traffic is multicast.

The architectural extension proposed by the IETF includes the following two elements:

■ The extended service model, identified by the acronym *IS* (Integrated Services)
■ Its possible implementation structure

We should clearly distinguish the model of service, which defines the external behavior, from one of its possible implementations, which can and should change during the life of the model of service itself.

11.1   The Integrated Services Model

The possibility of providing QoS is strictly related to the ability to administer the network resources (for example, the bandwidth). Introducing either resource reservation mechanisms or acceptance/refusal of service request mechanisms (*admission control*) is essential on the basis of the requested QoS and of available resources. A resource reservation accepted by the network guarantees a service whose quality meets the desired requirements and therefore guarantees the application will operate acceptably.

Nevertheless, the introduction of resource reservation mechanisms on the Internet is not accepted by everybody. Some people assert that the resource reservation is only a method to administer resource shortages; to allocate resources to a user means to deprive all other users and therefore to dissatisfy them. Network administrators will soon discover that the real solution consists of the availability of more resources, not in the introduction of reservation or invoice schemes.

Some detractors of this idea also produced the following arguments:

■ *In the future, the bandwidth will be infinite.* New transmission techniques—in particular, fiber optics—cause some people to think that in the near future the bandwidth will be so big, widespread, and cheap to be considered infinite. Therefore, reserving network resources wouldn't be necessary.

■ *Simple priority schemes are enough.* We have already seen that the IPv6 header has a Priority field used both to distinguish the real-time traffic from the best-effort traffic and to provide different types of real-time traffic with different priorities. The use of this field could only bring adequate real-time service in certain periods and under certain conditions. But the priority is an implementation mechanism, not a model of service!

■ *Applications can be adapted to the present traffic of the network.* Techniques can be used to develop real-time applications that can be adapted to the variations of the load on the network. These techniques have been little used until today, but they will be the basis of new multimedia applications.

It is the author's opinion that these items will undoubtedly have a considerable impact on networks in the future, but that they are not sufficient to guarantee real-time services on the entire Internet. In fact, on the one hand, it is true that in the United States the bandwidth will soon be practically infinite; on the other hand, it is true that the situation in Europe, due to the persistence of monopolies, is very different, and in other Eastern Europe or Asian countries, the situation is even worse.

The priority mechanism is not sufficient to guarantee the management of real-time traffic. In fact, if several packets with the same priority compete for resources, with a lack of reservations, the QoS cannot be guaranteed.

The development of adaptive real-time applications doesn't eliminate the need to reduce packet delivery time because the human need to interact and to understand limits, in some way, this capability of adaptation. For example, some voice applications can adapt themselves to delays of many seconds, but they have been shown to make the interaction between users impossible.

The logical conclusion is that routers should be able to reserve resources to provide the QoS and will therefore be modified to identify flows, to maintain state information about flows themselves, and to manage queues of packets separated by different flows. This evolution represents an important and basic change to the Internet model because the Internet architecture has been, till now, based on the concept that the state relevant to various flows should be managed by hosts only[4].

11.2   Coding of Multimedia Information

Before examining a possible implementation of the IS architecture, we need to analyze the adaptive applications mentioned in the preceding sections. The first step for the implementation of these multimedia applications is the elimination of the redundancy in the information, usually obtained through compression algorithms. A disadvantage of this operation, which is essential for reducing the bandwidth necessary for transmission, is that the compression unavoidably introduces delays. Therefore, the choice of the compression algorithm must take into account how much delay it introduces and which is the application typology. For applications such as television broadcasting (which is devoid of interactivity), the introduced delay can be also very high, allowing the use of compression schemes with high compression rates or that favor the quality of images. On the other hand, for videoconference applications (in which a good level of interactivity is necessary), low-delay compression schemes must be favored. Another factor to be considered is whether the compression scheme transmits exactly the same image it received (compression without loss) or an approximation of it (compression with loss). Compression schemes with loss are suitable for videoconference and entertainment applications, but if transmitting X-rays or other medical images is necessary, choosing a compression scheme without loss is advisable, to avoid the risk of wrong diagnoses.

After the redundancy is eliminated, we can reintroduce it in the form of error correction codes. In fact, real-time requirements of many multimedia applications make the retransmission of an erroneous packet impossible because the transmission will then be useless. The only possibility is to increase the redundancy of essential information through codes that allow automatic correction of a certain number of errors during the reception of the erroneous packet.

Until now, we have considered acceptable and unacceptable delays without providing numerical information. The ITU 114 standard "General Delay Recommendation" defines as acceptable delays up to 150 ms, delays between 150 and 400 ms acceptable for some applications, and those delays higher than 400 ms generally unacceptable.

The design of applications must take into account from the beginning that the QoS cannot be guaranteed in particular circumstances; therefore, the coding of the information must be designed to always provide a minimum service, even if a low-quality service.

This service can be implemented through *hierarchical coding*. Let's suppose we want to transmit a numerical flow of CD quality with a 44 KHz sample and samples on 16 bits. Instead of coding the sound as a unique flow of data, subdividing it into the following four subflows to be transmitted with decreasing priorities makes more sense:

- A basis flow coded at 5.5 KHz
- A flow containing differences between 5.5 KHz and 11 KHz
- A flow containing differences between 11 KHz and 22 KHz
- A flow containing differences between 22 KHz and 44 KHz

The network will try to transport all four flows to the destination in time. In case of congestion, however, the network will begin to discard packets belonging to the last flow, then to the next-to-last flow, and so on, guaranteeing the best possible service consistent with the state of congestion of the network.

11.3   Reference Implementation

We have seen that the router is the component that needs more modifications to implement IS Internet. Let's analyze the possible architecture of the router shown in Figure 11-1.

Notice that the router is ideally subdivided into two parts: the *forwarding path* (lower part) and the *background code* (upper part). The additional blocks, in comparison with a common router, are the *packet scheduler*, the *admission control agent*, the *classifier,* and the *reservation setup agent*. These blocks operate on data flows, and this concept is clearly present in IPv6 (see Sections 1.2.8 and 3.1.3).

Figure 11-1
Architecture of an IS router

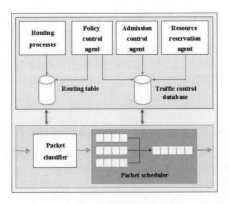

Current routers are designed for best-effort traffic; therefore, they treat packets with a simple FIFO (First In, First Out) queuing for each egress line (see Figure 11-2).

As for integrated services, a router must provide an appropriate QoS for each flow, and it must therefore be equipped with a module for the traffic control. This module consists of the following three submodules:

- The *packet scheduler* guarantees the QoS administering the transmission of packets through a mechanism for the periodical visit of a set of queues.

- The *packet classifier* recognizes which flow a packet belongs to and queues it on the corresponding queue. A queue can be associated with a single flow or to a class of flows.

- The *admission control* decides, in response to a request of resource reservation from the reservation agent, whether this packet can be accepted. The decision is made on the basis of resources reserved by other flows, of the network administration policies set through the control agent, and of globally available resources. In practice, this module checks whether the requested QoS can be provided without colliding with the guarantees of service provided to other flows.

The presence of a classification module and of a packet scheduler requires that each egress line be associated with a set of queues. An example of this association is shown in Figure 11-3.

The presence of a set of queues is a necessary, but not sufficient, characteristic to guarantee the QoS. It is, in fact, necessary that the scheduler guarantees that the frequency with which each queue is served is greater than or equal to that guaranteed during the resource reservation. This forces us to have a separate queue for each real-time flow (in the example, R1, R2, R3 e R4) and a shared queue for the best-effort traffic. The best-effort traffic will clearly be penalized, and it will be served only in the absence of real-time traffic.

The model of admission control is sometimes confused with the so-called *policing*, a control mechanism that checks packet by packet that a

Figure 11-2
A queue for each egress line

TX: transmitter on the output line

host doesn't violate traffic characteristics agreed upon by a previous QoS agreement. In this case, the packet scheduler provides the policing.

The fourth and last component is the resource reservation protocol, which is necessary to create and maintain the state of each flow on the routing path and which allows the interaction between reservation agents. The protocol chosen by the IETF is *RSVP (Resource reSerVation Protocol)*[5, 6].

The implementation for hosts is usually similar to that of routers, but with the addition of applications. Figure 11-4 shows the interconnection between a host and a router. The host's data are received by an application that, if needing QoS for a flow, must request it from the local reservation agent (the RSVP agent).

Figure 11-3
Set of queues associated with an exit

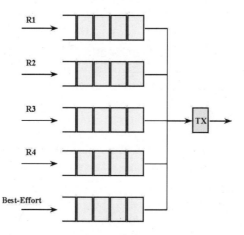

Figure 11-4
Connection between a router and a host in IS Internet

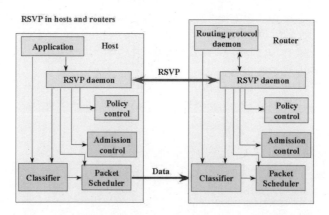

11.4   Traffic Control

Traffic control mechanisms implemented in traditional routers are very simple. But the tasks of the traffic control module of an IS router are unavoidably more complex. In particular, a network can administer its resources in two ways: through the packet scheduler and through buffer management.

11.4.1   The Packet Scheduler

The packet scheduler determines the order in which each packet is served (transmitted). It represents the main control function on how a network serves its users.

The simplest scheduling algorithm consists of ordering packets as a function of their priority. In this way, packets with higher priority are transmitted first. This method of transmission can cause an indefinite waiting period for lower priority packets if the traffic of higher priority data is very heavy.

Currently, the commonly used algorithm for the management of real-time traffic is WFQ (*Weighted Fair Queuing*)[7], which is based on a scheme similar to that shown in Figure 11-3. Each queue is associated with a weight proportional to the frequency it must be served. The packet scheduler uses weights to determine which queue must be served. The WFQ alternates the transmission of packets belonging to several flows, and for each of them, it works like a low-pass filter.

The WFQ algorithm is already available on several routers associated with a classifier; it uses information such as the protocol type or the type of application to which packets belong.

11.4.2   Buffer Management

The presence of buffers (queues) in the network is essential each time packets arrive at a speed higher than at which they can be retransmitted. Nevertheless, this setup can exist only in a transition period because, if packets arrive for a long period at a speed higher than at which they can be retransmitted, some of them must be discarded.

Packets to be discarded must not be chosen randomly, but as a function of the type of application and of services they require. These considerations, in addition to the meaning of packets discarded, raise the need for implementing specific buffer management mechanisms for different classes of packets.

In fact, for the TCP, the indication of a discarded packet is interpreted like a signal of network congestion; it induces the protocol itself to reduce the load on the network, thus reducing the speed of packet generation at the source. For real-time applications to discard a packet involves the possibility of maintaining the quality of the desired service; that is, it helps in correctly transmitting many other packets. In fact, if an output buffer is full, discarding a packet within the buffer shortens the delay of all other packets that follow the discarded one.

11.4.3   Packet Classification

The preceding discussion on packet scheduling and on buffer management assumes that the traffic has been subdivided into classes, each of which must be treated in a specific way.

The classification must be made by analyzing many fields of the packet. In fact, the only information relevant for the forwarding process to determine the packet routing is the destination address, and this information is not sufficient to correctly classify the packet received.

We have already seen how IPv6, to reduce the elaborate overhead, marks packets with a flow identification, called a *flow label*, inserted in the IP header. This identifier can be cached in routers and used for a quick classification of packets. This technique simplifies the classification when the source station differentiates flows by marking them with different flow labels.

Nevertheless, in the initial phase of the deployment of IPv6, many applications will transmit using the default flow label (flow label = 0); therefore, it is necessary to recognize data flows in routers, by analyzing, for example, the content of several fields in the packets header such as the source address, the protocol number, or the value of the UDP port. In this way, it is possible to recognize a flow of video information through a well-known port in the UDP header, for example, or to recognize an application from the joint analysis of the TCP header's source port and destination port. Moreover, a classification can be made on the basis of information contained in upper layer packets.

In this way, it is also possible to manage the QoS for already-existing applications, without modifying them, but trying to make decisions on the basis of the header content. This second approach presents a disadvantage, which brings about the introduction of the flow label in IPv6. In fact, finding the information on ports and on applications entails processing the whole chain of headers, with a considerable computing burden, and this process can be quite complicated if the payload is encrypted (see Section 8.1.3).

11.4.4 Access Control

The technique traditionally proposed for implementing access control consists of storing all service parameters of all previous requests and making a decision based on the worst characteristics discovered for each service.

This onerous method can be replaced by another one, which allows us to obtain a better use of links. This goal is reached when each router determines the use of links from existing packet flows, and the router uses this information to accept or not accept new flows entering the network. This technique exposes the system to a higher risk of overloading, balanced by a better use of the link.

We should notice that the need for an admission control function is required by the model of service, although its implementation is not specified. For this reason, manufacturers of routers and network devices are encouraged to find better solutions that, in comparison with their competitors' solutions, allow them to find better uses of the network and a lower risk of overload.

11.5 RSVP

A resource reservation protocol must be designed to allow the network to propagate the resources requested by the different applications. The protocol chosen by the IETF is RSVP *(Resource reSerVation Protocol)*[5, 6].

RSVP can operate in a multicast environment, consisting of a set of sources that send *data* to a particular set of receivers through a distribution tree (see Figure 11-5). The distribution tree is identified by the multicast address of the set of receivers.

RSVP supports resource reservations both for unicast applications and for multicast applications of the type "many to many," dynamically adapting itself both to variations in the composition of groups and to variations in routing paths.

RSVP is a protocol used by a host to request a specific QoS from an application. RSVP is also used by routers both to retransmit QoS requests along the entire data routing tree and to maintain the state information about flows in routers.

RSVP is a protocol for *simplex* data flows (the sender is treated in a different way from the receiver); therefore, the request of resources is unidirectional. RSVP is layered on IP (both version 4 and version 6); it doesn't transport data, but only control messages (*Path* and *Resv* messages in Figure 11-5).

In RSVP, the receiver is responsible for reservation requests (Resv messages). The sender limits itself to inform receivers about the type of transmission made through information messages (Path messages).

Moreover, a reservation setup protocol must provide a flexible control on the way resources allocated along multicast trees are shared among the different applications and manage very large multicast groups. Because these multicast groups are dynamic, being able to add or to eliminate stations to or from a group, as well as to allow the creation and the cancellation of groups, is therefore necessary.

In IPv6, these functions are provided by ICMP and OSPF. ICMP manages the participation of groups at a single link level (for example, a local area network), whereas OSPF maintains distribution trees of multicast groups among several different subnets (for example, for wide area networks).

Figure 11-5
Path and Resv Messages

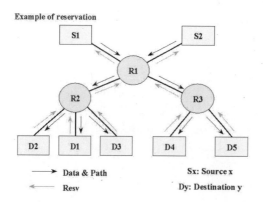

11.5.1   Flowspec and Filterspec

A reservation request must specify both the necessary resources, through a set of parameters called *flowspecs*, and the set of packets to which resources are allocated through a set of parameters called *filterspecs*.

If the admission control procedure gives a positive result, allowing the acceptance of the reservation request, the flowspec parameter is used to define a class of flows in the scheduler and to allocate the relative buffers. On the other hand, the filterspec parameter is used by the classifier to identify, among the packets received, those belonging to the given flow.

RSVP allows the creation and management of the necessary state information in a distributed form along the whole multicast tree. Flowspec and filterspec parameters are transported only by RSVP, leaving their interpretation to admission control functions.

11.5.2   Reservation Styles

RSVP can use different reservation styles. Differences among these styles depend on how the information about resources for a set of receivers is stored in different routers.

At present, the following three styles of reservation have been defined:

- Wildcard reservation
- Fixed filter reservation
- Shared filter reservation

The first method creates a single reservation shared by all senders' flows. We can think of this reservation like a shared channel whose size is equal to the maximum size requested by receivers and independent from the number of senders. In practice, the reservation uses the flowspec that requests the largest number of resources, among all those proposed by receivers.

This technique is particularly suitable for voice applications, such as the transmission of audioconferences, in which a limited number of sources are active at the same time and can share the same resources.

The other two methods use parameters that depend on transmission sources. These techniques are used for applications in which a determined receiver may decide to accept or not accept data flows from determined sources.

In the fixed filter reservation, the receiver requests a dedicated reservation for a particular sender that cannot be shared by other senders, even if belonging to the same multicast group. This reservation style is typically used for video flows.

In the shared filter reservation, the receiver requests a shared reservation for a set of senders that are explicitly identified. This style can be used as an alternative to the first one for voice applications.

11.5.3   Reservation by Receiver

In the RSVP protocol, resource reservation is receiver-initiated, allowing management of heterogeneous receivers in a simple way. In fact, each receiver sends a reservation request suitable to its characteristics and needs (*Resv* messages, in Figure 11-5). To do so, the receiver must have previously acquired source characteristics, in terms of flowspec, through information messages (*Path* messages, in Figure 11-5).

The reservation request is propagated on the network to sources, and each node traversed executes a resource allocation.

11.5.4   The Soft-State Approach

RSVP operates by the use of state information distributed in the routers within the network. This information is stored in special caches on routers, and these caches must be periodically updated by hosts, which must periodically repeat the reservation request.

In this way, useless information is automatically removed in case of errors with a time-out mechanism. In case the routing path has been changed, the suitable information will be automatically learned by new crossed routers by means of the periodical messages generated by RSVP.

This method is used to guarantee the robustness and the simplicity typical of the connectionless protocols used in the Internet.

11.5.5   Routing and Reservations

There is a strict connection between routing and reservation procedures because the latter requires the storage of state information along the path followed by packets. Clearly, in case of a routing change, the state information must be moved on the new path.

In general, RSVP has four main goals:

- To find a path allowing the resource allocation. This process entails the need to use a routing mechanism that differentiates the types of services.

- To find a path with enough resources for a new flow. This goal can be achieved in two different ways. The first requires a modification of routing protocols so that the new path is found on the basis of the most recent average load. The second method requires the redesign of the routing protocols to provide a series of alternative paths on which the reservation can be attempted. In both cases, obtaining dynamic routing based on the load of the network is difficult without creating instability problems. If, however, the dynamic routing is used only during the reservation, the instability doesn't create significant problems.

- To recover errors on the path. In case of failure of a node or of a link, the dynamic routing provides an alternative path. Refresh messages periodically sent by RSVP automatically request a reservation along the new path. This request can clearly fail because of the lack of available resources. This method entails an accurate management of the network configuration, that is due neither to routing protocols nor to reservation protocols used. The time necessary to create the reservation information on the new path shouldn't be too long, in order to avoid problems in the case of real-time applications.

- To implement a change of path not triggered by an error. In some cases, we also need to request a change of the path in the absence of errors. For example, this service can be used to allow the management of mobile stations within the network.

11.6 Integrated Services in an IP over ATM Architecture

Because problems of the use of IP over ATM have already been discussed in Chapter 9, in this section we will focus on aspects relevant to the QoS and in particular on analyzing how resource reservation mechanisms based on RSVP can work successfully with ATM's QoS, in a way similar to the one proposed in Figure 11-6. This description, which is based on

RFC 1821[8], analyzes only present problems without proposing organic solutions.

At a first glance, we can clearly see how the use of RSVP (and therefore of IP-QoS) by applications is much more general than the use of the ATM-QoS because it allows operation with a heterogeneous network.

The most significant issue, from the point of view of the reservation management, is that of the communication between two hosts, not directly connected to an ATM network, but using one or more ATM networks in some parts of the routing path. In this case, the entities connected to the ATM network are IP routers whose aim is to exploit different types of ATM-QoS, to guarantee the desired IP-QoS to the path between the two hosts.

IP routers, according to the description of IP-QoS, must determine whether an existing ATM connection can be used or whether a new one, with the desired characteristics, must be created.

From this example, we can deduce that the main aspects to be analyzed are the following:

- How the IP service model and the ATM service model are related

- How to translate RSVP reservation requests into ATM signaling packets

- How to execute the IP on ATM routing when QoS parameters are present

Figure 11-6
RSVP and ATM QoS

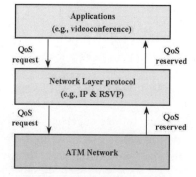

11.6.1   The Service Model

The main problem resides in the relationship between IP's QoS and ATM's QoS.

ATM provides five different classes of service:

- *CBR (Constant Bit Rate):* For applications requiring a fixed bandwidth and delays
- *VBR-real-time (Variable Bit Rate):* For real-time applications with variable bandwidth and with tightly constrained delays
- *VBR-non-real-time:* For variable bandwidth applications without tight delay constraints
- *UBR (Unspecified Bit Rate):* Class of service that approximates the best-effort service of IP
- *ABR (Available Bit Rate):* An evolved version of UBR able to control the loss rate by a flow control mechanism

The preceding classes oppose those provided by the IP model:

- *guaranteed:* Provides a guaranteed maximum delay bound
- *predictive:* Provides a probabilistic delay bound
- *controlled delay:* Provides several levels of delay from which applications can choose

When we decide the type of connection to be used to transport an IP flow, the QoS requests must be carefully evaluated. For example, we can decide to use a CBR class, or we can open a VBR connection to obtain a better use of the network resources because the IP traffic is usually burst traffic.

Another important element of the service model concerns the resource reservation. In fact, ATM uses only one signaling protocol (UNI 3.1 also called Q.2931) to request the connection and to allocate network resources at the same time. This protocol uses a sender-oriented approach—that is, requests are sent by sources. Moreover, it is based on a hard-state model, in which a connection's characteristics cannot be modified during the connection itself.

The main differences between the reservation protocol adopted by the IS Internet (RSVP) and that adopted by ATM (UNI) are as follow:

- In RSVP, the reservation request is sent by the receiver; whereas in ATM, it is sent by the sender.

- RSVP uses a soft-state approach that provides the possibility to dynamically modify the reservation. In ATM this approach is impossible.

- RSVP adopts a unidirectional allocation, whereas ATM uses a bidirectional allocation in the unicast case and a unidirectional allocation in the multicast case.

- RSVP allows the management of many senders in a unique multicast group. ATM cannot manage these operations.

In ATM, the routing and the reservation are implemented at the same time, unlike RSVP. The comparison will help us analyze the main problems to be solved:

- How to create ATM connections. Because these connections are bidirectional, the receiver could set up point-to-point connections. This solution is potentially wasteful of network resources because resources would be allocated for bidirectional transmission. The receiver must somehow request the sender to create a unidirectional point-to-multipoint connection. Because the QoS is associated with the connection, if different receivers request different QoSs, creating many point-to-multipoint connections with only one receiver is necessary. This approach, in the case of a very large multicast group, makes setting up a large number of connections necessary.

- ATM adopts a hard-state model. This means to take into account the possibility of opening and closing an ATM connection when the IP reservation is modified or released. Moreover, to optimize the use of the ATM network resources, the connection can be left open for use by other flows, or it can be closed. Frequently, the connection is left open for a subsequent use. If this connection is not sufficient to receive the new flow, a new connection can be opened to accommodate the extra traffic.

- RSVP uses control messages (Path) to convey information about sources to receivers before any data is transferred. In ATM, this solution requires a mechanism for setting up a connection whose QoS characteristics will be necessarily different from those that will probably be requested by the Resv message of RSVP.

- Finally, we need to develop security aspects to avoid a situation in which the differences between IP and ATM can allow nonauthorized users to reserve resources.

The main difficulty of implementing the IP routing on ATM in the presence of QoS parameters is that most routing protocols don't use the information about resources available on the network to determine the routing path. Some protocols, like OSPF, allow the determination of the routing depending on the ToS (Type of Service) value of the IPv4 header and on other metrics, but no protocol can manage the huge number of parameters provided by ATM.

The preceding items help us to understand the complexity of mapping the RSVP protocol on ATM.

A possible alternative consists of adapting a different protocol, called ST2[9], to ATM. It presents fewer problems than RSVP because it is based on a hard-state operation in which connections are set up by the sender, and the reservation is made during the connection setup.

The following problems must be solved to adapt ST2 on ATM:

- Managing changes to active stream reservations, which are allowed in ST2

- Avoiding the use of bidirectional connections for the management of point-to-point connections because ST2 uses unidirectional flows that would determine a waste of resources

REFERENCES

[1] ISO/IEC 13818-1, ITU H.220.0, *Information Technology—Generic Coding of Moving Pictures and Associated Audio.*

[2] S. Deering, *RFC 1112: Host Extensions for IP Multicasting*, August 1989.

[3] R. Braden, D. Clark, S. Shenker, *RFC 1633: Integrated Services in the Internet Architecture: an Overview*, June 1994.

[4] D. Clark, *The Design Philosophy of the DARPA Internet Protocols*, ACM SIGCOMM '88, August 1988.

[5] L. Zhang, S. Deering, D. Estrin, S. Shenker, D. Zappala, *RSVP: A New Resource ReSerVation Protocol*, IEEE Network, September 1993.

[6] R. Braden, L. Zhang, S. Berson, S. Herzog, S. Jamin, *Resource ReSerVation Protocol (RSVP)—Version 1 Functional Specification*, Internet Draft, November 1996.

[7] A. Demers, S. Keshav, S. Shenker, *Analysis and Simulation of a Fair Queuing Algorithm, Journal of Internetworking: Research and Experience*, 1, pp. 3-26, 1990, also in Proc. ACM SIGCOMM '89, pp. 3-12.

[8]M. Borden, E. Crawley, *RFC 1821: Integration of Real-time Services in an IP-ATM Network Architecture*, August 1995.

[9]L. Delgrossi, L. Berger, *RFC 1819 Internet Stream Protocol Version 2 (ST2) Protocol Specification—Version ST2+*, August 1995.

12

The Migration from IPv4 to IPv6

Migrating from IPv4 to IPv6 in an instant is impossible because of the huge size of the Internet and of the great number of IPv4 users. Moreover, many organizations are becoming more and more dependent on the Internet for their daily work, and they therefore cannot tolerate downtime for the replacement of the IP protocol. As a result, there will not be one special day on which IPv4 will be turned off and IPv6 turned on because the two protocols can coexist without any problems. The migration from IPv4 to IPv6 must be implemented node by node by using autoconfiguration procedures (see Section 6.7) to eliminate the need to configure IPv6 hosts manually. This way, users can immediately benefit from the many advantages of IPv6 while maintaining the possibility of communicating with IPv4 users or peripherals. Consequently, there is no reason to delay updating to IPv6!

We have already seen that some IPv6 characteristics are explicitly designed to simplify the migration. For example, IPv6 addresses can be automatically derived from IPv4 addresses, IPv6 tunnels can be built on IPv4 networks, and at least in the initial phase, all IPv6 nodes will follow the *dual stack* approach; that is, they will support both IPv4 and IPv6 at the same time.

This good level of compatibility between IPv4 and IPv6 may cause some users to think that the migration to IPv6 is useless. In the future, the choice of not migrating to IPv6 will limit the possibility of evolving because it will prevent users from accessing new implementations that, starting from 2000, will concern IPv6 only.

IPv6 has been accurately designed, discussed thoroughly, and tested in the field by the IETF and by many other research institutions. A project called *6-Bone* (described in Section 12.3) was created so that users could acquire experience and test the IPv6 protocol stacks.

The years from 1997 to 2000 will be characterized by the adoption of IPv6 by ISPs and users. During 1997, users could still have problems related to the newness of products, but starting from 1998, IPv6 will be part of mass-produced protocols distributed on routers, on workstations, and on PCs. At that point, organizations will begin to migrate, less or more gradually, to IPv6.

The key goals of the migration are as follow:

- IPv6 and IPv4 hosts must interoperate.

- The use of IPv6 hosts and routers must be distributed over the Internet in a simple and progressive way, with a little interdependence.

- Network administrators and end users must think that the migration is easy to understand and implement.

A set of mechanisms called *SIT (Simple Internet Transition)* has been implemented; it includes protocols and management rules to simplify the migration. The main characteristics of SIT are the following:

- *Possibility of a progressive and nontraumatic transition:* IPv4 hosts and routers can be updated to IPv6, one at a time, without requiring other hosts or routers to be updated simultaneously.

- *Minimum requirements for updating:* The only requirement for updating hosts to IPv6 is the availability of a DNS server to manage IPv6 addresses. No requirements are needed for routers.

- *Addressing simplicity:* When a router or a host is updated to IPv6, it can also continue to use IPv4 addresses.

■ *Low initial cost:* No preparatory work is necessary to begin the migration to IPv6.

Mechanisms used by SIT include the following:

■ A structure of IPv6 addresses that allows the derivation of IPv6 addresses from IPv4 addresses.

■ The availability of the dual stack on hosts and on routers during the transition—that is, the presence of both IPv4 and IPv6 stacks at the same time.

■ A technique to encapsulate IPv6 packets inside IPv4 packets (tunneling) to allow IPv6 packets to traverse clouds not yet updated to IPv6.

■ An optional technique that consists of translating IPv6 headers into IPv4 headers and vice versa to allow, in an advanced phase of the migration, IPv4-only nodes to communicate with IPv6-only nodes.

The SIT approach guarantees that IPv6 hosts can interoperate with IPv4 hosts initially on the entire Internet. When the migration is completed, this interoperability will be locally guaranteed for a long time. This capability allows for the protection of investments made on IPv4; simple devices that cannot be updated to IPv6—for example, network printers and terminal servers—will continue to operate with IPv4 until they are no longer used.

The possibility of a gradual migration allows manufacturers to integrate IPv6 in routers, operating systems, and network software when they think that implementations are stable and users to begin the migration at a time they consider the most appropriate.

Migration problems are described in RFC 1933[1]. The following sections of this chapter are dedicated to describing these problems.

12.1 Tunneling

As we mentioned in the introduction, while the IPv6 routing infrastructure is being deployed, the routing will continue to be based on IPv4. Tunneling techniques (see also Section 7.5.6) allow use of IPv4 networks to carry the IPv6 traffic.

Hosts and routers supporting the dual stack (also called IPv4/IPv6 nodes) can use tunnels to route IPv6 packets over IPv4 regions, as shown in the example in Figure 12-1.

In this example, host A sends the native IPv6 packet to router R1, which retransmits the packet in an IPv4 tunnel to router R2, which finally transmits it as a native IPv6 packet to host B. In this case, the tunnel is managed by R1 and R2.

From the encapsulation point of view, implementing a tunnel means encapsulating an IPv6 packet inside an IPv4 packet, as shown in Figure 12-2.

In the example shown in Figure 12-2, the IPv6 header will contain addresses A and B, and the IPv4 header will contain addresses R1 and R2.

12.1.1 Alternative Tunneling Schemes

During the migration, the tunneling technique can be used in the following ways:

- *Router-to-router:* IPv6/IPv4 routers interconnected by an IPv4 infrastructure can tunnel IPv6 packets between themselves. See Figure 12-3(a).

- *Host-to-router:* IPv6/IPv4 hosts can tunnel IPv6 packets to an intermediary IPv6/IPv4 router that can be reached via an IPv4 infrastructure. See Figure 12-3(b).

- *Host-to-host:* IPv6/IPv4 hosts that are interconnected by an IPv4 infrastructure can tunnel IPv6 packets between themselves. See Figure 12-3(c).

Figure 12-1
IPv6 over IPv4
Tunneling

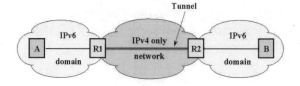

Figure 12-2
IPv6 over IPv4
Encapsulation

IPv6 packet without a tunnel

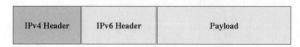

IPv6 packet in an IPv4 tunnel

■ *Router-to-host:* IPv6/IPv4 routers can use tunnels to reach an IPv6/IPv4 host via an IPv4 infrastructure. See Figure 12-3(d).

In the first two tunneling methods—router-to-router and host-to-router—the IPv6 packet is tunneled to a router; therefore, the endpoint of this type of tunnel is a router that must decode the IPv6 packet and forward it to its final destination. No relationship exists between the router address and the final destination address. For this reason, the router address that is the tunnel endpoint must be manually configured. This type of tunnel is called a *configured tunnel*.

In the last two tunneling methods—host-to-host and router-to-host—the IPv6/IPv4 packet is tunneled from a host or from a router to its destination host. In this case, the tunnel endpoint address and the destination host address are the same. If the IPv6 address used for the destination node is an IPv4-compatible address (see Section 4.6.8), the tunnel endpoint IPv4 address can be automatically derived from the IPv6 address, and therefore no manual configurations are necessary. These tunnels are also called *automatic tunnels*.

Figure 12-3
Tunneling schemes

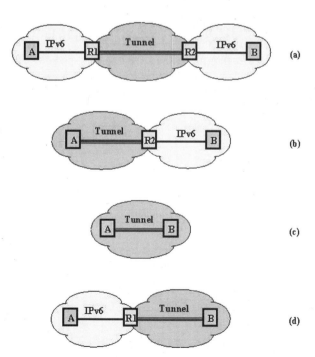

12.1.2 IPv6 Addresses with Embedded IPv4 Addresses

IPv6 addresses with embedded IPv4 addresses have the format shown in Figure 12-4, and they have a syntax of the type `::10.1.3.4` (see Section 4.6.8). They must not be confused with IPv4 addresses whose syntax is `10.1.3.4`.

12.1.3 MTU

The encapsulating node can also transmit large IPv6 packets (up to 65,535 20-octet packets, because the IPv4 header is 20 octets long) by delegating the fragmentation problem to the IPv4 level. This approach, even if theoretically possible, would be inefficient for the following reasons:

- It would result in more fragmentation than needed. In fact, the loss of an IPv4 fragment would cause the retransmission of the entire IPv6 packet and therefore also of fragments that correctly reached the destination.

- The fragmentation occurring at one endpoint of the tunnel should be removed at the other endpoint. For tunnels that terminate at a router, this process would require additional memory in the router to contain fragments waiting to be reassembled.

Therefore, the fragmentation at tunnel endpoints can be minimized by recording the tunnel's IPv4 Path MTU.

The algorithm used to deal with this problem is described in RFC 1933[1] and reported in Section A.5 of Appendix A.

Figure 12-4
IPv6 addresses with embedded IPv4 addresses

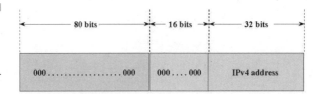

12.1.4   Hop Limit

In IPv6, a tunnel is like a single point-to-point link, and each tunnel corresponds to a hop. The Hop Limit field of the IPv6 header is therefore decremented by one when an IPv6 packet traverses a tunnel, independently from the number of IPv4 links the tunnel consists of.

12.1.5   Default Configured Tunnel

An IPv6 node connected to a purely IPv4 network can reach other IPv6 nodes only if a *default configured tunnel* has been defined. It is a tunnel toward an IPv6/IPv4 router that is configured in a way similar to a default route. All the IPv6 traffic will be sent to the IPv6/IPv4 router on the default configured tunnel. This type of tunnel allows testing of IPv6 even on a single host!

12.2   Dual Stack Approach

The dual stack approach consists of providing hosts and routers with IPv6 and IPv4 protocol stacks. In the case of an IPv6/IPv4 host, a possible organization of protocol stacks is shown in Figure 12-5.

The dual stack approach doesn't necessarily require the ability to create tunnels, whereas the ability to create tunnels requires the dual stack approach. In general, both approaches are provided by IPv6/IPv4 implementations.

The following is a simple description of the way the dual stack approach operates:

■ If the destination address used by the application is an IPv4 address, then the IPv4 protocols stack is used.

■ If the destination address used by the application is an IPv6 address with an embedded IPv4 address, then IPv6 is encapsulated inside IPv4.

■ If the destination address is an IPv6 address of another type, then IPv6 is used, possibly encapsulated in the default configured tunnel.

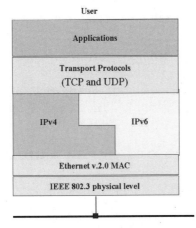

Figure 12-5
The dual stack approach

As a matter of fact, many more cases can be considered, and a more complete discussion of this topic can be found in a dedicated section of RFC 1933[1], reported in Section A.6 of Appendix A.

Moreover, we must consider that a user normally provides the application with a name, not with an address. This name must be translated into an address by using the DNS (see Section 2.11). In the DNS, only the IPv4 address (record A), only the IPv6 address (record AAAA), or both of them can be stored for each name. In the last case, deciding whether to use the IPv4 address or the IPv6 address is not easy, and the choice is the result of much consideration.

First, determining whether the node has an IPv6 direct connectivity is necessary. If not, the use of the IPv6 address will require the transmission of an IPv6 packet in an IPv4 tunnel. This approach can be less convenient than the use of native IPv4 or even impossible if the node cannot use tunnels.

12.3   6-Bone

The 6-Bone project (`http://www-cnr.lbl.gov/6bone/`) is a spontaneous derivation of the IETF IPng working group, and its aim is to implement and test IPv6 protocols with the final goal of replacing IPv4 with IPv6 on the Internet. 6-Bone is an informal collaboration between several research institutions located in Northern America, Europe, and Japan.

A strategic phase of the migration from IPv4 to IPv6 is represented by the implementation of an IPv6 backbone covering the entire Internet and able to transport IPv6 packets. As in the case of the present Internet IPv4 backbone, the IPv6 backbone will consist of many ISPs and of user networks interconnected to form the new Internet. Until protocols of the IPv6 stack will be widely available and tested, with particular reference to the interoperability of implementations, ISPs and users may not want to migrate production IPv4 routers to avoid risks. Therefore, identifying a way to provide an IPv6 connectivity on the entire Internet without modifying the present IPv4 Internet is necessary in order to test IPv6 protocols and to use them as soon as possible.

NOTE: *6-Bone, which is a virtual network layered on the present IPv4 Internet, provides the routing of IPv6 packets because not all routers currently available can correctly manage the IPv6 routing. The network consists of "islands" providing an IPv6 direct connectivity (usually LANs) interconnected by virtual point-to-point channels (tunnels). Tunnels' endpoints are either single workstations supporting IPv6 or routers supporting IPv6.*

6-Bone is a time-oriented project. In fact, as time goes by and with the growth of the reliability and routing of IPv6 packets on routers, IPv6 will be available by default on new routers and on updated software releases, and 6-Bone will disappear as agreed by its designers. It will be transparently replaced by an IPv6 global connectivity offered by ISPs and by user networks.

The goal of 6-Bone is to provide an environment in which the transport of IPv6 packets can be tested and users are allowed to gain the required experience. It isn't aimed at creating a new and permanent interconnection architecture.

6-Bone is trying to involve as many ISPs and users as it can to spread the experience on IPv6 as much as possible and to create an easy migration to IPv6 itself.

12.3.1   The 6-Bone Node at Politecnico di Torino

Figure 12-6 shows the 6-Bone node implemented at Politecnico di Torino, Italy, in September 1997.

Figure 12-6
The 6-Bone node at
Politecnico di Torino

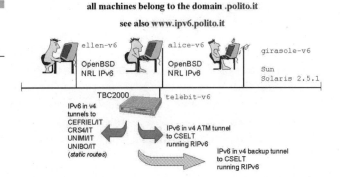

Figure 12-6
The 6-Bone node at Politecnico di Torino

Figure 12-7 shows a dump of the Telebit router in which we can see IPv6 addresses manually configured on the local network and those automatically learned through the RIP protocol. Furthermore, we can estimate the role of tunnels in 6-Bone.

12.3.2   Registration to RIPE-NCC

Organizations willing to participate in the 6-Bone experiment should register with the RIPE-NCC. Figure 12-8 shows, as an example, the registration form of Politecnico di Torino.

Figure 12-7
Dump of the Telebit
router

```
% use ip routing 3
% show ip v6route
Route to:                              Out Interface:    Metric: Source:
::130.192.26.253/128                        1.0          0 IGP Configured
::192.168.0.26/128                         atm.0         0 Configured path
3ffe:300::/24                          cselt.internet    5 IGP RIPv6
3ffe:301:dec0::/44                     cselt.internet   12 IGP RIPv6
3ffe:301:dec1::/48                     cselt.internet   12 IGP RIPv6
3ffe:400::/24                          cselt.internet    5 IGP RIPv6
3ffe:501:402:a00::/64                  cselt.internet    8 IGP RIPv6
3ffe:900::/24                          cselt.internet    4 IGP RIPv6
3ffe:a00::/24                          cselt.internet   12 IGP RIPv6
3ffe:c00::/24                          cselt.internet    4 IGP RIPv6
3ffe:c00:0:1::/64                      cselt.internet    7 IGP RIPv6
3ffe:f00::/24                          cselt.internet    3 IGP RIPv6
3ffe:1000::/24                         cselt.internet    3 IGP RIPv6
3ffe:1001:1::/80                       cselt.internet    3 IGP RIPv6
3ffe:1001:1:0:0:0:0:1/128              cselt.internet    1 IGP Configured
3ffe:1001:1:0:0:0:0:2/128              cselt.sirius      1 Configured Peer
3ffe:1011::/32                         default.1         1 IGP Static path
3ffe:1011:101:e00::/80                 default.1         1 IGP Configured
3ffe:1011:101:e00:0:bd:0:1111/128      default.1         0 IGP Configured
3ffe:1011:111:1111:0:1111:1111:1111/128  cselt.internet  0 IGP Configured
3ffe:1011:111:1111:0:2222:2222:2222/128  cselt.sirius    0 Configured path
3ffe:1011:111:2222:0:1111:2222:1111/128        unimi     0 IGP Configured
3ffe:1011:111:2222:0:1111:2222:2222/128        unimi     1 IGP Configured
3ffe:1011:111:2222:0:1111:3333:1111/128      unibo       0 IGP Configured
3ffe:1011:111:2222:0:1111:3333:2222/128      unibo       1 IGP Configured
3ffe:1011:200::/40                          unimi        1 IGP Static path
3ffe:1011:300::/40                          unibo        1 IGP Static path
3ffe:1100::/24                          cselt.internet    3 IGP RIPv6
3ffe:1200::/24                          cselt.internet    5 IGP RIPv6
3ffe:1300::/48                          cselt.internet    5 IGP RIPv6
3ffe:1300:1::/48                        cselt.internet    5 IGP RIPv6
3ffe:1d00:1::/48                        cselt.internet   12 IGP RIPv6
3ffe:1d00:1:100::/64                    cselt.internet   10 IGP RIPv6
3ffe:1dec::/32                          cselt.internet   12 IGP RIPv6
3ffe:2000:0:1:0:0:0:2/127              cselt.internet    8 IGP RIPv6
3ffe:2100::/24                          cselt.internet    4 IGP RIPv6
5f00::/8
```

(Continues)

Figure 12-7
Continued.

```
More (Y/N)?n

% show ip v4route
Route to:            Interface:      Metric: Source:         NextHop:
          0.0.0.0/0      default.2      1 IGP Static path
     130.192.0.0/16            1.0     22 IGP Own Domain
    130.192.26.0/24      default.2     20 IGP Configured
  130.192.26.253/32            1.0      0 IGP Configured
      192.168.0.0/24          atm.0     22 Own Domain
     192.168.0.26/32          atm.0      0 Configured path
```

Figure 12-8
Example of registration form to RIPE-NCC

```
ipv6-site:   POLITO
origin:      AS5456
descr:       Politecnico di Torino
descr:       Torino, ITALY
location:    45 03 52.2 N 07 39 43.2 E 250m
country:     IT
prefix:      5F15:5000::/32
application: ping girasole-v6.ipv6.polito.it
application: ping telebit-v6.ipv6.polito.it
application: ping ellen-v6.ipv6.polito.it
application: ping alice-v6.ipv6.polito.it
tunnel:      IPv6 in IPv4 telebit.ipv6.polito.it -> polo.cefriel.it    CEFRIEL STATIC
tunnel:      IPv6 in IPv4 telebit.ipv6.polito.it -> schubert.crs4.it    CRS4 STATIC
tunnel:      IPv6 in IPv4 telebit.ipv6.polito.it -> telebit.cselt.it    CSELT RIPng
tunnel:      IPv6 in IPv4 telebit.ipv6.polito.it -> sun1.spfo.unibo.it UNIBO STATIC
tunnel:      IPv6 in IPv4 telebit.ipv6.polito.it -> phoebe-v6.ip6.dsi.unimi.it UNIMI STATIC
contact:     SG389-RIPE
remarks:     OpenBSD/NRL, Sun Solaris, DEC RouteAbout Access EW/IPv6, Telebit
remarks:     Running Bind 4.9.5 on ns.ipv6.polito.it
remarks:     our modified NRL distribution is available at ftp.ipv6.polito.it
remarks:     ipv6-site is operational since 11/1996
url:         http://www.ipv6.polito.it
notify:      silvano.gai@polito.it
changed:     spera@csp.it 19970324
changed:     auto-dbm@ISI.EDU 19970331
changed:     rivetti@csp.it 19970609
changed:     spera@alp.net 19970917
source:      6BONE

% Rights restricted by copyright. See http://www.ripe.net/db/dbcopyright.html

person:      Silvano Gai
address:     Dip. Automatica e Informatica
address:     Politecnico di Torino
address:     Corso Duca degli Abruzzi 24
address:     I-10129 Torino
address:     Italy
phone:       +39 11 5647013
```

REFERENCES

[1] R. Gilligan, E. Nordmar, *RFC 1933: Transition Mechanisms for IPv6 Hosts and Routers*, April 1996.

[2] R. Hinden, J. Postel, *RFC 1897: IPv6 Testing Address Allocation*, January 1996.

13

Cisco and IPv6[1]

Cisco Systems, the premier IP vendor, is committed to the evolution of the Internet and of intranets and considers the next generation IP to be a key component of their growth. Cisco has taken a leadership role in the definition and implementation of the IPv6 protocols within the IETF and within its IOS™ software. Recognizing the magnitude of the migration involved, Cisco also is implementing techniques (discussed later in this chapter) that facilitate the transition from IPv4 to IPv6. Its current IOS™ implementation is in Beta, and Cisco expects to ship its comprehensive IOS IPv6 support near the end of 1998.

[1]This chapter was written with the help of Martin McNealis, IOS™ product line manager at Cisco Systems, Inc. Without his help, this chapter would not have been possible. The author wants to thank Martin for his contribution, his advice, and his friendship.

IOS runs on Cisco routers and is a very powerful router and switch operating system supporting more than 15,000 features and various protocols.

IPv6 will be one of the protocols supported by IOS, and it will be fully integrated into the operating system.

Leveraging its unparalleled experience in building the world's largest network including, of course, the Internet, Cisco has developed optimum layer 3 switching techniques such as *Cisco Express Forwarding* and *Tag Switching*, which will encompass support for IPv6.

Cisco's Express Forwarding (CEF) technology is a scalable, distributed, layer 3 switching solution designed to meet the future performance requirements of the Internet and Enterprise networks. CEF represents the ultimate advance in Cisco IOS switching capabilities, which include *NetFlow™ Switching* and *Distributed Switching*. CEF is also a key component of Cisco's *Tag Switching* architecture.

The position of Cisco—as premium IP vendor—is not to force the users to migrate to IPv6 but to enable users to decide the right moment to migrate based upon their unique network condition. For many customers, the transition to IPv6 is a decision that they won't need to make for several years. Cisco has already developed extensions to IPv4, incorporating in IPv4 many of the advantages of IPv6. For example:

■ *Classless Inter-Domain Routing* (CIDR) and *Network Address Translation* (NAT) provide an effective means of resolving the current limitations of IP address assignment.

■ *Virtual Private Networks* (VPNs) made with IPv4 tunnels are an effective solution for Enterprise networks and when integrated with NAT mitigate the lack of IPv4 address space.

■ IPSec available in IPv4 addresses the security concerns of network managers.

■ DHCP servers and relays address the need for user mobility and for plug-and-play configuration.

■ *Resource Reservation Protocol* (RSVP) and *Weighted Fair Queuing* (WFQ) are among the options available for defining quality of service on existing IP networks.

In particular, NAT [1] supports the connectivity in the presence of nonunique addresses. The NAT technology enables each organization connected to the Internet to reuse the same block of addresses (for example, the addresses defined in [2]), while requiring only a small number (relative to the total number of addresses used by the organization) of globally unique addresses for external connectivity.

Cisco recognises that continued growth of the Internet and demand for IP addressing will be fueled for example by the *Voice over IP* (VoIP), the new on-line devices such as *Personal Digital Assistants* (PDAs), hybrid mobile phones, and set-top boxes, all of which are becoming Network-aware and IP manageable and as such IPv6 provides a clear path to such expansion.

Of course, there are also some caveat and inefficiencies introduced by IPv6: while the regular and simple structure of the IPv6 header will simplify the streamline processing of packets without options, the larger header size will no longer make possible to fully contain a TCP ACK response in a single ATM cell (as in IPv4)—introducing a substantial overhead.

Another important advantage of IPv6 is the provider-based addressing, that will introduce an efficient aggregation hierarchy with the related benefits (there is a clear analogy with telephony network). With the current proposal of Top-Level Aggregator, Next-Level Aggregator, Site-Level Aggregator, etc., it is possible that the Internet core router would carry only 8,000 prefixes on the Internet backbone.

Cisco's strategy is to minimize the transition pain and leverage existing proven technology, like translation. The most likely deployment scenario will see the Enterprise first with Cisco routers performing translation for the backbone Internet until a major ISP seeks first-mover advantage.

Going forward, Cisco understands that both IPv4/NAT and IPv6 will coexist for a long period of time and, therefore, it is ready to support both of them in an integrated way in IOS.

Cisco maintains an official IPv6 web server at the following address: `http://www.cisco.com/IPv6`.

IPv6 in IOS™

At the time of writing, Cisco has a Beta version of IOS, which includes the IPv6 support. Information presented here is not based on the final implementation, and therefore, users are invited to read official Cisco manuals before configuring the router.

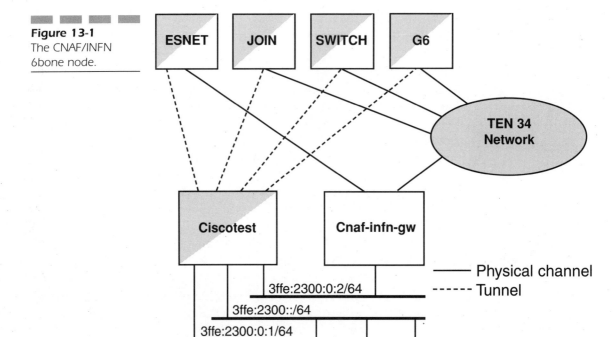

Figure 13-1
The CNAF/INFN
6bone node.

The explanation is based on an example courtesy of the backbone node of 6bone of the Italian research network (GARR), which is run in Bologna by CNAF/INFN[2]. Figure 13-1 depicts the architecture of the 6bone node present at CNAF/INFN (for details, see `http://www.cnaf.infn.it`).

Routers colored white and gray run both IPv4 and IPv6.

The following description is related to the node "CISCOTEST," a Cisco 7505 router, running an appropriate version of IOS.

Before going on with a description of the configuration, it is important to understand the IPv6 addressing plan of 6bone at the time of this writing.

---

[2] The author is in debt to the people of CNAF/INFN for their help and in particular to Antonia Ghiselli, Cristina Vistoli, and Luca dell'Agnello, who provided all the valuable information.

The CNAF/INFN asked of 6bone a *pseudo Top Level Aggregation Identifier* (pTLA) for GARR. The word "pseudo" means that this TLA will only be used during the testing phase of 6bone. 6bone is seen from IANA as a TLA, and IANA has assigned to 6bone the TLA-ID 0x1fe on 13 bits (see Figure 13-2). Adding the Aggregatable Address Format Prefix equal to 001 on 3 bits, we can derive the 6bone prefix **3ffe::/16** on 16 bits.

The first 8 bits of the *Next Level Aggregation* (NLA) identify all the IPv6 networks of GARR and have been set by 6bone equal to 0x23. Therefore, the IPv6 prefix of GARR is **3ffe:2300::/24**. GARR has assigned to CNAF/INFN the remaining 24 bits of the NLA equal to zero, and therefore the CNAF/INFN prefix is **3ffe:2300::/48**.

The router CISCOTEST has three Ethernet interfaces that run IPv6. A different IPv6 subnet using a different value in the SLA-ID field is associated to each Ethernet network. The three subnet prefixes are **3ffe:2300::/64**, **3ffe:2300:0:1::/64**, and **3ffe:2300:0:2::/64**.

Figure 13-3 lists the significant sections of the configuration file of the router CISCOTEST. The ellipsis indicates an omission of material not relevant to IPv6 configuration.

Figure 13-2
6bone Aggregatable
Address

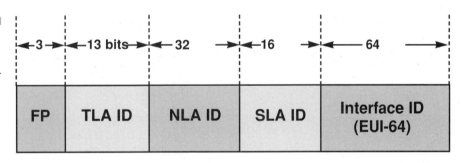

| FP | TLA ID | NLA ID | SLA ID | Interface ID (EUI-64) |

Figure 13-3
CISCOTEST configuration file.

```
!
...
hostname ciscotest
!
...
ipv6 unicast-routing
ipv6 bgp redistribute connected
ipv6 bgp neighbor 3FFE:700:20:2::9 remote-as 293
ipv6 bgp neighbor 3FFE:302:11:2:0:2:0:51 remote-as 1717
ipv6 bgp neighbor 3FFE:2000:0:1::61 remote-as 559
ipv6 bgp neighbor 3FFE:401::2C0:33FF:FE02:14 remote-as 1275
ipv6 bgp network 3FFE:2300::0/24 summary
```

continues

Figure 13-3
Continued.

```
interface Tunnel100
 description tunnel BGP4+ --> ESNET
 no ip address
 ipv6 address 3FFE:700:20:2::A/126
 tunnel source FastEthernet0/0/0
 tunnel destination 198.128.2.27
 tunnel mode ipv6ip
!
interface Tunnel101
 description tunnel BGP4+ --> IMAG
 no ip address
 ipv6 address 3FFE:302:11:2:0:2:0:52/124
 tunnel source FastEthernet0/0/0
 tunnel destination 129.88.26.7
 tunnel mode ipv6ip
!
interface Tunnel102
 description tunnel BGP4+ --> SWITCH
 no ip address
 ipv6 address 3FFE:2000:0:1::62/124
 tunnel source FastEthernet0/0/0
 tunnel destination 130.59.15.6
 tunnel mode ipv6ip
!
interface Tunnel103
 description tunnel BGP4+ --> JOIN
 no ip address
 ipv6 enable
 ipv6 address 3FFE:2300:0:FFFF::9/126
tunnel source FastEthernet0/0/0
 tunnel destination 128.176.191.66
 tunnel mode ipv6ip
!
interface Tunnel200
 description static tunnel --> UNIBO
 no ip address
 ipv6 address 3FFE:2300:0:FFFF::5/126
 tunnel source FastEthernet0/0/0
 tunnel destination 137.204.198.2
 tunnel mode ipv6ip
!
interface Tunnel201
 description static tunnel --> DEMOKRITOS
 no ip address
 ipv6 address 3FFE:2300:0:FFFF::D/126
 tunnel source FastEthernet0/0/0
 tunnel destination 192.108.114.29
 tunnel mode ipv6ip
!
...
interface FastEthernet0/0/0
 ip address 131.154.3.58 255.255.255.0
 ipv6 address 5F15:4100:839A:300:0:2E0:14C5:6B60/80
```

```
    ipv6 address 3FFE:2300::0/64 eui-64
!
interface Ethernet3/0
 ip address 131.154.100.1 255.255.255.0
 ipv6 address 3FFE:2300:0:2::0/64 eui-64
!
...
router bgp 137
!
...
ipv6 route 3FFE:401::2C0:33FF:FE02:14/128 Tunnel103
ipv6 route 3FFE:2300:31::0/48 Tunnel200
ipv6 route 3FFE:23FF::0/32 Tunnel201
!
...
                       end
```

IPv6 commands

Let's examine the most relevant commands of Figure 13-3 and also the output of some show commands.

show ipv6 route

```
show ipv6 route
```

This command displays the IPv6 routing table.

Figure 13-4
Output of show IPv6 route.

```
ciscotest>show ipv6 route
*** This output has been cut to fit into one page ***
IPv6 Routing Table - 120 entries
Codes: C - Connected, L - Local, S - Static, R - RIP, B -
     BGP
Timers: Uptime/Expires

B 3FFE:301:DEC2::0/48 [20/6]
   via FE80::C3F:5B96:B, Tunnel101, 00:01:27/never
B 3FFE:301:DEC0::0/44 [20/4]
   via FE80::C3F:5B96:B, Tunnel101, 02:01:30/never
L 3FFE:302:11:2:0:2:0:52/128 [0/0]
   via 3FFE:302:11:2:0:2:0:52, Tunnel101, 06:24:17/never
C 3FFE:302:11:2:0:2:0:50/124 [0/0]
   via 3FFE:302:11:2:0:2:0:52, Tunnel101, 06:24:17/never

...
```

continues

Figure 13-4
Continued.

```
L 3FFE:2300:0:2:2E0:14FF:FEC5:6B60/128 [0/0]
   via 3FFE:2300:0:2:2E0:14FF:FEC5:6B60, Ethernet3/0,
     06:24:30/never
C 3FFE:2300:0:2::0/64 [0/0]
   via 3FFE:2300:0:2:2E0:14FF:FEC5:6B60, Ethernet3/0,
     06:24:30/never
L 3FFE:2300:0:FFFF::5/128 [0/0]
   via 3FFE:2300:0:FFFF::5, Tunnel200, 06:24:19/never
C 3FFE:2300:0:FFFF::4/126 [0/0]
   via 3FFE:2300:0:FFFF::5, Tunnel200, 06:24:19/never
L 3FFE:2300:0:FFFF::9/128 [0/0]
   via 3FFE:2300:0:FFFF::9, Tunnel103, 06:24:19/never
C 3FFE:2300:0:FFFF::8/126 [0/0]
   via 3FFE:2300:0:FFFF::9, Tunnel103, 06:24:19/never
L 3FFE:2300:0:FFFF::D/128 [0/0]
   via 3FFE:2300:0:FFFF::D, Tunnel201, 06:24:19/never
C 3FFE:2300:0:FFFF::C/126 [0/0]
   via 3FFE:2300:0:FFFF::D, Tunnel201, 06:24:19/never
S 3FFE:2300:31::0/48 [1/0]
   via 0::0, Tunnel200, 06:24:19/never
S 3FFE:23FF::0/32 [1/0]
   via 0::0, Tunnel201, 06:24:19/never
L FE80::0/64 [0/0]
   via 0::0, Null0, 06:24:38/never
ciscotest>
```

show ipv6 tunnel

```
show ipv6 tunnel
```

This command displays, for each tunnel running IPv6, the tunnel unit number, the name of the dynamic routing protocol in use, the time of the last input, the number of input packets, and the description string.

Figure 13-5
Output of show IPv6
tunnel.

```
ciscotest>show ipv6 tunnel
Tun Route   LastInp   Packets Description
100   -     00:00:00    12356 tunnel BGP4+ --> ESNET
101   -     00:00:00     6992 tunnel BGP4+ --> IMAG
102   -     00:00:01     5841 tunnel BGP4+ --> SWITCH
103   -     03:55:00        9 tunnel BGP4+ --> JOIN
200   -     never           0 tunnel statico --> UNIBO
201   -     never           0 tunnel statico --> DEMOKRITOS
ciscotest>
```

show ipv6 neighbors

```
show ipv6 neighbors [<ipv6addr> | <interface>]
```

This command displays neighbor adjacency entries from the IPv6 *Neighbor Discovery* (ND) table (see Section 6.5). It includes the state of the adjacency entry, its lifetime, and the associated MAC and IPv6 addresses.

Figure 13-6
Output of show IPv6 neighbors.

```
ciscotest>show ipv6 neighbors
IPv6 Address                             Age MAC Address
      State Interface
3FFE:2300::2A0:24FF:FE99:DA7             24 00a0.2499.0da7 REACH
      FastEthernet0/0/0
FE80::2A0:24FF:FE99:DA7                  24 00a0.2499.0da7 REACH
      FastEthernet0/0/0
ciscotest>
```

show ipv6 interface

```
show ipv6 interface [<interface>]
```

This command displays IPv6 interface related parameters and addresses.

Figure 13-7
Output of show IPv6 interface.

```
ciscotest>  show ipv6 int FastEthernet0/0/0
FastEthernet0/0/0 is up, line protocol is up
  IPv6 is enabled, link-local address is
      FE80::2E0:14FF:FEC5:6B00
  Global unicast address(es):
    5F15:4100:839A:300:0:2E0:14C5:6B60, subnet is
     5F15:4100:839A:300::0/80
    3FFE:2300::2E0:14FF:FEC5:6B00, subnet is
     3FFE:2300::0/64
  Joined group address(es):
    FF02::1
    FF02::2
    FF02::1:FFC5:6B00
    FF02::1:FFC5:6B60
    FF02::1:14C5:6B60
    FF02::1:FEC5:6B00
  MTU is 1500 bytes
  ICMP error messages limited to one every 500 milliseconds
  ND advertised reachable time is 0 milliseconds
  ND advertised retransmit interval is 0 milliseconds
  ND router advertisements are sent every 200 seconds
  ND router advertisements live for 1800 seconds
  Hosts use stateless autoconfig for addresses.
ciscotest>
```

show ipv6 traffic

```
show ipv6 traffic
```

This command displays IPv6 related traffic statistics.

traceroute ipv6

```
traceroute ipv6 <destination>
```

This command traces the route for IPv6 packets between the node where the command is entered and the destination address.

ping ipv6

```
ping ipv6 <destination>
```

This command sends ICMPv6 echo request packets (see Sections 5.6.1 and 5.6.2) to `<destination>`, i.e., to an IPv6 host name or address.

ipv6 unicast-routing

```
ipv6 unicast-routing
```

This command enables the routing of IPv6 unicast packets. The default setting is disabled.

interface tunnel

```
interface tunnel
```

Tunneling provides a way to encapsulate arbitrary packets inside another protocol (see Section 12.2). It is implemented as a virtual interface to provide a simple configuration.

In the preceding example it is used to create an IPv6 tunnel over IPv4. The IPv4 end-points are specified with the commands:

■ tunnel source `<interface>`

■ tunnel destination `<IPv4 address>`

Because tunnels are point-to-point links, a separate tunnel is configured for each link.

The command `no ip address` specifies that there is no IPv4 address associated to this tunnel, while the command `ipv6 address <IPv6 address>` assigns an IPv6 address to the tunnel interface. Finally, the command `tunnel mode ipv6ip` configures a *static* tunnel interface (a "configured tunnel" according to RFC 1933 [1]). This interface can be used like any other interface (static routes can point to it or a dynamic routing protocol can run over it).

ipv6 address

```
[no] ipv6 address <ipv6addr>[/<prefix-length>]
```

This command enables IPv6 and configures an IPv6 address on the interface. Optionally, a prefix length may be specified. In this case the router will autoconfigure the remaining bits.

ipv6 address ... eui-64

```
[no] ipv6 address <ipv6prefix>/<prefix-length> eui-64
```

This command is used to enable IPv6 and to autoconfigure an IPv6 address on an interface using the EUI-64 style "Interface ID" (see section 4.10). If the `<prefix-length>` specified is greater than 64, the prefix bits will have precedence over the EUI-64 ID.

ipv6 unnumbered

```
[no] ipv6 unnumbered <interface>
```

It is also possible to enable and to configure an interface without requiring a global IPv6 address. The `<interface>` parameter must specify the name of an interface that does have a global IPv6 address. This command is used to reduce address administration for a network administrator.

ipv6 route

```
[no] ipv6 route <prefix> {<next-hop> | <interface>} [<dis-
    tance>]
```

This command configures a static IPv6 route. **<prefix>** specifies the IPv6 prefix for which the route is created. **<next-hop>** is the host name or IPv6 address of the next-hop to reach the destination prefix. **<inter-face>** can be used in place of **<next-hop>** for point-to-point interfaces like serial links or tunnels. The default value for **<distance>** is 1, which gives static routes precedence over any other type of route with the exception of directly connected routes.

ipv6 mtu

```
[no] ipv6 mtu <bytes>
```

This command configures the *Maximum Transmission Unit* (MTU) for IPv6 packets on an interface. The default value is the link MTU. If a non-default value is configured, an MTU option will be included in Router Advertisements (see Section 5.6.5).

ipv6 hop-limit

```
ipv6 hop-limit <value>
```

This command configures the router to use **<value>** as the IPv6 Hop Limit value used in Router Advertisements (see Section 5.6.5) and in all IPv6 packets generated within the router. The default value is 255.

ipv6 auto-tunnel

```
[no] ipv6 auto-tunnel
```

This command configures IPv6 in IPv4 automatic tunneling (see RFC 1933 [1]). Automatic tunneling is performed when a destination address in an IPv6 packet contains an IPv4 compatible IPv6 address (see section 4.7.8).

RIP Protocol

The Cisco implementation of IPv6 supports RIPv6 (see section 7.5.1). RIP routing is started whenever RIP is enabled on at least one interface. It is also possible to redistribute static routes over RIP.

BGP4+

During the standardization process of IPv6, it was decided to adopt IDRPv2 as Exterior Routing Protocol (see Section 7.5.2). This new protocol, derived from OSI, has been implemented by some companies, but it does not seem to gain acceptance among users. Cisco's decision to implement a generalized BGP rather than IDRP was based upon the fact that the Service Provider community preferred to leverage a time-proven/deployed protocol with integrated support for IPv4 and IPv6 rather than run another protocol in the ships-in-the-night mode. This was a very realistic, pragmatic approach to deployment which Cisco wholly endorsed with the support of BGP4+ or more formally "Multiprotocol Extensions for BGP-4" [2]. BGP4+ defines extensions to BGP-4 to enable it to carry routing information for multiple Network Layer protocols (e.g., IPv6, IPX, etc...). The extensions are backward compatible—a router that supports the extensions can interoperate with a router that doesn't support the extensions.

To configure BGP4+ it is therefore necessary first to configure and start the IPv4 BGP with the classical command:

```
router bgp <as-number>
```

The definition of IPv6 neighbors and parameters is however done in a different section of the configuration file. The principal commands used are described in the following sections.

ipv6 bgp redistribute connected

```
[no] ipv6 bgp redistribute connected
```

This command configures the redistribution of routing information learned on directly connected networks into bgp.

ipv6 bgp redistribute static

`[no] ipv6 bgp redistribute static`

This command configures the redistribution of static routes into bgp.

ipv6 bgp redistribute rip

`[no] ipv6 bgp redistribute rip`

This command configures the redistribution of routes learned via rip process into bgp.

ipv6 bgp neighbor

```
ipv6 bgp neighbor <IPv6 address> remote-as <as-num>
no ipv6 bgp neighbor remote-as
```

This command defines a BGP neighbor. External neighbors must be directly connected. Neighbors must be specified by global addresses.

ipv6 bgp network

`[no] ipv6 bgp network <prefix>`

This command originates a BGP route for each route found on the IPv6 routing table that matches with the given prefix.

NAT

Chapter 12 presents the migration from IPv4 to IPv6 and explains that NAT between IPv4 and IPv6 is not a mandatory feature according to IETF.

Cisco decided to provide the NAT feature related to both protocols and address translation between IPv6 and IPv4 in IOS from the beginning. This is an important value-added feature that will greatly simplify the introduction of IPv6 in Enterprise Networks.

NAT devices would enable the interconnection of hosts that have IPv6-only addresses (hosts that do not have IPv4-compatible addresses) with hosts that have IPv4-only addresses. If assigning globally unique IPv4 addresses would become impossible (due to the exhaustion of the IPv4 address space) before a sufficient number of the Internet hosts would transition to IPv6, then NAT devices would allow continuing (and completing) the transition, even in the absence of the globally unique IPv4 addresses.

Cisco IPv6 NAT is designed to allow an IPv6 network to access and be accessed by the IPv4 Internet.

CONCLUSIONS

With the design decision made in the implementation of IPv6, Cisco confirms to be the leading company in IP routing. The Internet is today mostly powered by Cisco routers and so are many Intranets. The Cisco implementation of IPv6 will greatly simplify the migration phase from IPv4 to IPv6 and the unavoidable coexistence of IPv4 and IPv6 nodes. From the end of 1998 IPv6 will be a standard feature of Cisco's strategic IOS-based routing and switching platforms.

REFERENCES

[1] P. Francis, K. Egevang, *The IP Network Address Translator (NAT)*, RFC 1631, May 1994.

[2] Y. Rekhter, B. Moskowitz, D. Karrenbergde, G. Groot, E. Lear, *Address Allocation for Private Internets*, RFC 1918, February 1996.

[3] R. Gilligan, E. Nordmar, *RFC 1933: Transition Mechanisms for IPv6 Hosts and Routers*, April 1996.

[4] T. Bates, R. Chandra, D. Katz, Y. Rekhter, *Multiprotocol Extensions for BGP-4*, <draft-bates-bgp4-multiprotocol-03.txt>, July 1997.

Appendix A

Excerpts from RFCs

A.1   Routing Header Pseudo Code

This section contains the pseudo code for the processing of the Routing header, excerpted from the RFC 1883.[1] See also Section 3.2.5.

```
if Segments Left = 0 {
    proceed to process the next header in the packet, whose
    type is identified by the Next Header field in the
    Routing header
}
else if Hdr Ext Len is odd or greater than 46 {
        send an ICMP Parameter Problem, Code 0, message to
        the Source Address, pointing to the Hdr Ext Len
        field, and discard the packet
}
else {
    compute n, the number of addresses in the Routing
    header, by dividing Hdr Ext Len by 2

    if Segments Left is greater than n {
        send an ICMP Parameter Problem, Code 0, message to
        the Source Address, pointing to the Segments Left
        field, and discard the packet
    }
    else {
        decrement Segments Left by 1;
        compute i, the index of the next address to be
        visited in the address vector, by subtracting
        Segments Left from n

        if Address [i] or the IPv6 Destination Address is
        multicast {
            discard the packet
        }
        else {
            swap the IPv6 Destination Address and Address[i]

            if bit i of the Strict/Loose Bit map has value 1
            and the new Destination Address is not the
            address of a neighbor of this node {
                send an ICMP Destination Unreachable - Not a
                Neighbor message to the Source Address and
                discard the packet
            }
```

```
else if the IPv6 Hop Limit is less than or equal
to 1 { send an ICMP Time Exceeded - Hop Limit
Exceeded in Transit message to the Source Address
and discard the packet
}
else {
    decrement the Hop Limit by 1

    resubmit the packet to the IPv6 module for
    transmission to the new destination
}
      }
   }
}
```

A.2   Example of Routing Header Processing

This section contains an example of the application of the algorithm reported in Appendix A.1, excerpted from the RFC 1883. [1] Let's consider the case of a node S that transmits to a node D by using a Routing header that forces the packet being routed through intermediate nodes I1, I2, and I3. The following are significant values assumed by the IPv6 header and by the Routing header fields while the packet propagates:

As the packet travels from S to I1:

```
Source Address = S                Hdr Ext Len = 6
Destination Address = I1          Segments Left = 3
                                     Address[1] = I2
(if bit 0 of the Bit Map is 1,       Address[2] = I3
 S and I1 must be neighbors;         Address[3] = D
 this is checked by S)
```

As the packet travels from I1 to I2:

```
Source Address = S                Hdr Ext Len = 6
Destination Address = I2          Segments Left = 2
                                     Address[1] = I1
(if bit 1 of the Bit Map is 1,       Address[2] = I3
 I1 and I2 must be neighbors;        Address[3] = D
 this is checked by I1)
```

As the packet travels from I2 to I3:

```
Source Address = S                    Hdr Ext Len = 6
Destination Address = I3         Segments Left = 1
                                           Address[1] = I1
(if bit 2 of the Bit Map is 1,   Address[2] = I2
 I2 and I3 must be neighbors;     Address[3] = D
 this is checked by I2)
```

As the packet travels from I3 to D:

```
Source Address = S                    Hdr Ext Len = 6
Destination Address = D          Segments Left = 0
                                           Address[1] = I1
(if bit 3 of the Bit Map is 1,   Address[2] = I2
 I3 and D must be neighbors;     Address[3] = I3
 this is checked by I3)
```

A.3   Processing of ICMPv6 Packets

This section contains a description of the processing of ICMPv6 packets, excerpted from the RFC 1885. [2] See also Section 5.3.

Implementations MUST observe the following rules when processing ICMPv6 messages (from [3]):

a   If an ICMPv6 error message of unknown type is received, it MUST be passed to the upper layer.

b   If an ICMPv6 informational message of unknown type is received, it MUST be silently discarded.

c   Every ICMPv6 error message (type < 128) includes as much of the IPv6 offending (invoking) packet (the packet that caused the error) as will fit without making the error message packet exceed 576 octets.

d   In those cases where the internet-layer protocol is required to pass an ICMPv6 error message to the upper-layer protocol, the upper-layer protocol type is extracted from the original packet (contained in the body of the ICMPv6 error message) and used to select the appropriate upper-layer protocol entity to handle the error.

If the original packet had an unusually large amount of extension headers, it is possible that the upper-layer protocol type may not be present in the ICMPv6 message, due to truncation of the original packet to meet the 576-octet limit. In that case, the error message is silently dropped after any IPv6-layer processing.

e   An ICMPv6 error message MUST NOT be sent as a result of receiving:

1   an ICMPv6 error message, or

2   a packet destined to an IPv6 multicast address (there are two exceptions to this rule: (1) the Packet Too Big Message—Section 3.2 —to allow Path MTU discovery to work for IPv6 multicast, and (2) the Parameter Problem Message, Code 2—Section 3.4—reporting an unrecognized IPv6 option that has the Option Type highest-order two bits set to 10), or

3   a packet sent as a link-layer multicast, (the exception from e.2 applies to this case too), or

4   a packet sent as a link-layer broadcast, (the exception from e.2 applies to this case too), or

5   a packet whose source address does not uniquely identify a single node—e.g., the IPv6 Unspecified Address, an IPv6 multicast address, or an address known by the ICMP message sender to be an IPv6 anycast address.

f   Finally, to each sender of an erroneous data packet, an IPv6 node MUST limit the rate of ICMPv6 error messages sent, in order to limit the bandwidth and forwarding costs incurred by the error messages when a generator of erroneous packets does not respond to those error messages by ceasing its transmissions.

There are a variety of ways of implementing the rate-limiting function, for example:

1   Timer-based—for example, limiting the rate of transmission of error messages to a given source, or to any source, to at most once every T milliseconds.

2   Bandwidth-based—for example, limiting the rate at which error messages are sent from a particular interface to some fraction F of the attached link's bandwidth.

The limit parameters (e.g., T or F in the above examples) MUST be configurable for the node, with a conservative default value (e.g., T = 1 second, NOT 0 seconds, or F = 2 percent, NOT 100 percent).

A.4   Addresses to Be Used During the Testing Phase

Addresses to be used during IPv6 tests and in particular in 6bone (see also Chapter 12 and Appendix C, Section C.6) are described in the RFC 1887 [4] of which this appendix contains the most significant part.

The address format for the IPv6 test address is consistent with the provider-based unicast address allocation which is as follows:

```
| 3 |   5 bits   |  16 bits | 8 |   24 bits   | 8 |     64 bits     |
+---+-----------+----------+---+-------------+---+-----------------+
|010|RegistryID|ProviderID|RES|SubscriberID|RES|Intra-Subscriber|
+---+-----------+----------+---+-------------+---+-----------------+
```

The specific allocation of each field of the test address format is as follows:

```
| 3 |   5 bits   |  16 bits | 8 |   24 bits   | 8 | 16 bits|48 bits|
+---+-----------+----------+---+-------------+---+--------+-------+
|   |           |Autonomous|   |    IPv4     |   | Subnet | Intf. |
|010|   11111   | System   |RES|  Network    |RES|        |       |
|   |           | Number   |   |  Address    |   | Address|  ID   |
+---+-----------+----------+---+-------------+---+--------+-------+
```

where:

010   This is the Format Prefix used to identify provider-based unicast addresses.

11111   This is a Registry ID reserved by the IANA. The initial use of addresses in this Registry ID for IPv6 testing is temporary. All users of these addresses will be required to renumber at some time in the future.

Autonomous System Number   This is the current autonomous system number assigned to the provider providing internet service to an IPv6 testers organization. For example for IPv6 testers receiving internet service from BBN Barrnet would use autonomous system number 189. This would be coded in the autonomous system field of the address as follows:

0000 0000 1011 1101 (binary)

The values for the autonomous system number of an organization's provider can be obtained from that provider, or can be looked up in the "whois" database maintained by the internic.net.

RES   This field is reserved and must be set to zero.

IPv4 Network Address   This is based on the current IPv4 routable address for the subscriber which the interface is connected. It is formed by taking the high order 24 bits of the IPv4 address. For example for an IPv4 address (in IPv4 syntax):

IPv4 Address
 39.11.22.1

the value to put in this field of IPv6 address is:

IPv4 Format	Hex
39.11.22	270B16

This technique for generating values for this field only works for subscribers which have IPv4 subscriber prefixes less than equal to 24 bits long. There may be subscribers using IPv4 addresses with longer subscriber prefixes, but this conflict is expected to be very rare. Subscribers with subscriber prefixes larger than 24 bits should use the remaining bits in the IPv4 prefix as the high order bits in the Subnet Address field.

Subnet Address   The Subnet ID identifies a specific physical link on which the interface is located. There can be multiple subnets on the same physical link. A specific subnet can not span multiple physical links. The assignment of values for this field is left to an individual subscriber. One possible algorithm to generate values for this field is to use the bits in the IPv4 address which identify the IPv4 subnet.

Interface ID   This is the unique identifier of the interface on the link, usually the 48-bit IEEE 802 MAC address of the interface if available.

The following registration form to 6bone contains an example of the application of the techniques described previously:

```
site:              Politecnico di Torino
location:          Torino, ITALY
loc-string:        45 03 52.2n 07 39 43.2e 250m
prefix:            5f15:5000::/32
ping:              5f15:5000:82c0:0e00:bd:800:2bb5:a7a8
tunnel:            130.192.26.254 204.123.2.236 DIGITAL-CA
tunnel:            130.192.26.254 131.175.5.37   CEFRIEL
tunnel:            130.192.26.254 156.148.3.24   CRS4
tunnel:            130.192.26.254 163.162.17.77 CSELT
contact:           silvano.gai@polito.it
status:            operational since 11/1996
remark:            OpenBSD/NRL, DEC RouteAbout Access EW/IPv6
remark:            locally using Bind 4.9.3
changed:           rivetti@csp.it, spera@csp.it 19961220
source:            RIPE
```

The address **5f15:5000:82c0:0e00:bd:800:2bb5:a7a8** is coded following the rules of RFC 1887 [4] and the result is as follows:

- 5f ♦ FP = 010, Registry ID = 11111;

- 1550 ♦ AS = 5456;

- 00 ♦ Reserved;

- 82c00e ♦ IPv4 Network Address = 130.192.15;

- 00 ♦ Reserved;

- bd ♦ Subnet Address = 189;

- 800:2bb5:a7a8® MAC Address.

A.5   MTU of a Tunnel and Fragmentation

Tunnels are widely used during the migration from IPv4 to IPv6 (see Chapter 12). This section contains the algorithm to transmit an IPv6 packet over a tunnel, when the packet is longer than the tunnel's MTU. This algorithm is described in the RFC 1933 [5].

The encapsulating node can employ the following algorithm to determine when to forward an IPv6 packet that is larger than the tunnel's path MTU using IPv4 fragmentation, and when to return an IPv6 ICMP "packet too big" message:

```
if (IPv4 path MTU - 20) is less than or equal to 576
        if packet is larger than 576 bytes
                Send IPv6 ICMP "packet too big" with
                MTU = 576.
                Drop packet.
        else
                Encapsulate but do not set the Don't
                Fragment flag in the IPv4 header. The
                resulting IPv4 packet might be fragmented
                by the IPv4 layer on the encapsulating
                node or by some router along the
                IPv4 path.
        endif
else
        if packet is larger than (IPv4 path MTU - 20)
                Send IPv6 ICMP "packet too big" with
                MTU = (IPv4 path MTU - 20).
                Drop packet.
        else
                Encapsulate and set the Don't Fragment
                flag in the IPv4 header.
        endif
endif
```

Encapsulating nodes that have a large number of tunnels might not be able to store the IPv4 Path MTU for all tunnels. Such nodes can, at the expense of additional fragmentation in the network, avoid using the IPv4 Path MTU algorithm across the tunnel and instead use the MTU of the link layer (under IPv4) in the above algorithm instead of the IPv4 path MTU.

In this case the Don't Fragment bit must not be set in the encapsulating IPv4 header.

A.6   Transmission of IP Packets

During the migration from IPv4 to IPv6 many nodes will adopt the dual-stack approach (see Chapter 12). When an application requests the dual-stack to transmit a packet, determining whether to transmit an IPv4 packet or an IPv6 packet and whether to use tunnels is necessary. A possible algorithm to make these decisions is described in the RFC 1933[5] and reported in the following.

> This section presents a combined IPv4 and IPv6 sending algorithm that IPv6/IPv4 nodes can use. The algorithm can be used to determine when to send IPv4 packets, when to send IPv6 packets, and when to perform automatic and configured tunneling. It illustrates how the techniques of dual IP layer, configured tunneling, and automatic tunneling can be used together. Note this is just an example to show how the techniques can be combined; IPv6/IPv6 implementations may provide different algorithms. This algorithm has the following properties:

- Sends IPv4 packets to all IPv4 destinations.

- Sends IPv6 packets to all IPv6 destinations on the same link.

- Using automatic tunneling, sends IPv6 packets encapsulated in IPv4 to IPv6 destinations with IPv4-compatible addresses that are located off-link.

- Sends IPv6 packets to IPv6 destinations located off-link when IPv6 routers are present.

- Using the default IPv6 tunnel, sends IPv6 packets encapsulated in IPv4 to IPv6 destinations with IPv6-only addresses when no IPv6 routers are present.

> The algorithm is as follows:
> 1 If the address of the end node is an IPv4 address then:
>   1.1 If the destination is located on an attached link, then send an IPv4 packet addressed to the end node.
>   1.2 If the destination is located off-link, then;
>   1.2.1 If there is an IPv4 router on link, then send an IPv4 format packet. The IPv4 destination address is the IPv4 address of the end node. The datalink address is the data-link address of the IPv4 router.

1.2.2 Else, the destination is treated as "unreachable" because it is located off link and there are no on-link routers.

2 If the address of the end node is an IPv4-compatible Pv6 address (i.e. bears the prefix 0:0:0:0:0:0), then:

2.1 If the destination is located on an attached link, then send an IPv6 format packet (not encapsulated). The IPv6 destination address is the IPv6 address of the end node. The datalink address is the datalink address of the end node.

2.2 If the destination is located off-link, then:

2.2.1 If there is an IPv4 router on an attached link, then send an IPv6 packet encapsulated in IPv4. The IPv6 destination address is the address of the end node. The IPv4 destination address is the low-order 32-bits of the end node's address. The datalink address is the datalink address of the IPv4 router.

2.2.2 Else, if there is an IPv6 router on an attached link, then send an IPv6 format packet. The IPv6 destination address is the IPv6 address of the end node. The datalink address is the datalink address of the IPv6 router.

2.2.3 Else, the destination is treated as "unreachable" because it is located off-link and there are no on-link routers.

3 If the address of the end node is an IPv6-only address, then:

3.1 If the destination is located on an attached link, then send an IPv6 format packet. The IPv6 destination address is the IPv6 address of the end node. The datalink address is the datalink address of the end node.

3.2 If the destination is located off-link, then:

3.2.1 If there is an IPv6 router on an attached link, then send an IPv6 format packet. The IPv6 destination address is the IPv6 address of the end node. The datalink address is the datalink address of the Ipv6 router.

3.2.2 Else, if the destination is reachable via a configured tunnel, and there is an IPv4 router on an attached link, then send an IPv6 packet encapsulated in IPv4. The Ipv6 destination address is the address of the end node. The IPv4 destination address is the configured IPv4 address of the tunnel endpoint. The datalink address is the data-link address of the IPv4 router.

3.2.3 Else, the destination is treated as "unreachable" because it is located off-link and there are no on-link IPv6 routers.

A summary of these sending rules are given in the table below:

End Node Address Type	End Node On Link?	IPv4 Router On Link?	IPv6 Router On Link?	Packet Format To Send	IPv6 Dest Addr	IPv4 Dest Addr	DLink Dest Addr
IPv4	Yes	N/A	N/A	IPv4	N/A	E4	EL
IPv4	No	Yes	N/A	IPv4	N/A	E4	RL
IPv4	No	No	N/A	UNRCH	N/A	N/A	N/A
IPv4-compat	Yes	N/A	N/A	IPv6	E6	N/A	EL
IPv4-compat	No	Yes	N/A	IPv6/4	E6	E4	RL
IPv4-compat	No	No	Yes	IPv6	E6	N/A	RL
IPv4-compat	No	No	No	UNRCH	N/A	N/A	N/A
IPv6-only	Yes	N/A	N/A	IPv6	E6	N/A	EL
IPv6-only	No	N/A	Yes	IPv6	E6	N/A	RL
IPv6-only	No	Yes	No	IPv6/4	E6	T4	RL
IPv6-only	No	No	No	UNRCH	N/A	N/A	N/A

Key to Abbreviations

N/A:	Not applicable or does not matter.
E6:	IPv6 address of end node.
E4:	IPv4 address of end node (low-order 32-bits of IPv4-compatible address).
EL:	Datalink address of end node.
T4:	IPv4 address of the tunnel endpoint.
R6:	IPv6 address of router.
R4:	IPv4 address of router.
RL:	Datalink address of router.
Ipv4:	IPv4 packet format.
Ipv6:	IPv6 packet format.
Ipv6/4:	IPv6 encapsulated in IPv4 packet format.
UNRCH:	Destination is unreachable. Don't send a packet.

References

[1] S.E. Deering, R. Hinden, *RFC 1883: Internet Protocol, Version 6 (IPv6) Specification,* December 1995.

[2] A. Conta, S. Deering, *RFC 1885: Internet Control Message Protocol (ICMPv6),* December 1995.

[3] S.E. Deering, *RFC 1112: Host extensions for IP multicasting,* August 1989.

[4] Y. Rekhter, T. Li, *RFC 1887: An Architecture for IPv6 Unicast Address Allocation,* December 1995.

[5] R. Gilligan, E. Nordmar, *RFC 1933: Transition Mechanisms for IPv6 Hosts and Routers,* April 1996.

Appendix B

Analysis of IPv6 Packets

B.1 · Introduction

This appendix presents some IPv6 packets captured on the 6bone network of Politecnico di Torino (see Section 12.3.1) by the protocol analyzer Radcom RC-100 WL[1]. For each packet, first its hexadecimal format is shown, and then its decoding is shown.

Packets have been captured on an IEEE 802.3 network, and they have an Ethernet v.2.0 encapsulation, according to the description in Section 2.9. In particular, the encapsulation used is shown in Figure 2-6a.

The hexadecimal format consists of a certain number of lines containing 16 couples of hexadecimal digits. Each couple of digits represents an octet; therefore, a line represents 128 bits. The last line typically contains a number of couples lower than 16 to take into account the real length of the IPv6 packet. The hexadecimal format ends with the IPv6 PDU; the Ethernet FCS is not shown.

B.2 Example of Decoding

Figure B-1 shows an example of decoding of the hexadecimal format.

The Ethernet header must be decoded with reference to Figure 6-2a and begins with source and destination addresses both on 6 octets, followed by the Protocol Type field on 2 octets that contain the value 86DD (hexadecimal). This value indicates that an IPv6 header follows, which must be decoded with reference to Figure 3-1. In the IPv6 header, the second word and the destination IPv6 address are highlighted in gray.

---

[1]The protocol analyzer RC-100 WL is manufactured by RADCOM Ltd. (Israel). See `http://www.radcom-inc.com/` or send e-mail to: **info@radcom.co.il**. The author thanks this company for its collaboration.

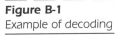

Figure B-1
Example of decoding

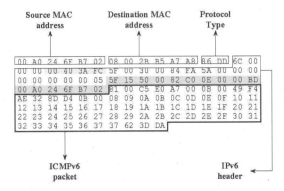

In the second part, we find the value 3A (hexadecimal) in the third octet—that is, 58 (decimal)—that indicates that the Next Header is ICMPv6.

The destination IPv6 address is followed by the ICMPv6 packet, which must be decoded with reference to Figure 5-1. It presents a Type = 81 (hexadecimal)—that is, 129 (decimal)—that classifies it like an Echo Reply packet, that is, as a reply to the ping.

Figure B-2 shows the complete decoding of the packet made by the analyzer Radcom RC-100 WL.

Figure B-2
Complete decoding
of the packet

```
Captured at:    50.227925
Length: 122     Status: Ok
Ethernet: Destination Address 00A0246FB702   <00A0246FB702>
Ethernet:    Individual Address
Ethernet:    Universal Address
Ethernet: Source Address DecNetB5A7A8   <08002BB5A7A8>
Ethernet:    Individual Address
Ethernet:    Universal Address
Ethernet: Ethernet V.2, Type IPv6   <86DD>
IPv6: Version: 6                  <6C>
IPv6: Priority: 12
IPv6: Flow Label: 0x000000 (Packet Do Not Belong To a Flow Carry)  <000000>
Pv6: Payload Length: 64           <0040>
IPv6: Next Header: 58 Internet Control Message Protocol  <3A>
IPv6: Hop Limit: 252              <FC>
IPv6: Source Address:  5F00:3000:84FA:5A00::5
IPv6: Destination Address: 5F15:5000:82C0:E00:BD:A0:246F:B702
ICMPv6: Type: 129 Echo Reply (IPv6 Ping Message)   <81>
ICMPv6: Code: 0                   <00>


ICMPv6: Checksum: 0xC5E0          <C5E0>
ICMPv6: Identifier: 42752         <A700>
ICMPv6: Sequence Number: 2816     <0B00>
User Data
OFFST DATA                                            ASCII
003E: 49 F4 AE 32 8D D4 0B 00 08 09 0A 0B 0C 0D 0E 0F  I..2...........
004E: 10 11 12 13 14 15 16 17 18 19 1A 1B 1C 1D 1E 1F  ................
005E: 20 21 22 23 24 25 26 27 28 29 2A 2B 2C 2D 2E 2F  !"#$%&'()*+,-./
006E: 30 31 32 33 34 35 36 37                          01234567
Frame Tail
OFFST DATA                                            ASCII
0076: 37 62 3D DA                                       7b=.
```

B.3 TCP Packet

This section shows an IPv6 packet containing a TCP packet. To better understand the decoding, please refer to Section 3.1. (See Figures B-3 and B-4.)

Figure B-3
TCP packet in hexadecimal

```
Captured at:    08.116772
Length: 261     From: Network       Status: Ok
OFFST DATA                                              ASCII
0000: 00 A0 24 6F B6 A3 00 A0 24 6F B7 02 86 DD 60 00   ..$o....$o....`.
0010: 00 00 00 CB 06 40 5F 15 50 00 82 C0 0E 00 00 BD   .....@_.P.......
0020: 00 A0 24 6F B7 02 5F 15 50 00 82 C0 0E 00 00 BD   ..$o.._.P.......
0030: 00 A0 24 6F B6 A3 23 3F 04 06 63 A9 BC 4A 1E 41   ..$o..#?..c..J.A
0040: B0 80 80 18 43 80 74 8A 00 00 01 01 08 0A 00 0A   ....C.t.........
0050: 96 D9 00 00 14 D5 4C 61 73 74 20 6C 6F 67 69 6E   ......Last login
0060: 3A 20 54 75 65 20 4A 61 6E 20 20 37 20 31 37 3A   :  Tue Jan  7 17:
0070: 30 33 3A 34 36 20 66 72 6F 6D 20 61 6C 69 63 65   03:46  from alice
0080: 2D 76 36 2E 69 70 76 36 0D 0A 57 61 72 6E 69 6E   -v6.ipv6..Warnin
0090: 67 3A 20 6E 6F 20 4B 65 72 62 65 72 6F 73 20 74   g: no Kerberos t
00A0: 69 63 6B 65 74 73 20 69 73 73 75 65 64 2E 0D 0A   ickets issued...
00B0: 4F 70 65 6E 42 53 44 20 31 2E 32 20 28 49 50 4E   OpenBSD 1.2 (IPN
00C0: 47 4B 45 52 29 20 23 31 3A 20 46 72 69 20 4E 6F   GKER) #1: Fri No
00D0: 76 20 31 35 20 30 38 3A 30 33 3A 34 32 20 50 53   v 15 08:03:42 PS
00E0: 54 20 31 39 39 36 0D 0A 0D 0A 57 65 6C 63 6F 6D   T 1996....Welcom
00F0: 65 20 74 6F 20 4F 70 65 6E 42 53 44 2E 0D 0A 0D   e to OpenBSD....
0100: 0A A3 5F 44 A9                                     .._D.
```

Figure B-4
Decoded TCP packet

```
Captured at:    08.116772
Length: 261     Status: Ok
Ethernet: Destination Address 00A0246FB6A3   <00A0246FB6A3>
Ethernet:    Individual Address
Ethernet:    Universal Address
Ethernet: Source Address 00A0246FB702   <00A0246FB702>
Ethernet:    Individual Address


Ethernet:    Universal Address
Ethernet: Ethernet V.2, Type IPv6   <86DD>
IPv6: Version: 6                     <60>
IPv6: Priority: 0 Uncharacterized Traffic
IPv6: Flow Label: 0x000000 (Packet Do Not Belong To a Flow  Carry)
<000000>
IPv6: Payload Length: 203            <00CB>
IPv6: Next Header: 6 Transmission Control Protocol    <06>
IPv6: Hop Limit: 64                  <40>
IPv6: Source Address:   5F15:5000:82C0:E00:BD:A0:246F:B702
IPv6: Destination Address: 5F15:5000:82C0:E00:BD:A0:246F:B6A3
TCP: Source Port = 9023              <233F>
TCP: Destination Port = 1030         <0406>
TCP: Sequence Number = 1672068170   <63A9BC4A>
TCP: Acknowledgement Number = 507621504   <1E41B080>
TCP: HLEN = 32 [Bytes]               <80>
TCP: Flags: 0x18    ACK  PSH             <18>
```

Figure B-4
Continued

```
TCP: Window = 17280                      <4380>
TCP: CheckSum = 0x748A                   <748A>
TCP: Option = 1 [No Operation]           <01>
TCP: Option = 1 [No Operation]           <01>
TCP: Option = 8
TCP: Padding = 100101502170020213   <0A000A96D9000014D5>
User Data
OFFST DATA                                          ASCII
0056: 4C 61 73 74 20 6C 6F 67 69 6E 3A 20 54 75 65 20   Last  login: Tue
0066: 4A 61 6E 20 20 37 20 31 37 3A 30 33 3A 34 36 20   Jan   7 17:03:46
0076: 66 72 6F 6D 20 61 6C 69 63 65 2D 76 36 2E 69 70   from alice-v6.ip
0086: 76 36 0D 0A 57 61 72 6E 69 6E 67 3A 20 6E 6F 20   v6..Warning: no
0096: 4B 65 72 62 65 72 6F 73 20 74 69 63 6B 65 74 73   Kerberos tickets
00A6: 20 69 73 73 75 65 64 2E 0D 0A 4F 70 65 6E 42 53   issued...OpenBS
00B6: 44 20 31 2E 32 20 28 49 50 4E 47 4B 45 52 29 20   D 1.2 (IPNGKER)
00C6: 23 31 3A 20 46 72 69 20 4E 6F 76 20 31 35 20 30   #1:  Fri Nov 15 0
00D6: 38 3A 30 33 3A 34 32 20 50 53 54 20 31 39 39 36   8:03:42 PST 1996
00E6: 0D 0A 0D 0A 57 65 6C 63 6F 6D 65 20 74 6F 20 4F   ....Welcome to O
00F6: 70 65 6E 42 53 44 2E 0D 0A 0D 0A                  penBSD.....
Frame Tail
OFFST DATA                                          ASCII
0101: A3 5F 44 A9                                         ._D.
```

B.4   UDP Packet

This section shows an IPv6 packet containing an UDP packet. To better understand the decoding, please refer to Section 3.1. (See Figures B-5 and B-6.)

Figure B-5
UDP packet in
hexadecimal

```
Captured at:    50.024340
Length: 90     Status: Ok
OFFST DATA                                          ASCII
0000: 33 33 00 00 00 09 08 00 2B B5 A7 A8 86 DD 67 00   33......+.....g.
0010: 00 00 00 20 11 FF FE 80 00 00 00 00 00 00 00 00   ... ...........
0020: 08 00 2B B5 A7 A8 FF 02 00 00 00 00 00 00 00 00   ..+............
0030: 00 00 00 00 00 09 02 09 02 09 00 20 21 A1 01 01   .......... !...
0040: 00 00 00 00 00 00 00 00 00 00 00 00 00 00 00 00   ...............
0050: 00 00 00 00 00 10 F2 9B F3 73                     .........s
```

Figure B-6
Decoded UDP packet

```
Captured at:    50.024340
Length: 90     Status: Ok
Ethernet: Destination Address 333300000009   <333300000009>
Ethernet:    Multicast Address
Ethernet:    Local Address
Ethernet: Source Address DecNetB5A7A8   <08002BB5A7A8>
Ethernet:    Individual Address
Ethernet:    Universal Address
```

Figure B-6
Continued

```
Ethernet: Ethernet V.2, Type IPv6    <86DD>
IPv6: Version: 6                     <67>
IPv6: Priority: 7 Internet Control Traffic
IPv6: Flow Label: 0x000000 (Packet Do Not Belong To a Flow  Carry)
<000000>
IPv6: Payload Length: 32             <0020>
IPv6: Next Header: 17 User Datagram Protocol   <11>
IPv6: Hop Limit: 255                 <FF>
IPv6: Source Address:  FE80::800:2BB5:A7A8
IPv6: Destination Address:  FF02::9
UDP: Source Port = RIPng             <0209>
UDP: Destination Port = RIPng    <0209>
UDP: Length = 32                     <0020>
UDP: CheckSum = 0x21A1               <21A1>
RIPng: Command:1 Request             <01>
RIPng: Version No.:1                 <01>
RIPng: Must Be Zero:0x0000           <0000>
RIPng:  Entry No. :1
RIPng:    IPv6 Prefix:0x00000000000000000000000000000000  [Default Route]
        <00000000000000000000000000000000>
RIPng:    Route Tag:0x0000           <0000>
RIPng:    Prefix Length:0            <00>
RIPng:    Metric:16                  <10>
Frame Tail
OFFST DATA                                       ASCII
0056: F2 9B F3 73                                   ...s
```

B.5   Router Solicitation Packet

This section shows an IPv6 packet containing a Router Solicitation ICMP packet. To better understand the decoding, please refer to Section 5.5.4. (See Figures B-7 and B-8.)

Figure B-7
Router Solicitation
in hexadecimal

```
Captured at:    15.017728
Length: 66      Status: Ok
OFFST DATA                                       ASCII
0000: 33 33 00 00 00 02 00 A0 24 6F B7 02 86 DD 6F 00  33......$o....o.
0010: 00 00 00 08 3A FF FE 80 00 00 00 00 00 00 00 00  ....:...........
0020: 00 A0 24 6F B7 02 FF 02 00 00 00 00 00 00 00 00  ..$o............
0030: 00 00 00 00 00 02 85 00 A1 25 00 00 00 00 3D BE  .........%....=.
0040: 4C 0B                                            L.
```

B.6   Router Advertisement Packet

This section shows an IPv6 packet containing a Router Advertisement
ICMP packet. To better understand the decoding, please refer to Section
5.5.5. (See Figures B-9 and B-10.)

Figure B-8
Decoded Router
Solicitation

```
Captured at:    15.017728
Length: 66     Status: Ok
Ethernet: Destination Address 333300000002   <333300000002>
Ethernet:    Multicast Address
Ethernet:    Local Address
Ethernet: Source Address 00A0246FB702   <00A0246FB702>
Ethernet:    Individual Address
Ethernet:    Universal Address
Ethernet: Ethernet V.2, Type IPv6   <86DD>
IPv6: Version: 6                     <6F>
IPv6: Priority: 15
IPv6: Flow Label: 0x000000 (Packet Do Not Belong To a Flow Carry)   <000000>
IPv6: Payload Length: 8              <0008>
IPv6: Next Header: 58 Internet Control Message Protocol   <3A>
IPv6: Hop Limit: 255                 <FF>
IPv6: Source Address:   FE80::A0:246F:B702
IPv6: Destination Address:   FF02::2
ICMPv6: Type: 133 Router Solicitation    <85>
ICMPv6: Code: 0                      <00>
ICMPv6: Checksum: 0xA125             <A125>
ICMPv6: Reserved: 0x00000000         <00000000>
Frame Tail
OFFST DATA                                          ASCII
003E: 3D BE 4C 0B                                    =.L.
```

Figure B-9
Router Advertisement
in hexadecimal

```
Captured at:    15.500171
Length: 122     Status: Ok
OFFST DATA                                          ASCII
0000: 33 33 00 00 00 01 08 00 2B B5 A7 A8 86 DD 6F 00   33......+.....o.
0010: 00 00 00 40 3A FF FE 80 00 00 00 00 00 00 00 00   ...@:...........
0020: 08 00 2B B5 A7 A8 FF 02 00 00 00 00 00 00 00 00   ..+.............
0030: 00 00 00 00 00 01 86 00 07 BD 40 00 07 08 00 00   ..........@.....
0040: 75 30 00 00 27 10 01 01 08 00 2B B5 A7 A8 05 01   u0..'.....+.....
0050: 00 00 00 00 05 DC 03 04 50 40 FF FF FF FF 00 09   ........P@......
0060: 3A 80 00 00 00 00 5F 15 50 00 82 C0 0E 00 00 BD   :....._.P.......
0070: 00 00 00 00 00 00 19 10 05 C0                     ..........
```

Figure B-10
Decoded Router
Advertisement

```
Captured at:    15.500171
Length: 122     Status: Ok
Ethernet: Destination Address 333300000001   <333300000001>
Ethernet:   Multicast Address
Ethernet:   Local Address
Ethernet: Source Address DecNetB5A7A8   <08002BB5A7A8>
Ethernet:   Individual Address
Ethernet:   Universal Address
Ethernet: Ethernet V.2, Type IPv6   <86DD>
IPv6: Version: 6                  <6F>
IPv6: Priority: 15
IPv6: Flow Label: 0x000000 (Packet Do Not Belong To a Flow  Carry)
<000000>
IPv6: Payload Length: 64          <0040>
IPv6: Next Header: 58 Internet Control Message Protocol   <3A>
IPv6: Hop Limit: 255              <FF>
IPv6: Source Address:  FE80::800:2BB5:A7A8
IPv6: Destination Address:  FF02::1
ICMPv6: Type: 134 Router Advertisement   <86>
ICMPv6: Code: 0                       <00>
ICMPv6: Checksum: 0x07BD             <07BD>
ICMPv6: Cur Hop Limit: 64            <40>
ICMPv6: M Flag: 0                    <00>
ICMPv6: O Flag: 0
ICMPv6: Reserved: 0
ICMPv6: Router Lifetime (sec) : 1800  <0708>
ICMPv6: Reachable Time (millisec): 0:0:30:0
ICMPv6: Retrans Timer (millisec): 0:0:10:0
ICMPv6: Option Type: 1 Source Link-Layer Address   <01>
ICMPv6: Option Length: 1 (8*bytes) <01>
ICMPv6:    Link-Layer Address: DecNetB5A7A8   <08002BB5A7A8>
ICMPv6: Option Type: 5 MTU          <05>
ICMPv6: Option Length: 1 (8*bytes) <01>
ICMPv6:    Reserved: 0               <0000>
ICMPv6:    MTU: 0x000005DC          <000005DC>
ICMPv6: Option Type: 3 Prefix Information   <03>
ICMPv6: Option Length: 4 (8*bytes) <04>
ICMPv6:    Prefix Length: 80         <50>
ICMPv6:    L Flag: 0                 <40>
ICMPv6:    A Flag: 1 Prefix Can Be Use For Autonomous Address  Configuration
ICMPv6:    Reserved(1): 0
ICMPv6:    Valid Lifetime (sec): 4294967295  <FFFFFFFF>
ICMPv6:    Preferred Liftime (sec): 604800  <00093A80>
ICMPv6:    Reserved(2):0x00000000   <00000000>
ICMPv6:    Prefix: 0x5F15500082C00E0000BD    <5F15500082C00E0000BD>
ICMPv6:    Pad: 0x000000000000       <000000000000>
Frame Tail
OFFST DATA                                            ASCII
0076: 19 10 05 C0                                     ....
```

B.7   Neighbor Solicitation Packet

This section shows an IPv6 packet containing a Neighbor Solicitation
ICMP packet. To better understand the decoding, please refer to Section
5.5.6. (See Figures B-11 and B-12.)

Figure B-11
Neighbor Solicitation
in hexadecimal

```
Captured at:   40.244537
Length: 90    Status: Ok
OFFST DATA                                                ASCII
0000: 33 33 24 6F B7 02 08 00 2B B5 A7 A8 86 DD 6F 00    33$o....+.....o.
0010: 00 00 00 20 3A FF FE 80 00 00 00 00 00 00 00 00    ... :...........
0020: 08 00 2B B5 A7 A8 FF 02 00 00 00 00 00 00 00 00    ..+.............
0030: 00 01 24 6F B7 02 87 00 CB 4C 00 00 00 00 5F 15    ..$o.....L...._.
0040: 50 00 82 C0 0E 00 00 BD 00 A0 24 6F B7 02 01 01    P.........$o....
0050: 08 00 2B B5 A7 A8 95 8F 01 B1                      ..+.......
```

Figure B-12
Decoded Neighbor
Solicitation

```
Captured at:   40.244537
Length: 90    Status: Ok
Ethernet: Destination Address 3333246FB702   <3333246FB702>
Ethernet:    Multicast Address
Ethernet:    Local Address
Ethernet: Source Address DecNetB5A7A8   <08002BB5A7A8>
Ethernet:    Individual Address
Ethernet:    Universal Address
Ethernet: Ethernet V.2, Type IPv6   <86DD>
IPv6: Version: 6                     <6F>
IPv6: Priority: 15
IPv6: Flow Label: 0x000000 (Packet Do Not Belong To a Flow  Carry)   <000000>
IPv6: Payload Length: 32             <0020>
IPv6: Next Header: 58 Internet Control Message Protocol   <3A>
IPv6: Hop Limit: 255                 <FF>
IPv6: Source Address:   FE80::800:2BB5:A7A8
IPv6: Destination Address:   FF02::1:246F:B702
ICMPv6: Type: 135 Neighbor Solicitation    <87>
ICMPv6: Code: 0                      <00>
ICMPv6: Checksum: 0xCB4C             <CB4C>
ICMPv6: Reserved: 0x00000000         <00000000>
ICMPv6: Target Address: 5F15:5000:82C0:E00:BD:A0:246F:B702
ICMPv6: Option Type: 1 Source Link-Layer Address   <01>
ICMPv6: Option Length: 1 (8*bytes)   <01>
ICMPv6:    Link-Layer Address: DecNetB5A7A8   <08002BB5A7A8>
Frame Tail
OFFST DATA                                                ASCII
0056: 95 8F 01 B1                                         ....
```

B.8   Neighbor Advertisement Packet

This section shows an IPv6 packet containing a Neighbor Advertisement ICMP packet. To better understand the decoding, please refer to Section 5.5.7. (See Figures B-13 and B-14.)

Figure B-13
Neighbor Advertisement in hexadecimal

```
Captured at:    40.244896
Length: 90    Status: Ok
OFFST DATA                                                          ASCII
0000: 08 00 2B B5 A7 A8 00 A0 24 6F B7 02 86 DD 6F 00   ..+.....$o....o.
0010: 00 00 00 20 3A FF 5F 15 50 00 82 C0 0E 00 00 BD   ... :._.P.......
0020: 00 A0 24 6F B7 02 FE 80 00 00 00 00 00 00 00 00   ..$o............
0030: 08 00 2B B5 A7 A8 88 00 26 69 60 00 00 00 5F 15   ..+.....&i`..._.
0040: 50 00 82 C0 0E 00 00 BD 00 A0 24 6F B7 02 02 01   P.........$o....
0050: 00 A0 24 6F B7 02 BE 3E 40 51                     ..$o...>@Q
```

Figure B-14
Decoded Neighbor Advertisement

```
Captured at:    40.244896
Length: 90    Status: Ok
Ethernet: Destination Address DecNetB5A7A8   <08002BB5A7A8>
Ethernet:   Individual Address
Ethernet:   Universal Address
Ethernet: Source Address 00A0246FB702   <00A0246FB702>
Ethernet:   Individual Address
Ethernet:   Universal Address
Ethernet: Ethernet V.2, Type IPv6   <86DD>
IPv6: Version: 6                      <6F>
IPv6: Priority: 15
IPv6: Flow Label: 0x000000 (Packet Do Not Belong To a Flow  Carry)
<000000>
IPv6: Payload Length: 32             <0020>
IPv6: Next Header: 58 Internet Control Message Protocol  <3A>
IPv6: Hop Limit: 255                 <FF>
IPv6: Source Address:   5F15:5000:82C0:E00:BD:A0:246F:B702
IPv6: Destination Address:   FE80::800:2BB5:A7A8
ICMPv6: Type: 136 Neighbor Advertisement   <88>
ICMPv6: Code: 0                      <00>
ICMPv6: Checksum: 0x2669             <2669>
ICMPv6: R Flag: 0                    <60000000>
ICMPv6: S Flag: 1 Advertisement is Response to Neighbor  Solicitation From
        Des.Add
ICMPv6: O Flag: 1 Advertisement Override Existing Cache Entry  And Update
        Cached Lin1
ICMPv6: Reserved: 0x0
ICMPv6: Target Address: 5F15:5000:82C0:E00:BD:A0:246F:B702
ICMPv6: Option Type: 2 Target Link-Layer Address   <02>
ICMPv6: Option Length: 1 (8*bytes)  <01>
ICMPv6:   Link-Layer Address: 00A0246FB702   <00A0246FB702>
Frame Tail
OFFST DATA                                                          ASCII
```

Appendix C

How to Obtain More Information

C.1 Author's Address

The author of this book can be contacted, preferably by e-mail, at the following address:

Silvano Gai

Dipartimento di Automatica e Informatica

Politecnico di Torino

Corso Duca degli Abruzzi, 24

10129 Torino

ITALY

e-mail: `Silvano.Gai@polito.it`

or: `silvano@ip6.com`

C.2 Author's WWW Address

The author administers WWW servers on the Internet in which he gathers information about computer networks. The servers' addresses are

`http://www.ip6.com`

`http://www.layer3.com`

`http://www.polito.it/~silvano`

C.3 Mailing List

The author administers a moderate mailing list in Italian on the Internet in which topics relevant to computer networks are discussed, with particular reference to LANs and to the IPv6 protocol. The registration is free. Applications can be sent by e-mail to

    `Silvano.Gai@polito.it`

There is also an official mailing list in English on IPv6, and applications can be sent by e-mail to `Majordomo@sunroof.eng.sun.com` by inserting in the text of the message the line `subscribe IPng`. Other useful words that can be inserted in the message are `help`, `info IPng`, and `who IPng`.

The archives of messages can be accessed by sending e-mail to `majordomo@sunroof.eng.sun.com` and by inserting in the text of the message the line

    `get ipng ipng.YYMM`

where `YY` are the last two digits of the year and `MM` are the two digits of the month. To obtain the index of available archives, insert the following line in the text of the message:

    `index ipng`

C.4   Where You Can Find RFCs and Internet Drafts

RFCs and Internet drafts can be copied free from the relative databases in the Internet through e-mail, FTP, or WWW. The starting point at the worldwide level is as follows:

    `http://www.isi.edu/rfc-editor/`

The following main databases operate through the FTP protocol:

    `ds.internic.net`
    `nis.nsf.net`
    `nisc.jvnc.net`
    `ftp.isi.edu`
    `wuarchive.wustl.edu`
    `src.doc.ic.ac.uk`
    `ftp.ncren.net`
    `ftp.sesqui.net`
    `nis.garr.it`

C.5   The Playground Server

The official server of the IETF working group on IPv6 is

```
http://www.ietf.cnri.reston.va.us/html.charters/
ipngwg-charter.html
```

The most updated server with the latest news on IPv6 is

```
http://playground.Sun.COM/pub/ipng/html/
```

In particular, it has two very important areas:

- `http://playground.Sun.COM/pub/ipng/html/ipng-implementations.html`, which keeps track of IPv6 implementations on hosts and routers;
- `http://playground.Sun.COM/pub/ipng/html/specs/specifications.html`, which keeps track of the progress of standards.

C.6   6-Bone

6-Bone is a pilot project of a backbone using the IPv6 protocol created to experiment with the introduction and the migration of the Internet to IPv6. 6-Bone administers a WWW server that keeps track of the progress of the project at the following address:

```
http://www-cnr.lbl.gov/6bone/
```

6bone nodes are registered in the RIPE-NCC register at the address:

```
ftp://ftp.ripe.net/ipv6/ip6rr/
```

6-Bone administers a mailing list at which you can register by e-mail to `majordomo@isi.edu` by inserting in the text of the message the line `subscribe 6bone`. Other useful commands that can be inserted in the message are `help`, `info 6bone`, and `who 6bone`.

C.7   Other WWW Servers

Other WWW addresses where you can find interesting information are as follow:

```
http://www.digital.com/info/ipv6/
http://www.wide.ad.jp/wg/ipv6/misc.html
http://www.urec.fr/IPv6/G6-english.html
http://www.ipv6.nas.nasa.gov/
http://www.process.com/ipv6/default.htp
http://www.cert.dfn.de/eng/team/ue/fw/ipv6fw/
http://web.mit.edu/network/isakmp/
http://www.computermethods.com/IPng/IPNG.htm
http://snad.ncsl.nist.gov/itg/ipv6.html
http://www.tbit.dk/
http://info.denet.dk/
http://www.ieee.org/comsoc/stallings.html
http://www.rs6000.ibm.com/ipv6/
http://www.ftp.com/product/whitepapers/wp-ipv6.htm
http://www.cisco.com/IPv6
http://www.research.microsoft.com/research/os/
http://ganges.cs.tcd.ie/4ba2/ipng/index.html
http://www.mentat.com/
http://www.join.uni-muenster.de/JOIN/ipv6/texte-
englisch/welcome.html
http://www.cpcug.org/user/jaubert/ipv6.html
http://www.canarie.ca/ntn/ipv6.html
http://www.interaus.net/old/dec/ipv6.html
http://www.ipv6.nas.nasa.gov/
http://www.tbit.dk/mdp/ipnk.html
http://www.yahoo.com/Computers_and_Internet/...
```

Some of these addresses may no longer be valid when you read this appendix. I apologize in advance, but in the Web world, such changes are unavoidable.

Appendix D

Glossary

3DES: Algorithm using the DES three times to increase the encryption security.

AAAA: Type of record used in DNS servers to store an IPv6 address.

AAL (ATM Adaptation Layer): Set of ATM-based protocols that provide different transmission services (voice, video, data, and so on) to ATM network users.

AAL 5: The AAL normally used to support connection-oriented VBR services and used prevalently for the classical IP over ATM traffic.

access control: A function used to decide whether a given request for a resource can be accepted.

ACK (acknowledgment): Notification sent from one network to another to acknowledge that some event (for example, receipt of a message) has occurred; acknowledgments can be present in different layers of the OSI reference model.

adaptive routing: See **dynamic routing**.

address: An identifier of an interface or a set of interfaces.

address mask: See **netmask**.

address resolution: Process to determine the relationship between an IP address and a link layer address (for example, in the LAN's case, a MAC address).

adjacent nodes: Nodes reachable by a single hop.

advertisement: Broadcast message used to notify all nodes of the availability of a certain service.

AFI (Authority and Format Identifier): In the OSI reference model, the first of the two parts into which the IDP field of the NSAP address is subdivided; it identifies the authority that issued the address and its format.

agent: A server or a relay.

AH: See **Authentication Header**.

All-Node: The multicast address (`FF02::1`) of all nodes connected to a link.

All-Router: The multicast address (`FF02::2`) of all routers connected to a link.

ANSI (American National Standard Institute): Voluntary organization composed of corporate, government, and other members that coordinate standard-related activities in the fields of, among other things, communications and networking. ANSI is a member of the IEC and of the ISO.

anycast: The unicast address of a group of interfaces belonging to different nodes. A packet that is sent to an anycast address is delivered to only one interface of the group (the nearest to the source, coherently to routing metrics).

API (Application Programming Interface): A set of functions used to access the network services independently from the implementation.

APNIC (Asia-Pacific Network Information Center): The service center for Internet information in the Asia and Pacific area.

application: A program that performs a function directly for a user. Examples of applications are Telnet, FTP, and mail.

area: Hierarchical partition of a network identified by a field of the layer 3 address (network).

ARP (Address Resolution Protocol): A protocol of the IPv4 architecture used to map an IPv4 address to a Data Link layer address (frequently MAC). ARP can be implemented only on physical networks that support the broadcast. See also **address resolution**.

ARP server: Server used to implement the ARP Protocol on NBMA networks. See also **ATMARP**.

AS: See Autonomous System.

asymmetric reachability: A type of asymmetrical link in which it is correct to reach node B from node A, but not node A from node B.

ATM (Asynchronous Transfer Mode): CCITT standard used to convey, through fixed-length cells, different kinds of information (data, voice, video, and so on). In the Internet world, this abbreviation is frequently synonymous with Another Terrible Mistake.

ATM switch: A multiport hardware set used to switch ATM cells. Cells are transferred from one physical connection to another, sometimes undergoing a variation in VCI/VPI fields.

ATMARP (ATM Address Resolution Protocol): Modified version of the ARP protocol, operating on a server, that can handle the mapping between IP addresses and ATM addresses.

Authentication: The verification of the identity of a person or a process.

Authentication Header (AH): Header with the function of guaranteeing the authenticity and the integrity of a packet. It guarantees that the packet-fixed fields have not been modified during the transmission.

automatic tunnel: Tunnel IPv6 on IPv4 where the endpoint of the IPv4 tunnel is determined by the IPv6 address with an embedded IPv4 address.

Autonomous System (AS): A set of routing domains under a common administration. See also **routing domain**.

backbone: The top level in a hierarchical network.

bandwidth: The difference between the highest and the lowest frequencies available for network signals. The term is also used to describe the rated throughput capacity of a given network medium or protocol.

Bellman-Ford: Alternative name used for distance vector algorithms.

best-effort: The behavior of some connectionless protocols, such as IP, that make their "best effort" to deliver a packet without guaranteeing the delivery itself or how long the packet will take to reach its destination.

BGP (Border Gateway Protocol): Path vector routing protocol, standardized by the IETF, used by exterior routers of an autonomous system to announce the network's addresses.

B-ICI (Broadband Inter-Carrier Interface): NNI between different public networks.

BIND (Berkeley Internet Name Daemon): Implementation of a DNS server developed and distributed by the University of California at Berkeley.

binding cache: A cache where the mapping between home addresses and care-of addresses of mobile hosts are stored.

B-ISDN (Broadband ISDN): A wide band version of ISDN that can offer transmission speed up to a 622 Mb/s.

black hole: A network configuration that discards packets without signaling it. The presence of black holes is detected by the Neighbor Unreachability Detection procedure.

BOOTP (BOOTstrap Protocol): TCP/IP network architecture protocol that allows a diskless machine to bootstrap on a local network.

border router: A synonym for **exterior router**.

bps: Bits per second, speed unit in data transmissions.

bridge: Routing device that operates at the Data Link layer (Layer 2) of the OSI reference model. MAC-bridges are frequently used to interconnect local networks.

broadband: A high-speed transmission, usually higher than 2 Mb/s.

broadcast: Data packet that will be sent to all nodes on a network.

brouter: A network device that bridges some packets and routes other packets. The bridge/route decision is based on different protocols.

BSD (Berkeley System Development): An implementation of the UNIX operating system developed and distributed by the University of California at Berkeley.

buffer: A storage area used to compensate for differences in processing speed between source and destination.

cache: A small storage area used in a node to store information temporarily.

care-of address: The IPv6 address acquired by a mobile host by connecting to a foreign network.

CATNIP: An alternative proposal for the IPv6 standard, dropped during the selection phase.

CCITT (Consultative Committee for International Telegraph and Telephone): The most important international organization responsible for the development of telephone and data communication systems standards. This organization is now part of the International Telecommunications Union, which recently reorganized, and CCITT was renamed the ITU-TSS.

cell: Short packet with fixed length (in ATM, 53 octets).

Cell Switching Router (CSR): Internetworking device that integrates routing IP and switching ATM functions.

CERT (Computer Emergency Response Team): Organization that works with the Internet community to improve and guarantee the security of the network.

CIDR (Classless Inter-Domain Routing): Technique that allows routers to group routes together to cut down on the quantity of routing information carried by the core routers.

circuit switching: Commutation technique to transmit digital data or analog signals that allow transmission systems to create a short delay and constant bandwidth temporary circuit.

Classifier: A part in an internetworking device in which packets are classified by their belongings to flows.

client: A host that requests a service of another host.

client-server: Interaction model in a distributed system in which a program sends a request to another program and waits for a reply. The program that requests is called a *client*; the one that replies to the request is called a *server*.

CLNP (ConnectionLess Network Protocol): OSI network layer protocol that does not require a circuit to be established before data are transmitted, as documented in ISO 8473.

CLNS (ConnectionLess-mode Network Service): OSI network layer service that does not require a circuit to be established before data are transmitted (also called *datagram protocol*). The delivery of the packet is not guaranteed, and the correction of errors procedures must be implemented by upper layers.

CMI (Cluster Member Identifier): In MARS, a station in a multicast group.

configured tunnel: IPv6 over IPv4 tunnel where the endpoint of the IPv4 tunnel is determined by the information configured on the node performing the encapsulation.

congestion: Traffic in excess of network, device, or circuit capacity.

connectionless-mode service: Service implemented by a connectionless protocol that doesn't guarantee the PDU's delivery.

connection-mode service: Reliable service implemented by a connected protocol.

CONS (COnnection-mode Network Service): Network layer reliable service where PDUs are exchanged through a connection protocol.

core gateway: The primary router in Internet. A synonym for **core router**.

core router: TRD's router.

cost: Metric associated to a link or to a path.

CRC (Cyclic Redundancy Check): Binary string computed on a packet to test its integrity during the reception phase.

CSR: See **Cell Switching Router**.

cut-through: In NBMA networks, a kind of routing that doesn't take into account LLG borders.

cyberspace: A term coined by William Gibson in his fantasy novel *Neuromancer* to describe the world of computers and the society that gathers around them.

datagram: packets transmitted by a connectionless protocol. Also a synonym for **IP packet**.

datagram service: See **connectionless-mode service**.

data link: The second layer of the OSI reference model. This layer provides reliable transit of data across a physical link.

DCC (Data Country Code): One of the possible formats of OSI NSAP addresses for use by private networks. Adapted from the subnetwork model of addressing in which the ATM layer is responsible for mapping network layer addresses into ATM addresses.

DCE (Data Communication Equipment): A term used in CCITT standards to identify devices and connections of a communication network that comprise the network end of the user-to-network interface; modems and interface cards are examples of DCEs, which connect to DTEs.

default route: Routing table entry that is used to direct frames for which a next hop is not explicitly listed in the routing table.

deprecated address: An address associated with an interface whose use by upper layer protocols is deprecated.

DES (Data Encryption Standard): Standard encryption algorithm used for data encryption.

DES-CBC (DES Cipher Block Chaining): A particular use mode of DES standard.

DHCP (Dynamic Host Configuration Protocol): Server-based protocol for the automatic configuration of IP networks (for example, addresses and prefixes).

distance vector: Distributed routing algorithm that computes routing tables based on an iterative exchange of routing tables between adjacent routers. Also called **Bellman-Ford** algorithm.

distributed routing: Dynamic routing technique in which routing tables are computed by an algorithm distributed on routers.

DLCI (Data Link Connection Identifier): Value that specifies a PVC or an SVC in a Frame Relay network.

DNS (Domain Name Server): Service for the translation of names into addresses and vice versa in the TCP/IP network architecture, based on a distributed and replicated database.

dotted decimal notation: Used for TCP/IP addresses, it refers to the common notation for addresses in the form <*n.n.n.n.*>, where each number *n* represents, in decimal, 1 byte of the 4-byte IP address.

downstream: From source to destination.

DSAP (Destination Service Access Point): Acronym used to identify the destination address in the OSI reference model.

DSP (Domain Specific Part): In the OSI reference model, the second of the two parts into which the NSAP address is subdivided.

DTE (Data Terminal Equipment): Term used in the CCITT standards for devices such as computers, protocol translators, and multiplexers; DTEs are usually connected to DCEs.

dual IP layer: Network architecture that allows hosts to use IPv4 and IPv6 protocol stacks at the same time.

Dual IS-IS: See **integrated IS-IS**.

dual stack: See **Dual IP layer**.

DVMRP (Distance Vector Multicast Routing Protocol): Routing protocol for IP multicast traffic, based on a distance vector philosophy and used in Mbone.

dynamic routing: Technique to dynamically compute and update routing tables as a function of the state and topology of the network.

E1: The 2.048 Mb/s transmission channel in the European plesiochronous hierarchy.

E3: The 34.368 Mb/s transmission channel in the European ple-siochronous hierarchy.

EGP (Exterior Gateway Protocol): The first EGP protocol. See also **Exterior Gateway Protocol.**

egress router: Router that connects an NBMA network to another network (for example, to a LAN).

EIGRP (Extended IGRP): extended version of the IGRP protocol.

e-mail: Electronic mail.

encapsulation: Technique used by protocols in which a lower layer adds information to the upper layer PDU by adding a header.

Encrypted Security Payload: Encapsulation technique using encryption to guarantee that only the receiver can read the data field.

Encryption: Manipulation of a data packet to guarantee that only the real receiver can extract its content. It is implemented by using standard algorithms, such as DES.

End Routing Domain (ERD): A routing domain in which routes are computed primarily to provide intra-domain routing services.

ES (End System): OSI term used to identify a node that can act only as a source or a final destination of the user's data and that doesn't feature the routing functions.

ES-IS (End System to Intermediate System): OSI protocol, specified in ISO 9542, for the neighbor greetings between router and end node and to associate Network layer addresses to Data Link layer addresses.

ESP: See **Encrypted Security Payload**.

Ethernet: Local network CSMA/CD; sometimes it is used for an IEEE 802.3 LAN.

extension header: A header, in addition to the IPv6 header, providing additional services (for example, fragmentation and source routing). It is placed between the IPv6 header and the upper layer header.

Exterior Gateway Protocol (EGP): Generic term applied to each protocol used to advertise reachability and routing information among different ASs. The term *gateway* is obsolete, and the term *router* is preferred.

exterior router: A router that connects different ASs.

FCS (Frame Check Sequence): Check information to test whether a CRC-based PDU is correct.

FDDI (Fiber Distributed Data Interface): Ring topology LAN, specifying a 100-Mbps token-passing network using fiber optic cable.

FIB (Forward Information Base): A synonym for **routing table**.

FIFO (First-In, First-Out): A storage buffer in which the first packet in is the first to go out. These buffers are useful to manage data bursts, allowing a computer to elaborate data at a constant, homogeneous, and average speed instead of at peak speed.

filterspec: In RSVP, a process that screens network traffic based on predefined criteria.

firewall: A computer or a router designated as a buffer between any connected public network and a private network to implement security.

flooding: Nonadaptive routing protocol in which a router sends packets out to all adjacent routers.

flow: Stream of IP packets that have some common characteristics (for example, the same source and destination addresses and the same application).

flow control: Technique to guarantee that a transmitting entity does not overwhelm a receiving entity with data, by reducing or stopping the transmission of new data on links.

flow label: Field of the IPv6 header used to identify the flow with the source address.

flowspec: In RSVP, the way to specify the QoS parameters.

foreign network: A network to which a mobile host can connect while traveling.

fragment: A piece of a larger packet that has been subdivided into smaller units.

frame: Generic term for a Data Link layer PDU.

frame relay: Standard for the implementation of public or private packet switching networks, based on a connected Data Link layer protocol in which virtual permanent circuits are defined.

FTP (File Transfer Protocol): Application protocol, part of the TCP/IP protocol stack, used for transferring files between network nodes.

gated (gate daemon): A software program that implements different routing protocols (available on the public domain at anonymous FTP server `gated.cornell.edu`). See also **EGP**, **OSPF**, **RIP**, and **routed**.

gateway: Device used to connect two different network architectures through the conversion of some application protocols of an architecture into the homologous protocols of another one. In the TCP/IP protocol, the term is improperly used as a synonym for **router**.

global address: A worldwide unique address.

hacker: A person who fraudulently tries to access a network and the hosts connected to it.

HBH (Hop By Hop): A particular kind of Extension Header used to transmit options that must be processed by all the nodes of the path.

HDLC (High-level Data Link Control): Data Link layer protocol used in WANs derived from SDLC and belonging to a family of protocols including LAP-B, LAB-D, LAP-F, and LLC.

header: First part of a PDU containing control information.

hierarchical coding: Technique for information coding used in multimedia applications that can adapt themselves to the bandwidth available on the network.

hierarchical routing: Technique to manage the routing in a wide network by subdividing it into several hierarchical levels (for example, inter-area routing and intra-area routing).

home address: The network address of a mobile host when at home.

home agent: A router answering to Neighbor Discovery messages on behalf of another node (for example, in the case of mobile nodes).

home network: The network to which a mobile host is connected when at home.

hop: The passage of a data packet between two network nodes (for example, between two routers). Frequently used as routing metric in the Network layer.

host: In the IP network architecture, every node that isn't a router.

HTML (HyperText Markup Language): Language used to create hypertext documents on WWW servers and accessible through the HTTP protocol.

HTTP (HyperText Transfer Protocol): The protocol used by WWW to transfer HTML files.

hub: LAN concentrator, usually with repetition functions.

hypertext: Electronically stored text, written with particular languages (for example, HTML), that allows direct access to other text by way of encoded links.

IAB (Internet Architecture Board): Board of internetwork researchers who discuss issues pertinent to Internet architecture.

IANA (Internet Assigned Number Authority): Technical organization that delegates authority for IP address-space allocation and domain-name assignment on the Internet to other organizations.

ICMP (Internet Control Message Protocol): In the TCP/IP network architecture, a Network layer protocol used with neighbor greetings functions, to report errors and to provide other information relevant to packet processing.

ICMPv6 (ICMP version 6): Version 6 of the ICMP protocol to be used with IPv6.

IDI (Initial Domain Identifier): In the OSI reference model, the second of the two parts into which the IDP field of the NSAP address is subdivided.

IDP (Initial Domain Part): In the OSI reference model, the first of the two parts into which the NSAP address is subdivided.

IDPR (Inter-Domain Policy Routing): An IETF proposal for a routing algorithm between link state autonomous systems that allows the implementation of the policy routing.

IDRP (Inter-Domain Routing Protocol): Inter-domain path vector routing protocol derived from BGP.

IEC (International Electrotechnical Commission): The European Union commission that issues and distributes standards for electrical products and components.

IEEE (Institute of Electrical and Electronics Engineers): Professional organization whose activities include the development of communications and network standards. IEEE LAN standards are the predominant LAN standards in use today.

IEEE 802: The IEEE committee working in the field of standardization of LANs that also defined the worldwide used MAC addresses on 48 bits.

IESG (Internet Engineering Steering Group): Steering committee for the Internet engineering.

IETF (Internet Engineering Task Force): ISOC working group responsible for the standardization and the development of the TCP/IP network architecture.

IGMP (Internet Group Management Protocol): Protocol used in IPv4 for multicast groups management. In IPv6, IGMP functions are included in ICMPv6.

IGP: See **Interior Gateway Protocol**.

IGRP (Interior Gateway Routing Protocol): IGP routing protocol developed by Cisco Systems to address the problems associated with routing in large, heterogeneous networks.

IKMP (Internet Key Management Protocol): Protocol for the encryption keys management.

Initialization Vector: Binary string used in association DES-CBC to introduce a casualness factor in the encryption process.

Integrated IS-IS (previously called **Dual IS-IS**): Routing protocol based on the OSI IS-IS routing protocol but supporting IP and other protocols; integrated IS-IS propagates reachability information of all protocols through the same LSP at the same time.

Integrated Service Internet: Proposal to extend the Internet architecture to support multimedia traffic.

inter-area routing: The routing between two or more logical areas.

interface: The device used to interconnect a node to a link.

interface token: A link layer interface identifier that is unique (at least) at the link layer. Usually derived from the interface's MAC address.

Interior Gateway Protocol (IGP): Generic term applied to each protocol used to advertise reachability and routing information within an AS. The term *gateway* is obsolete; it is replaced by *router*.

interior router: A router managing connections only within an AS.

internet: When used with lowercase *i,* it is short for *internetwork,* which is implemented by routers.

Internet: The largest global internetwork, based on the TCP/IP network architecture.

Internet draft: The preliminary issue of a document, to be discussed by the Internet community. Internet drafts circulate for six months, after which they expire or they are revised or they become RFCs.

Internet protocol suite: The network architecture best known as TCP/IP.

INTERNIC (INTERnet Network Information Center): The Northern American service center providing information about the Internet.

intra-area routing: Routing within a logical area.

Intranet: A company's private network based on the Internet model.

invalid address: an address not assigned to any interface.

IP (Internet Protocol): In TCP/IP network architecture, the Network layer data protocol.

IPAE (IP Address Encapsulation): A temporary solution toward SIP.

IP in IP: A temporary proposal toward IPv6.

IPng (IP new generation): Term used for IPv6 during the standardization phase.

IP spoofing: Counterfeiting of the source address in order to attack the security of an IP node.

IP Switch: Internetworking device that integrates routing IP and switching ATM functions.

IP Switching: Integrated technique for ATM switching and IP routing, based on the use of IP switches.

IPv4 (IP version 4): The only IP version used until 1996.

IPv4 address: The 32-bit address assigned to host and router interfaces using the IPv4 network architecture; written in dotted decimal format.

IPv6 (IP version 6): The new IP version described in this book.

IPv6 address: The 128-bit address assigned to host and router interfaces using the IPv6 network architecture; written as eight hexadecimal digits separated by **:** (colon).

IPv6 address compatible IPv4: An IPv6 address algorithmically derived from an IPv4 address.

IPv6 over IPv4 tunneling: Encapsulation of IPv6 packets in IPv4 packets to allow the IPv6 packets to be transmitted in IPv4 routing infrastructures. Two kinds of tunnels are available: configured and automatic.

IPv7: An alternative proposal for the IPv6 standard, dropped during the selection phase.

IPX (Internetwork Packet eXchange): Network layer protocol used by Novell; it is similar to XNS and IP.

IS (Intermediate System): OSI term used for a node (usually a router) that can route layer 3 messages to other nodes.

ISDN (Integrated Service Digital Network): An evolution of the telephone network, based on the digital technology, that allows telephone networks to transport data, voice, and other source data from 64 kbps to 2 Mb/s.

IS Internet: See **Integrated Service Internet**.

IS-IS (Intermediate System to Intermediate System): in the OSI network architecture, the interdomain Network layer protocol to compute the routing tables.

ISO (International Standard Organization): International organization that is responsible for a wide range of standards, including those relevant to networking. The ISO developed the OSI reference model.

ISOC (Internet SOCiety): Organization for the development of the Internet network and of the TCP/IP network architecture.

ISO-IP: Old name of the ISO CLNP protocol.

ISO-TP4 (ISO Transport Protocol class 4): Layer 4 protocol (transport) standardized by the ISO.

ISP (Internet Service Provider): A public or a private organization that provides Internet services. Often simply called *provider*.

ITU (International Telecommunication Union): United Nations agency that develops worldwide standards for telecommunications technologies.

ITU-T (ITU Telecommunications): Organization that carries out the functions of the former CCITT.

IV: See **Initialization Vector**.

label swapping: Routing technique used in connection protocols and, in particular, in ATM. Each packet is labeled as belonging to a connection or to a flow by a label used by switches/routers to route packets to their destinations. As the meaning of the label is univocal only at the single link layer, the label is replaced (swapped) by each switch/router.

LAN (Local Area Network): High-speed, low-error data network covering a relatively small geographic area (up to a few thousand meters). LANs connect workstations, peripherals, terminals, and other devices in a single building or other geographically limited area.

LAN emulation: Technique to emulate LAN IEEE 802.3 or IEEE 802.5 functions on an ATM network.

LAP (Link Access Procedure): Data Link layer protocol in the HDLC protocol stack.

LAP-B (LAP Balanced): LAP protocol used in X.25 networks.

LAP-D (LAP Data): LAP protocol used in ISDN networks.

LAP-F (LAP Frame): LAP protocol used in Frame Relay networks.

layer: A tier in the design of the modern network architecture. Each layer performs typical functions laying on lower layers and using protocols. The TCP/IP architecture consists of five layers, and the OSI consists of seven layers.

LEC (LAN Emulation Client): An ATM station emulating IEEE 802.3 or IEEE 802.5 station functions.

LECS (LAN Emulation Configuration Server): A software process of an ATM network that enables configuration of the emulation of one or more IEEE 802.3 or IEEE 802.5 LANs.

LES (LAN Emulation Server): A software process associated to a LAN on ATM emulation service with the main function of mapping MAC addresses into ATM addresses.

link: In hypertext, a pointer that can be used to access text or an application.

link: A communication channel over which nodes can transmit at the Data Link layer (that is, at the Layer 2 of the ISO/OSI reference model). Examples of links are Ethernet, PPP, X.25, Frame Relay, and ATM, or tunnels on other protocols such as IPv4 or IPv6.

link layer address: A layer 2 (Data Link) interface address.

link local address: IPv6 addresses valid only within a link.

link MTU: The MTU (that is, the maximum packet size) that can be transported on a link without being fragmented.

link state: Distributed routing algorithm to compute the routing tables where a router informs all other network routers about the state of links directly connected to it, by means of an LSP packet.

LIS (Logical IP Subnetwork): IP subnetwork defined by the netmask parameter; a physical network is associated to each LIS to allow all stations connected to that LIS to transmit directly (without using routers).

LLC (Logical Link Control): In IEEE 802 standard, the higher of the Data Link layer sublayers; protocol of the HDLC stack.

LLC/SNAP (LLC SubNetwork Access Protocol): A particular form of type 1 LLC encapsulation used for non-OSI protocols, such as IPv4 and IPv6.

LLG (Logical Link Group): A set of IPv6 stations that share the same prefixes and are connected to the same ATM network.

load splitting: Balancing of the load on alternative paths.

longest prefix match: The process to determine which prefix covers a given IPv6 address. In the case that more than one prefix covers the address, the longest one is chosen.

LSA (Link State Advertisement): A synonym for **LSP**.

LSP (Link State Packet): Multicast packet used by link-state protocols. This packet contains information about neighbors and path costs; it contains the list of the adjacent nodes.

MAC (Medium Access Control): The lower of two sublayers of the Data Link layer that arbitrates the access to shared media; the MAC sublayer provides the Logical Link Control sublayer with connectionless services.

MAC address: Data Link layer address, MAC sublayer, used in LANs, 48 bits long, and assigned by the network card manufacturer; it is written as six hexadecimal couples divided by the - character.

MAN (Metropolitan Area Network): High-speed network that spans a metropolitan area.

MARS (Multicast Address Resolution Server): A server that registers the participation of nodes to multicast groups on an NBMA network.

MBONE (Multicast backBONE): A network designed by point-to-point tunnels on the Internet to experiment with multicast applications.

MCS: See **MultiCast Server**.

MD (Message Digest): Summary of a packet computed by applying to the packet itself a function similar to a CRC. It is used to solve authentication problems.

MD2, MD4, MD5 (Message Digest 2, 4, 5): Algorithms used to compute the message digest.

MODEM (MOdulator-DEModulator): Device for the transmission of digital data over analog communication facilities (telephone lines) by an appropriate conversion (for example, FSK, QAM, DPSK).

MOSPF (Multicast OSPF): OSPF extension to manage IP multicast packets.

MPEG (Moving Picture Experts Group): Algorithm for the compression of video images.

MTU (Maximum Transmission Unit): Maximum packet size, in bytes, that a particular interface can manage.

multicast: A single address for a set of interfaces belonging to different nodes. A packet sent to a multicast address is delivered to all interfaces belonging to the set.

multicast link: A multiple access link that allows the sending of a packet to all nodes (or to a subset of them) by a single transmission at the link layer.

multicast server: A server associated to an NBMA network that receives packets on a point-to-point VC and retransmits them to all members of the multicast group by a point-to-multipoint VC.

multihomed: A network belonging to many routing domains; a host with more than a connection to a network but not acting as a router.

name: String of digits that univocally identify an entity.

NBMA (Non Broadcast Multiple Access): Term describing a multiaccess network where, from a station, it is possible to reach all others, but that either does not support broadcasting or in which broadcasting is not feasible. An example of NBMA is given by X.25 and ATM networks.

ND: See **neighbor discovery**.

neighbor advertisement: Message of the ICMPv6 protocol in reply to a request to translate an IPv6 address into a link layer address.

neighbor discovery: Process of the ICMPv6 protocol for the automatic configuration of neighbor relations on a link.

neighbor greetings: Definition frequently used to describe protocols exchanging packets with neighbors.

neighbors: Nodes connected on the same link.

neighbor solicitation: Message of the ICMPv6 protocol to request the mapping of an IPv6 address into a link layer address.

neighbor unreachability detection: Process to test the reachability of neighbor nodes and for the detection of black holes.

netmask: A 32-bit mask used in IPv4 to specify the subnetwork address.

network: Collection of computers, printers, routers, switches, and other peripherals and devices that can communicate with each other over some transmission medium. It can be made of a combination of LANs and WANs.

network address: In IPv4, the part of the IP address identifying the network. The network address can belong to A, B, and C classes.

network architecture: Design, organization, and set of rules that govern the design and functions of hardware and software components of a computer network.

network mask: See **netmask**.

next hop: The next node toward which to transmit a packet. The node must be reachable at link layer (that is, must be on-link) and therefore must be a neighbor.

NFS (Network File System): Protocol developed by Sun Microsystems, based on the TCP/IP network architecture that allows a set of computers to share the file systems.

NHRP (Next Hope Resolution Protocol): Similar to the ARP protocol, this protocol is used by routers to dynamically discover the MAC address of other routers and hosts connected to NBMA networks (for example, ATM networks).

NHS (Next Hop Server): A server used by the NHRP protocol.

NIC (Network Information Center): Organization that serves network users by providing user assistance, documentation, training, and other services.

NIS (Network Information Service): A set of services provided by a NIC to the users of a network. Also a protocol developed by Sun Microsystems for the administration of network-wide databases.

NNI (Network to Network Interface): Interface between two ATM switches. The two types of NNI are the P-NNI and the B-ICI.

NNTP (Network News Transfer Protocol): The protocol used to request, copy, and send articles to News.

NOC (Network Operations Center): Organization responsible for maintaining a network.

node: A device that uses the IP protocol.

NSAP (Network Service Access Point): Network layer address in the OSI architecture.

NTP (Network Time Protocol): A protocol used to synchronize the clock of computers connected to a network with millisecond precision.

octet: OSI term to describe a string of 8 bits (that is, a byte).

off-link: An IPv6 address not assigned to any interface connected to the link.

on-link: An IPv6 address assigned to an interface connected to the link.

OOB: See **Out Of Band**.

OSI (Open System Interconnect): International standard program created by the ISO to develop standards for data networking that facilitate multivendor equipment interoperability. It consists of seven layers: Physical, Data Link, Network, Transport, Session, Presentation, and Application. This standard is described in the ISO document 7498.

OSPF (Open Shortest Path First): Link state protocol to compute routing tables used in the TCP/IP network architecture.

OUI (Organization Unique Identifier): The three octets assigned by the IEEE to an organization operating in the field of networks.

Out Of Band: The technique for the distribution of encryption keys outside the frequencies or channels normally used for information transfer.

overhead: A worsening of performance due to the need to process and/or transmit more information.

packet: Term normally used to indicate a PDU. In this book, *packet* is synonymous with *PDU* at the IP layer.

packet sniffing: Reading of transmission packets to learn their content, for network diagnostics reasons or to try to access reserved information fraudulently.

packet switching: Commutation technique to group digital data in PDUs and to route them on transmission media shared by network nodes.

Pad1: A one octet padding option.

PadN: A two or more octets padding option.

path: An ordered set of links that connect a source with a destination.

path MTU: The minimum link MTU of all the links in the path between source and destination.

payload: The data field of an IP packet or of an ATM cell.

PC: Personal Computer.

PDH: See **Plesiochronous Digital Hierarchy**.

PDU (Protocol Data Unit): Set of data transmitted between entities of the same layer, usually called *packet*.

PID (Protocol IDentifier): Protocol identifier on two octets, used in the LLC/SNAP enveloping.

PING (Packet InterNet Groper): A program used to test the reachability of an IP node.

PIP (Paul's Internet Protocol): A proposal for the IPv6 protocol merged with SIPP.

Plesiochronous Digital Hierarchy (PDH): Hierarchy for multiplexing almost synchronous numerical signals. In Europe, the following levels have been defined: E1 = 2048 Mbps, E2 = 8448, E3 = 34.368, and E4 = 139.264 Mbps. In the U.S., the following levels are used: T1 = 1544 Mbps and T3 = 44.736 Mbps.

P-NNI (Private NNI): NNI interface to be used on private networks. It defines the physical aspects, the signaling procedures to create and to pull down SVCs, and the ways to determine SVCs routings.

point-to-point: A kind of link interconnecting exactly two interfaces.

policy routing: Routing scheme that forwards packets to specific interfaces based on user-configured policies.

POP (Point Of Presence): Physical access point to a long distance carrier interchange.

POP (Post Office Protocol): Protocol used to manage the electronic mail in a client-server mode.

port: Point of access to application protocols in the TCP/IP network architecture.

PPP (Point-to-Point Protocol): Data Link layer protocol of the HDLC stack for point-to-point links with multiplexing capacity among Network layer protocols, standard in multivendor environments.

pps (packets per second): Also written p/s.

preferred address: An address associated with an interface for which use by upper layer protocols is allowed without limitations.

preferred lifetime: The time an address remains preferred (that is, the time before it becomes deprecated).

prefix: The first part of an IPv6 address common to all nodes belonging to the same subnet (connected to the same link).

probe: Neighbor Solicitation packets sent to a neighbor node to test its reachability.

protocol: Formal description of a set of rules and conventions that govern how devices on a network exchange information.

protocol stack: A set of related communications protocols organized by layers that cooperate to provide some network functions.

protocol type: Field of the Ethernet v.2.0 frame that indicates the upper layer protocol contained in the data field.

provider: See **ISP**.

provider-based address: IPv6 global addresses obtained from an ISP.

proxy: An entity that participates with protocols on behalf of another entity.

proxy ARP: Technique that allows the subdivision of an IPv4 subnet into two physical networks. The router connecting physical networks responds to the queries from the ARP on behalf of nodes connected to other physical networks.

proxy server: A server responding to the messages from application protocols on behalf of another node (for example, in the case of the HTTP protocol).

PTT (Post, Telephone, and Telegraph): Government agency that provides telecommunications within one nation.

PVC (Permanent Virtual Connection): Virtual circuit that is permanently established by the network administrator.

QoS (Quality of Service): In OSI and ATM architectures, the measure of performance for a transmission system that reflects its transmission quality and service availability.

random delay: A delay introduced before the transmission of a packet to prevent the transmission of different nodes at exactly the same time.

RARP (Reverse Address Resolution Protocol): Protocol in the TCP/IP stack that provides a method to obtain a Network layer address starting from a Data Link layer address.

reachability: Whether the one-way "forward path" to a node is functioning properly.

real time: Type of traffic, usually associated with multimedia applications, that needs limited and constant delays.

reassembly: The reconstruction of a packet after it has been fragmented by either the source or an intermediate node.

redirect: A message of the ICMPv6 protocol generated by a router to advertise a better hop toward a given destination.

relay: A node that acts as an intermediate device in the transmission of a packet between other two nodes (for example, between client and server).

relaying: Transmitting a PDU between two entities of the same layer in the same node (for example, in bridges, the transmission of a MAC PDU between MAC layers of two LAN cards).

RFC (Request For Comments): Document series used as the primary means for communicating information about the Internet. Some RFCs are designated as standards about the TCP/IP network architecture.

RH: See **Routing Header**.

RIP (Routing Information Protocol): Protocol to compute routing tables, suitable for small networks.

RIPE-NCC (Réseaux IP Européens Network Information Centre): European service center for information about the Internet.

route: Routing path; in IP routers, each reachable subnet has a route.

routed (route daemon): A software program that implements the routing protocol RIP. See also **gated**.

router: A node that can route packets to the nodes at IP layer.

router advertisement: Message of the ICMPv6 protocol to inform nodes that a router connected to the link exists.

router solicitation: Message of the ICMPv6 protocol to request routers to announce themselves on a link.

routing: The process of finding a path to a destination host; the path that an IP packet must traverse to reach its destination.

routing by network address: Routing technique mainly used in connectionless protocols.

routing domain: A hierarchical partition of the network containing a group of hosts and routers; routers share the same routing information, compute tables using the same IGP, and are managed by a common administrator.

routing domain confederation: A set of routing domains seen as a unique entity and identified by a unique IPv6 prefix.

routing header: Extension header used to implement the source routing in IPv6.

routing layer 1: See **intra-area routing**.

routing layer 2: See **inter-area routing**.

routing QoS based: A routing technique that determines paths on the basis of the kind of service requested.

routing table: A table containing useful information for routing algorithms such as, for each destination, the line to be used, its cost, and the number of hops.

RPC (Remote Procedure Call): The extension of the conventional call procedure that allows execution of the procedure called on a remote node.

RSA: The encryption algorithm by public key invented by Rivest, Shamir, and Adleman, from whom the acronym comes.

RSVP (Resource reSerVation Protocol): Protocol used in IP networks to reserve network resources.

SA (Security Association): Agreement between two or more nodes about security algorithms and about the related parameters to be used during the packets exchange. Every SA is identified by the SPI.

SAP (Service Access Point): Point where a layer provides upper layer services.

SAR (Segmentation And Reassembly): One of the two sublayers of the AAL, responsible for dividing into cells (at the source) and reassembling a message from cells (at the destination).

Scheduler: Function of an internetworking device that decides which packet to transmit among those queued, to guarantee the QoS.

SDH: Synchronous Digital Hierarchy.

SDU (Service Data Unit): Unit of information from an upper layer protocol that defined a service request to a lower layer protocol.

SEAL (Simple and Efficient ATM Adaptation Layer): Old name of AAL 5.

server: A host that offers a specific service to another host.

service provider: A company that installs telecommunications networks to provide users with a set of public services (such as telephone, cable TV, data transmission, and so on).

shared media: A kind of link that allows the communication between many nodes but where nodes are configured without a complete prefixes list; for this reason, nodes connected to the shared medium can ignore neighbors. Examples of shared media are SMDS and B-ISDN.

singlecast: A synonym for **unicast**.

SIP (Simple IP): A proposal for the IPv6 protocol, which was then combined with PIP and became SIPP.

SIPP (Simple IP Plus): The proposal on which the IPv6 protocol is based; born from the fusion of SIP and PIP.

site local address: IPv6 address valid only within a site (a set of subnetworks belonging to an organization).

SLIP (Serial Line IP): A protocol used to transport IP on serial connections. Predecessor of PPP.

SMDS (Switched Multi Megabit Data Service): A public service for data transmission at speeds between 1.5 and 45 megabits per second.

SMTP (Simple Mail Transfer Protocol): In the TCP/IP network architecture, the protocol providing electronic mail services.

SNMP (Simple Network Management Protocol): TCP/IP protocol to manage network devices; became a *de facto* standard.

socket: The interface used by UNIX BSD to access network services.

SONET: Synchronous Optical NETwork; the U.S. version of SDH.

source routing: Routing technique mainly used in IBM architectures and in IEEE 802.5; it consists of the specification, during the PDU generation, of the sequence of nodes that the PDU will traverse.

SPF (Shortest Path First): Term frequently used to describe Dijkstra's algorithm, in which all paths to all destinations are computed starting from the network graph; used by link state packet routing protocols.

SPI (Security Parameter Index): The SA to be used in a packet exchange. Used both by AH and by ESP.

SSAP (Source Service Access Point): Abbreviation used to describe the source address.

static route: An entry in a static routing table, manually written by the network administrator.

static routing: Routing technique in which routing tables are statically determined during the network configuration. See also **static route**.

station: Term used in LANs to describe an ES or an IS, stressing their functions at the Data Link layer.

stub network: A network transporting packets only for nodes belonging to the network itself and therefore not admitting the transition traffic.

subnet: A subset of nodes identified by addresses with a common prefix to which a physically independent network segment corresponds.

subnet address: In IPv4, IP address bits that identify the subnet.

subnet mask: See **netmask**.

SVC (Switched Virtual Connection): Virtual circuit that is dynamically established on demand and is explicitly closed when transmission is complete.

switch: Multiport device able to commute frames at the Data Link layer.

Synchronous Digital Hierarchy (SDH): Numerical transmission system defined by the ITU-T and chosen to implement the transmission infrastructure of B-ISDN. Currently, it operates at the following speeds: 155 Mb/s, 622 Mb/s, 2.4 Gb/s, and 9.6 Gb/s.

system: Term frequently used in computer networks as a synonym for **node**.

T1: In U.S. plesiochronous hierarchy, the transmission channel at 1.544 Mbps.

T3: In U.S. plesiochronous hierarchy, the transmission channel at 44.736 Mbps.

tag: A synonym for **label**.

tag switch: Switch that routes packets by using tag information. Tag switches perform the tag swapping. See also **label swapping**.

tag switching: Fast routing approach proposed by Cisco Systems in which traffic is routed in the function of tags associated to packets. It uses tag switches.

target: An address searched through a process of address resolution or the address of the first hop obtained through the redirection process.

TCP (Transmission Control Protocol): In the TCP/IP network architecture, a connection-oriented transport layer protocol that provides reliable and full-duplex data transmission. TCP is part of the TCP/IP protocol stack.

TCP/IP (Transmission Control Protocol/Internet Protocol): The network architecture developed in the 1970s to support the construction of worldwide internetworks, the best known of which is the Internet; it is a market and *de facto* standard.

TDP: Tag Distribution Protocol. Protocol used by Cisco Systems for tag distribution.

Telnet: In the TCP/IP network architecture, standard terminal emulation protocol used for remote terminal connection, enabling users to log in to remote systems and to use resources as though they were connected to a local system.

tentative address: An address whose uniqueness is tested within a link before it is assigned to an interface.

TFTP (Trivial File Transfer Protocol): Simplified version of the FTP protocol, mainly used for downline loading on diskless stations.

throughput: Rate, usually in pps, of the real transmission capacity of a network or a part of it.

TIB (Tag Information Base): Table filled by the TDP and used by tag switches.

TOS (Type Of Service): In IPv4, similar to Quality of Service.

TP/IX: A proposal for the IPv6 protocol, rejected during the selection phase.

traceroute: A program available on many computers showing the routing path followed by a packet to reach a given destination.

TRD (Transit Routing Domain): A routing domain in which routes are computed primarily to carry transit (that is, inter-domain) traffic.

triple DES: See **3DES**.

TTL (Time To Live): A field in the IPv4 header used to limit the life of packets temporarily in case of loops in the network.

TUBA (TCP and UDP over Bigger Addresses): A proposal, based on the OSI standard, for the IPv6 protocol, rejected during the selection phase.

tunnel: Encapsulation of a protocol A into a protocol B. A considers the protocol B as if it were an IP link (that is, a Data Link layer protocol).

tunneling: Technique for packet transmission by using tunnels.

UDP (User Datagram Protocol): In the TCP/IP network architecture, a connectionless transport layer protocol used, for example, by NFS and SNMP.

UNI (User to Network Interface): Interface between a station and an ATM switch. The UNI standard defines both the physical aspects and the signaling procedures to create and reduce SVCs.

unicast: The address of a single interface. A packet sent to a unicast address is delivered only to the interface identified by that address.

UNIX: Operating system developed in 1969 at Bell Laboratories. Widely used in computers connected to the Internet.

upper layer: A protocol that operates at a higher layer in the OSI reference model. Examples are the transport protocols TCP and UDP, the control protocols such as ICMP, routing protocols such as OSPF, or protocols tunneled over IP (for example, IPX and AppleTalk).

upstream: From destination to source.

valid address: A preferred or deprecated address.

valid lifetime: The period of validity of an address.

variable MTU: A type of link without a well-defined MTU.

VCI (Virtual Circuit Identifier): A 16-bit field in the header of an ATM cell.

Virtual circuit: A circuit, implemented through a cell or packet switching network, that offers the simulation of a point-to-point connection between two points.

VPI (Virtual Path Identifier): An 18-bit field in the header of an ATM cell.

VPN (Virtual Private Network): Frequently implemented by tunneling on IP.

W3: A synonym for **WWW**.

WAN (Wide Area Network): Data communications network that serves users across a broad geographic area and often uses transmission devices provided by common carriers.

well-known port: In the TCP/IP network architecture, ports pre-assigned to main application protocols.

WFQ (Weighted Fair Queuing): Algorithm used to implement scheduling policies on internetworking devices.

Winsock: In Windows systems, a sockets library.

WWW (World Wide Web): Servers used to provide hypertext information on the Internet.

X.25: ITU-T standard for the homonymous packet switching network. Originally designed to connect terminals to computers, the X.25 offers a reliable and low-speed data flow service.

XDR (eXternal Data Representation): Standard developed by Sun Microsystems for the data representation independent from the computer architecture.

INDEX

E

F

G

H

I

ABOUT THE AUTHOR

Silvano Gai is a Professor of Electrical and Computer Engineering at the Polytechnic Turin, Italy. Professor Gai is a recognized pioneer in several areas, including IP and ATM, LAN emulating, ATM and IP multicasting, RSVP, and Tag and IP switching. He has served on the Italian National Council for Scientific Research and as President of a European Union project on the Information Society. While writing this book, he was on sabbatical at Cisco Systems in San Jose, California, as a distinguished guest scholar and researcher.